T0320841

Entropy Law, Sustainability, and Third Industrial Revolution

Entropy Law, Sustainability, and Third Industrial Revolution

RAMPRASAD SENGUPTA

OXFORD
UNIVERSITY PRESS

OXFORD
UNIVERSITY PRESS

Oxford University Press is a department of the University of Oxford.
It furthers the University's objective of excellence in research, scholarship,
and education by publishing worldwide. Oxford is a registered trademark of
Oxford University Press in the UK and in certain other countries.

Published in India by
Oxford University Press
22 Workspace, 2nd Floor, 1/22 Asaf Ali Road, New Delhi 110 002

ISBN-13 (print edition): 978-0-19-012114-3
ISBN-10 (print edition): 0-19-012114-9

ISBN-13 (eBook): 978-0-19-099050-3
ISBN-10 (eBook): 0-19-099050-3

Typeset in Dante MT Std 10.5/13
by Tranistics Data Technologies, Kolkata 700 091
Printed in India by Rakmo Press, New Delhi 110 020

To Sheila

Contents

Tables

Figures

Abbreviations

BAU	business as usual
BIG	baseline inclusive growth
CAGR	compound annual growth rate
CFI	Consolidated Fund of India
CIESIN	Centre for International Earth Science Information Network
CSP	consolidated solar power
C-WET	Centre for Wind Energy Technology
DNI	direct normal irradiance
EFI	ecological footprint index
EPI	environmental performance index
GDP	gross domestic product
GHG	greenhouse gas
GMM	generalized method of moments
GNI	gross national income
GNP	gross national product
GSDP	gross state domestic product
GST	goods and service tax
GW	gigawatt
HDI	human development index
HDR	*Human Development Report*
ICSSR	Indian Council of Social Sciences Research
IEA	International Energy Agency
INR	Indian National Rupee

IPCC	Intergovernmental Panel on Climate Change
LCIG	low carbon inclusive growth
MDG	millennium development goal
MGNREGA	Mahatma Gandhi National Rural Employment Guarantee Act
MOSPI	Ministry of Statistics and Programme Implementation
MPI	multidimensional poverty index
NCEEF	National Clean Energy & Environment Fund
NSS	National Sample Survey
NSSO	National Sample Survey Office
OSDI	overall sustainable development indicator
PFCE	private financial consumption expenditure
PPP	purchasing power parity
SC/ST	Scheduled Castes/Scheduled Tribes
SSI	social sustainability index
SVL	statistical value of life
T&D	transmission and distribution
TERI	The Energy and Resources Institute, Delhi
TSLS	two-stage least square
UNDP	United Nations Development Programme
USD	United States Dollar
WHO	World Health Organization
WISE	World Institute of Sustainable Energy
YCELP	Yale Centre for Environmental Law and Policy

Acknowledgements

I thank the Indian Council of Social Sciences Research (ICSSR), Delhi, for providing funding support for the basic study on which this book is based by awarding me the Mahatma Gandhi National Fellowship of the ICSSR during 2016–18. I also thank the Centre for Studies in Social Sciences Calcutta (CSSSC), West Bengal, and especially its former and present directors, Professors Tapati Guha Thakurta and Rosinka Chaudhuri, for permitting me to affiliate myself with the CSSSC and supporting my taking up the fellowship and carrying out the research work at the centre. I must make here a special mention of the very kind help and support that I received from Dr Debarshi Sen, registrar at the CSSSC, for providing all the administrative and infrastructural support for my work, without which this book would not have been possible.

During my stay at the CSSSC as a National Fellow, I had very stimulating and helpful academic interactions with all my colleagues in the economics group of the faculty at the Centre—specifically, Professor Sugata Marjit, Professor Jyotsna Jalan, Dr Sandip Sarkar, Dr Sattwik Santra, Dr Pranab Kumar Das, Dr Saibal Kar, and Dr Tushar Nandi. I thank all of them. I would further like to thank Abhijit Ghosh and his colleague Debajyoti Das for their prompt help with IT and computer-related matters. I would further like to thank the staff members managing the library, archives, and general administration of the CSSSC for their help and cooperation.

Besides these, I must thankfully acknowledge the great help and many useful suggestions I received from Professor Dipankor Coondoo, retired professor at the Indian Statistical Institute, Kolkata, West Bengal, regarding the econometric analyses involved in the study. I would also like to mention the many useful and productive discussions on the study that I had with Dr Dipak Dasgupta, who has been lead economist at the World Bank for India and principal economic adviser to the Ministry of Finance, Government of India. I also benefitted from some research ideas suggested by Satya Das, an energy journalist from Edmonton, Canada, on the Green Climate Fund.

Furthermore, I received immense help from Dr Somit Dasgupta, member of the Central Electricity Authority (CEA), and Dr Chetana Chaudhuri, consultant for the Institute of Economic Growth (IEG), who provided me data, which was of critical importance to this study and very useful suggestions regarding their use. I must also acknowledge the great encouragement that I received from Professor Manoj Panda, director of the IEG, for the study.

I must thank Sovik Mukherjee (assistant professor at St. Xavier's University, Kolkata) for providing me excellent research assistance. I greatly appreciate his sincere, meticulous, and thoughtful work. I would also like to thank Dr Shalini Saksena (associate professor at Delhi College of Arts and Commerce, University of Delhi) and Moumita Deb (formerly research assistant at India Development Foundation, Gurgaon) for their useful research assistance in some background studies on the theme of this book which helped my work.

Finally, I take this opportunity to thank my wife, Sheila Sengupta, for being my constant source of moral support and encouragement during this study.

Ramprasad Sengupta
14 January 2020
Kolkata

Foreword

In 1962, *Silent Spring* by Rachel Carson appeared. Carson drew attention, in a poetic manner, to the long-run impact of human actions on the environment.

> We stand now where two roads diverge. But, unlike the roads in Robert Frost's familiar poem, they are not equally fair. The road we have long been travelling is deceptively easy, a smooth superhighway on which we progress with high speed, but at its end lies disaster. The other fork of the road, the one 'less travelled by'—offers our last, our only chance to reach a destination that assures the preservation of our earth. (277)

Subsequent movements on sustainable development can be thought of as tentative steps along the other road. Both in the academic world and in numerous periodic meetings on the world stage beginning with Stockholm (1972) and Rio de Janeiro (1992), attempts have been made to identify some of the fundamental, complex, and interrelated issues that, if left unattended, will threaten the planet, people, prosperity, peace, and partnership. The journey has been marked with controversies, partly due to the difficulties of quantification, measurement, and prediction. The meaning of 'sustainability' too has evolved over time. The 2002 World Summit on Sustainable Development at Johannesburg stressed the need to go beyond a narrow view and to assume 'a collective responsibility to strengthen the interdependent and mutually reinforcing pillars of sustainable development, economic development, social development, and environmental protection at local, national and global levels' (UN 2002).

It is now obvious that nature cannot be taken for granted as the source of support, and the sink to absorb the wastes, in our quest for prosperity. Our commitment to the future generation dictates the creation of appropriate policies to avoid irreparable damage to our ecosystem that will limit consumption possibilities or drastically disrupt quality of life. The design of policies will differ from country to country, and will involve some theoretical analysis and careful monitoring of the indicators for sustainability in the broadest sense (elaborated, for example, at the United Nations Sustainable Development Summit of 2015 in New York).

Professor Ramprasad Sengupta is a seasoned researcher; a scholar for all seasons. He has written widely on sustainability in an engaging style, navigating effortlessly between themes, both analytical and empirical. In this book, the first part seeks to identify entropy as a unifying theme in alternative approaches to sustainability, reviving Georgescu-Roegen (1971). The second part, most fascinating to me, focusses on India's transition to green technology. That our future journey will involve major changes in consumption and production patterns has long been accepted. At the heart of such changes, of course, is a switch to new technologies, which are less reliant on exhaustible resources as the choice of input and less damaging to the environment in its generation of outputs. For readers interested in sustainability and development, Professor Sengupta has presented a highly thought-provoking monograph.

Mukul Majumdar
H.T. Warshow and Robert Irving Warshow Professor of Economics
Department of Economics
Cornell University, Ithaca, USA

Introduction

The role of entropy law and the finiteness of our planetary ecosystem in the economic processes of development are of fundamental importance in view of their wide-ranging impact on our society and economy. However, this had been neglected for long by most of the mainstream economists until Georgescu-Roesen's seminal work *The Entropy Law and the Economic Processes* (1971) highlighted the unsustainability of the indefinite scale of expansion of an economic system. This work subsequently gave rise to much research, debate, and discussion on the issue of the limits to growth. The present book sets out to examine and explore how the analyses of the key issues of sustainability—economic, environmental, and social—of the development process, can be unified under the idea of entropy, which is at the root of all scarcities of resources—natural, and human or social. The book also looks into the long-term implications of entropy law in respect of development of India's electrical energy sector, which is of critical importance for both India's energy security to support its economic growth process as well as ensuring environmental security in the context of global climate change.

Scheme of the Book

The book is divided into two parts. While Part I revisits sustainable development, as defined in the book, as a derivative of the idea of entropy in the operational context of economic development process, Part II examines the potential of India's ability to transition into a green energy regime, which is the anticipated outcome of the Third Industrial Revolution. Part I defines the concept of entropy in a finite, closed system and points out how economic processes are affected by entropy law, resulting in the scarcity of bio-physical resources, which constitute the foundation of the production system of any economy. In view of the openness of the planetary system with reference to the outer space, it also addresses (*i*) the question of whether solar energy flow can delimit or offset the impact of entropy law and (*ii*) whether the growth of human knowledge can abate the pressure applied by the system on entropy to rise along the development path. The discussions show the role of time in characterizing how the functioning of the economic system and that of nature's regeneration process is a critical determinant of sustainability of the concerned processes. The massive challenge in respect of sustainability that we are facing today arises from the fact that we are extracting resources—natural as well as human or social—from a finite pool of a closed system, causing increasing disorder or a rise in entropy of the resource system. The speed of extraction of resources and their uses with various technologies has fundamentally become unsustainable today because it has exceeded the capacity of resource regeneration as well as that of waste absorption of the natural ecosystem per unit of time.

The book further shows the relevance and wider applicability of the concept of entropy in the context of the functioning of the social system beyond that of the natural, physical, and economic system. Resource scarcity—a major fallout of entropy law—is, in fact, the root cause of inequality in the distribution of ownership or command over natural resources or distribution of the social product produced by these resources among the people of a society. As the people of a society who enjoy socio-economic and political advantage, in terms of initial endowment of resources, can manage to appropriate a greater share of resources, this leads to absolute or relative deprivation of the people of the society. The latter can be translated in terms of social welfare loss, which provides us a metric for the measure of social tension caused by such deprivation. The issue of social sustainability connects such social tensions arising from inequalities or poverty with violence and crime, which are evidences of the unsustainability of a social state. The concept of entropy, thus, plays a true role of a common unifying principle or an ultimate limiting factor for analysing sustainable development in all its dimensions.

In the context of sustainable development, the chapters of Part I discuss the issues of alternative approaches to development economics and have focused on three different aspects of sustainability of the development process—economic, social, and environmental. The individual chapters of this part (*i*) trace the pathways of connectivity between entropy and any of these individual aspects of sustainability, (*ii*) develop indicators for the three different types of sustainability and an overall indicator of development, and (*iii*) estimate the relations of interdependence among the different components of this overall development indicator representing the different aspects of sustainability. Most of the conclusions in these regards are based on econometric or statistical analysis of cross-country and interstate Indian data. In the context of analysis of social sustainability, the relations between crimes of various kinds (murder, property-related crime, riots, left-wing insurgencies) and the alternative indicators of social unsustainability, such as inequality, poverty, social tension, and religious and social divisiveness, have been estimated using multivariate generalized method of moments (GMM).

Part II, on the other hand, addresses the greatest challenge that we are facing today, a fallout of entropy law: climate change, which is the case of greatest market failure in the economic history of mankind. We of course limit ourselves to the issue of choices left to India in sharing the responsibility of controlling climate change and the losses arising from it. We specifically elaborate on the test case of Third Industrial Revolution in India, which is based on moving away from generating electricity using fossil fuels and transitioning to a green energy regime that relies on new renewable energy–based electricity generation. Apart from showing how such a shift to renewables is doable for India, Chapters 6, 7, and 8 highlight the challenges that are to be faced for the realization of such transition. The following is the chapter-wise layout of the two parts of the book.

Chapter-wise Layout

Part I: Entropy Law and Revisiting Sustainable Development

In Part I, Chapter 1 begins by discussing the concept and intuitive explanation of entropy law and the issues of sustainability—economic, social, and environmental. We have already pointed out that the ultimate limiting factors of economically sustainable, socially sustainable, or environmentally sustainable processes of development are the entropy law and finite nature of our planetary ecosystems. However, the conditions of combining the social and the environmental sustainability of a growth process would require a theory of social policy of development to take care of social and ecological equity and justice for sustainability. This warrants a social investment perspective of development that, along with welfare statism, ensures the realization of the sustainable development as discussed. In this connection, in Chapter 1, I have reviewed the outline of history of welfare statism since the early years of the Swedish Welfare State in the last century (Cronert and Palme 2017; Morrel 2012; Myrdal and Myrdal 1934) according to which expenditure on social welfare schemes is not consumption but rather investment in the development of productivity of human resources by raising their level of well-being. We have traced how this was followed by the rise of neoliberalism since the depression of the 1970s due to the oil shocks. We again point to the return of realization of the importance of social investment perspective of economic growth since the turn of the century, particularly in the aftermath of the latest crisis of the last decade and the relevance of the millennium development goals (MDGs) in making the growth process inclusive as well as socially and environmentally resilient and durable.

This book then focuses on the indicators of social and environmental sustainability in Chapters 2 and 4. The issue of measuring social sustainability can be approached in two ways: (i) basing the indicators of the extent of deprivation of the people on the basic needs contributing towards unsustainability, or (ii) basing it on the extent of attainment of human capability and development, which would determine how far the people can have access to a decent life and contribute towards social sustainability of the growth process. The latter approach is in fact the obverse of the former.

We have reviewed in Chapter 2 the issues of income, poverty, and deprivation, and traced the relationship between deprivation—in both absolute and relative senses—and social tension conceived as social welfare loss according to some social welfare function that underlies any indicator of development. We have then analysed the state of poverty, inequality, and estimated social tension using the state-level data for India-level analysis in order to assess the social sustainability of the Indian economic system. The social tension measure as induced by the Gini coefficient measure of inequality as well as the one induced by the poverty gap as implicit in the income distribution of the different states within India have been separately estimated. Such estimates of measures of social tension have not been estimated and made readily available in other works on the subject in the Indian context. The chapter further goes on not only to estimate the correlation between the alternative tension measures and their basic determinants of poverty or inequality but to describe also the distribution of income and social tension across states to depict the developmental landscape of India.

In Chapter 3, we digress to focus further on the social sustainability aspect of development by analysing the inter-relationships among crime, deprivation, and resulting social tension in Indian context. The chapter estimates the relationship of violent crimes such as homicide, property-related crime—dacoity, burglary, and robbery—with economic inequality (calculated using the Gini coefficient) or poverty ratio and poverty-induced social tension along with other developmental variables such as state of education, infrastructural development, urbanization, and so on in the Indian context. Interestingly, it has been found that poverty is a more consequential factor than inequality in respect of these crimes, although the focus of existing literature in the context of other countries has been on the determining role of inequality and not poverty on such crimes. The analysis of the results have also pointed to the relative importance of developmental factors vis-à-vis deprivation in determining the rate of crime. Besides, we have also covered riots and left-wing extremism in our analysis of the Indian crime situation. We have used panel data and both simple correlation analysis as well as multiple regression model–based analysis using panel data in its different dimensions of use and treatment. The multiple regression analysis has used the GMM to avoid any endogeneity problem that is quite likely to arise in the analysis of such data. The analysis of the determinant social factors of riots considered the share of religious minorities, that of the Scheduled Castes/Scheduled Tribes (SC/ST) in the population, as well as religious polarization among others. The results in respect of the role of religious *polarization* are, in fact, of important significance in Indian policy context. This chapter is a major new contribution to the understanding of the social developmental aspect of the Indian economy from the viewpoint of economic analysis of crime and violence arising from deprivation, discrimination, and polarization in the case of riots.

In Chapter 4, we introduce the issue of multidimensional poverty and review its method of measurement and estimation. We next review the notion of a human development indicator as the obverse of such multidimensional deprivation in terms of attainment of human capability. On the other hand, Chapter 4 also takes up the issues and indicators of environmental sustainability. There have also developed two types of measures to capture environmental unsustainability or sustainability (as its obverse indicator) in the chapter. We have reviewed the concept of ecological footprint, which is a measure of stress caused by human demands on the ecosystem in terms of appropriation of land area of primary productivity expressed in some normalized standard unit. In view of the importance of the climate change issue, which has the largest share in this total measure of stress, the carbon dioxide (CO_2) emission as carbon footprint can, alternatively, also be taken as a measure of unsustainability of the ecosystem, with the human system as its subsystem. We have also reviewed, on the other hand, the environmental performance indicator, which indicates the extent of performance of environmental conservation and protection in terms of abatement of damage to the ecosystem, which are driven by human policy initiatives as an obverse of the footprint measure.

We finally try to develop an overall sustainable development indicator (OSDI) based on the three components of sustainability in Chapter 4. For the choice of indicator of the economic aspect of development we choose an inequality adjusted per capita income–based index as the indicator. Since we consider income as a separate component of development, we have chosen non-income human development index (HDI) as the social sustainability indicator to avoid any double counting and over emphasis on the income aspect of development. Lastly, so far as the environmental aspect of sustainability is concerned, we have taken an unweighted mean of the ecological footprint index (EFI) and the environmental performance index (EPI) as the overall environmental sustainability indicator, giving equal weightage to environmental stress and policy-induced environmental protection.

The OSDI has been finally chosen to be a geometric mean of these three indicators of development: economic, social, and environmental. We give our estimates of the OSDI for most of the countries, their rank as per this index, and also the difference between the OSDI and per capita income–based conventional indicator (without any inequality adjustment).

In order to round up the analysis of the different dimensions of sustainability, Chapter 5 finally points to the interactive nature of the different aspects of sustainability of development and investigates the interrelations among different components of the OSDI using cross-country data with the help of a simple econometric model of quadratic regression. These econometric results of the models throw light on the interdependence of the various facets of development or sustainability. Furthermore, the chapter more deeply analyses the dynamic links between human development, the natural environment, and economic growth. It has been developed and estimated as a simultaneous equation econometric model (mostly of two-stage least square type), the results being useful for understanding the relative roles of economic growth, human development, and environmental conservations in the sustainability of the development process. These models have been estimated at the global level using cross-country data at different time periods.

Part II: New Renewable Energy and Third Industrial Revolution

As already pointed out, the results of sustainability analysis of development economics as emanating from a common source of ecological limitations due to entropy law point to the need for a social policy perspective when making investments in the economy—for implementing the lessons learnt from the chapters in Part I of this book. While the chapters of Part I discusses at length the conceptual issues of the different dimensions of sustainability, Part II focuses on the same issues as arising in the context of energy supply and use, particularly for the development of the power and energy sector in India. It may be noted here that entropy law makes its impact felt immediately and, most importantly, through the working of the process of the energy sector of an economy. The law impacts a range of issues such as energy security, energy poverty and equity in energy distribution, energy conservation, and energy resource or fuel substitution, particularly in the power and the transport sector. Energy security is not only concerned with the adequacy of supply for fueling the macroeconomic growth process, but also with the provision of adequate clean fuel for households' consumption of energy for cooking, lighting, mobility, and communication. However, the biggest impact of entropy law has been through energy use and its large carbon footprint because of predominance of fossil fuel in the energy resource mix at both the Indian and global levels. A Third Industrial Revolution is now envisaged to bring about a big transition from the present fossil fuel–based high carbon regime to a new renewables-based low carbon regime of economy. To effect such transition, the policy measures call for a revolutionary change in technology—its philosophy and architecture—with reference to resource use, along with its attendant social, economic, and organizational transformations. The global history of the last almost 300 years have seen two major revolutionary changes based on new energy and communication technologies: first, coal- and steam-based mechanical energy (steam locomotives, steam-powered printing press, and so on) followed by the second revolution based on hydrocarbons and electricity, using much more efficient energy technologies. The latter further revolutionized both transportation and communication, accelerating the pace of economic development. The twentieth century saw further the waves of electronic and internet revolution riding on the wave of electricity driven revolution, which had far-reaching and wide impact on human life and society due to automated control and electronic power conditioning. This facilitated fast rise in the productivity of labor without further sharp rise in the entropy level. The Third Industrial Revolution, based on new renewable resources-based (wind, solar, biomass, and so on) energy and further electronic conditioning of energy transmission and distribution through smart grid development, is expected to change the face of our life and society by making it clean and green. The ultimate aim should be to moderate the rise of entropy to ensure a healthier and a peaceful world free of multidimensional poverty. Part II of this book deals with energy security and energy poverty, and transition from fossil fuel to green power regime in India.

Part II of the book, containing three chapters, in fact, illustrates the issues of sustainability as raised in the context of energy sector development in India. Chapter 6 in this part introduces the subject of energy in the context of sustainable development, pointing out how energy supply of various fuels are critical for energy security for supporting macroeconomic growth as well as social sustainability by meeting the basic needs of energy of the households for cooking, lighting, and so on.

The chapter also points to the large carbon footprint of most of the economies due to the use of fossil fuel as the major energy resource which poses the most serious threat ever faced by the humanity in terms of its consequence of global warming and climate change. The chapter also provides international comparison of India with China, USA, and the world as a whole in respect of composition, pattern of primary energy use, fuel access to clean cooking energy and access to electricity for the households of the developing countries. It also points to the comparative over all measures of energy security, energy dependence, and energy efficiency in terms of a few broad indicators for a limited number of countries.

Chapter 6 further discusses energy poverty in the Indian context with reference to the cooking and lighting needs of the household sector and provides some results based on the analysis of National Sample Survey (NSS) household level data. This gives some insight in the state of equity in the distribution of energy in India.

However, as an introductory background to the larger issues of energy and climate change in the following chapters, the discussions in Chapter 6 point to the difference in perspectives of the developed and the developing countries in respect of visualizing the relation between inclusive economic growth and climate control. It argues to show how the issue of growth in the poor countries for poverty removal and that of control of climate change can have important complementariness instead of necessarily conflicting with each other. Similarly it also argues the use of fossil fuel and those of new renewables need not be viewed as competing options and may have complementarities in inter-temporal use under appropriate condition. The use of fossil fuel can support, if not accelerate economic growth immediately, and can give rise to the generation of substantive volume of Hotelling's resource rent. The state can mobilize such resource rents and deposit them in a climate fund for subsequent use in developing the backstop technologies, such as new renewables-based power development—wind, solar, biomass and micro-hydel power, including the related R&D activities. The latter is of critical importance not only for the development of technologies of power generation, but also for the development of a smart grid, which can only ensure electronic power conditioning for transmission and distribution. Considering the coordination required for matching of load demand and supply from generators that are widely dispersed spatially in a renewables-based regime, where both supply of energy resources for power generation and load demand are fluctuating and intermittent in nature, the development of such a smart grid becomes imperative.

Since the book intends to cover the sustainability issue of energy development in the context of power sector of India, Chapter 7 describes both the primary energy resource mix and the technology-wise gross generation mix of electrical energy in India as in 2015–16. It also describes in details the potential of all the renewable energy resources and carbon-free nuclear resources in terms of power generation capacity. It also points out the limitation of storage hydro and nuclear power in the Indian geological and political economic context. So far as the carbon-free solar and wind power potentials are concerned, the chapter explains the basis of the estimates of the new power capacity potentials and also provides the power generated utilizing these resources and the cumulative capacity built till 2012. These comparative figures indicate the huge potential of new capacity creation in future for each of such technology-based power. The chapter also discusses the natural resource requirement of these new renewables-based technologies on the one hand and gives comparative estimates of environmental cost and the true total resource cost for coal thermal power on the other. It also provides the technology-wise structure of power capacities as in India (2014–15) on the base of which the following Chapter 8 provides the projections of alternative power energy scenarios of India in the time horizon up to 2041–42.

The Chapter 8 provides model-based technology-wise projections of the following items for the different scenarios for the time horizon of 2021–22, 2031–32 and 2041–42 with 2014–15 as base:

a. gross generation of electrical energy;
b. capacity requirement for each type of resource based technology;
c. financial resource requirement for additional capacity build up for the different time horizons;
d. what resource rent can be generated from the use of fossil fuels; and
e. CO_2 emissions for the fossil fuel uses.

The model has been simulated on the basis of the alternative assumptions of policy-forced conservation of electrical energy by way of technical change, and the alternative rates of introduction of new renewables technologies replacing mainly coal thermal power. The chapter defines four scenarios of simulation including one of business as usual (BAU), the comparison with which would indicate relative benefit and financial resource cost of fuel substitution. Besides, the results would also show how the fossil fuel resource rents can suffice the financing of development of capacities of the new renewables-based technology in future for the time horizon. The chapter also gives the background and interpretation of the existing coal cess and analyse its adequacy for the financial resource requirement of building up new capacity for renewables over the time horizon of our period of future projection. Besides these, the chapter also gives comparative assessment of results of this study and those of other studies on strategies of Low Carbon economic Growth of India, particularly with reference to the Planning Commission report of 2014(b).

Finally, in Chapter 8, we have concluded by summarizing what big-bang changes are required to meet the challenges of development for transitioning from a fossil fuel to a new renewables-based power system in India. Social perspective of investment would in fact require accommodating policy measures required for changes. We have elaborated here the requirements of development of technology for the storage of electric power, development of flexibility in operations of thermal technologies for ramping up and down the intensity of generation, and of smart grid development. We have also elucidated what kind of financial support and human resource development measures may have to be arranged within the framework of social perspective of investment for facilitating the revolutionary development of eco-efficiency of India's economic system from the impending Third Industrial Revolution.

Concluding Observations

Finally in the epilogue of the book, the author argues for using consumption, and not production, as the basis for sharing responsibility of global emission control in the interest of its effectiveness and equity. This would require policies to drive re-composition of aggregate consumption depending on the emission intensities of the different goods and services in order to reduce the aggregate emission. This would also lead to philosophical issues regarding the value system on which the concept of well-being is to be founded and normative consumption to be decided for pollution control. The book ends by pointing to the necessity of a sufficiency theory of social well-being to guide development aiming at the goal of overall achievement of a qualitatively improved socio-economic system based on the consideration of all the three major aspects of development as highlighted in the book, rather than a larger one.

PART I

ENTROPY LAW AND REVISITING SUSTAINABLE DEVELOPMENT

Disorder increases with time because we measure time in the direction in which disorder increases.

—Stephen Hawking
(*A Brief History of Time*)

Entropy Law, Social Sustainability, and Development Policy

Entropy Law and Sustainability

Chapter 1 begins by discussing the concept and intuitive explanation of entropy law and shows how it plays a unifying role in the sustainability of the processes of development—economic, social, and environmental. The massive challenge in respect of sustainability that we are facing today arises fundamentally from the fact that we are extracting resources— natural as well as human/social—from a finite pool of a closed system, causing increasing disorder or rise in entropy of the resource system. It is the rate of outflow of resources from the ecosystem to the economic system and the return flow of waste that today substantively exceeds the natural environment's capacity to provide the respective resource regeneration and waste absorption services per unit of time, rendering the process of economic growth unsustainable in the long run.

The chapter further shows how the conditions of combining social and environmental sustainability of a growth process would require a theory of social policy of development to take care of social and ecological equity or justice. This warrants a social investment perspective of development along the lines of welfare statism for the realization of sustainable development. In this context, the outline in this chapter traces the history of welfare statism since the early years of the Swedish welfare state in the last century, which was followed by eras of Keynesianism, and neoliberalism, and finally returned to the realization of the importance of a social investment perspective of economic growth in the interest of social and environmental inclusiveness and resilience.

Understanding Entropy, Economic Processes, and Sustainability

The role of entropy law and the finiteness of our planetary ecosystem in the economic processes of development and their wide-ranging impact on our society and economy are fundamental, but were neglected for a long time by most mainstream economists. It was Georgescu-Roesen (1971) who first pointed out in his book *Entropy Law and Economic Processes* the unsustainability of indefinite expansion of an economic system due to the role of entropy law. Ayres (1978), Cleveland (1987), Daly (1973; 1991), Brown (2001), Dasgupta (2001), Dasgupta and Maeler (2000), Costanza (1991), Costanza and Daly (1987), Karl Goran-Maeler (1991), and others followed the theme of this pioneering work by further exploring the scope of influence of the law and its impact in greater detail through both theoretical and applied works. These volumes have made us conscious of the consequences of entropy law in adversely affecting the flow of resources from the natural ecosystem to the economy, as also the flowing back of waste from the economy to the ecosystem. The adverse impacts of the law can, however, be abated to some extent if the strategies and policies of growth and development take these flows of resources into account. Many of the stories from history about the discovery of new continents and countries, wars and migration, and colonization are believed to have resulted from the search for resources and the scramble for their ownership by their physical appropriation due to the fundamental limitedness of the eco-services. The rude shock that global capitalism had suffered from the two oil crises of the 1970s gave rise to a sense of deep concern among economists regarding the exhaustibility of all resources. The examples of the intensification of conflict between economy and ecosystem are now abundant in various forms, such as global climate change, dust storms in China, burning rainforests in Indonesia, collapsing fisheries in the North Sea, falling crop yield in Africa, a lowering of the water table in India, and desertification in various parts of the world. All these can be traced to the unsustainably growing demand on the ecosystem, causing overharvesting of nature's resources by the global economy.

In this context, some basic questions as well as their answers are posed below to explain how entropy fundamentally affects economic processes and sustainability.

What Is the Notion of Entropy and How Are Economic Processes Related to the Operation of Entropy Law?

Entropy is a concept that places a finite limit on the extent to which resources can be used in any closed system. In contrast, mainstream economics mostly neglect the problem, assuming that only labour, capital, and technology are essential and that the required energy and material resources could be simply drawn indefinitely from the natural environment to give us more of our wants, without cost. Unfortunately, we now know that this is not the case: this is because of the fundamental effect of entropy, from the second law of thermodynamics in physics, which affects all economic production processes.

In the natural ecosystem or in the human economy, there are innumerable processes of change that are continuously taking place. In the most generalized sense, the concept of entropy evolved to capture the irreversibility of such changes. A system is characterized by the existence of some energy contained in it—bio-physical particles with their chemical properties and a level of entropy. Thermodynamics, in fact, is the science of energy, which studies how heat and movement convert into each other in such a system and enables us to study the level of efficiency with which energy can do useful mechanical work. The energy of a given system, while interacting with the chemical properties of the particles, drives mechanical transformation, which can be measured in terms of work done. The efficiency of such transformation depends on the orderliness of the molecular structure of the particles. The performance process of such mechanical work, however, results in a break in the order of the molecular structure of particles of matter and energy resources such that it involves irreversible change, causing dissipation of the original energy as waste heat, which vastly reduces the scope of efficiency (even bringing it down to zero) in further doing such work. In an isolated system there is no inflow or outflow of material. As entropy can be taken to represent the degree of disorder of the molecular structure of the particles of material and energy resources in the system, it represents the potential ability or efficiency of doing work at any given state of the system.

In the simplest terms, entropy can alternatively be defined as a measure of bound or unavailable energy in a closed thermodynamic system. Energy exists in two qualitative states—available or free energy, which human beings can command for use, and bound energy, which is unavailable or which man cannot access for use. The chemical energy contained in a litre of oil, which can be transformed into heat to do some mechanical work is free energy, while the fantastic heat energy contained in the hydrogen content of sea water is bound energy. When a piece of coal or a litre of oil is burnt, the initial free energy (often simply called energy) gets transformed into heat energy, gases such as CO_2 and nitric oxide, and some unburnt particles as well, which are all wastes for the purpose of rendering similar energy service. In such use, the initial energy gets partly transformed into work done and the remaining part gets dissipated as useless waste heat when the work is completed; and the system reaches a new equilibrium, making such a process of change irreversible. Entropy is the measure of this disorder of the structure of a material or energy resource, which therefore attains its maximum at the new equilibrium. The second law of thermodynamics characterizes such transformation of energy and matter as unidirectional, the level of entropy always strictly increasing in an irreversible transformation and remaining constant in a reversible transformation. This concept of disorder or entropy fits the description of use of non-energy materials as well in production processes. For example, iron ore is an ordered structure of low-entropy material with reference to the distribution or concentration of the basic element, Fe, in the ore.

As there exists a bio-physical foundation of all production activities, low-entropy natural resources are inevitably required in all such processes as inputs, and their use is inevitably entropic. Abiotic material resources such as iron ore, bauxite, or copper would be transformed into a product of a more ordered structure, such as steel, aluminium, or copper sheets with even lower entropy, in order to be consumed. However, the concerned metallic conversion process uses a large amount of low-entropy energy and other resources such as fluxing and refining materials, which can end up as high-entropy chaotically dissipated materials and waste heat of a much higher disorder. The aggregate effect would be that the stock of low-entropy material/energy would go down and the proportion of high entropy would go up in the concerned system. The use of biotic resources in the production process can also be similarly shown to be entropic. And finally, any use of output of the production process for consumption or capital use would involve degradation due to the gradual dissipation of the basic constituent elements of the material product compound into higher disorder in their structural forms in the transformed state at the end of their life cycle. Such entropic conceptualization of economic processes is at the root of the resource and energy crisis facing the world today. The rising entropy with the indiscriminate use of energy and material resources explains the reality of development, which is confronted with significant constraints both in terms of natural and technical processes.

How Does Entropy Affect Biological Processes?

The consumption of food by humans, like any other species, also involves movement along the entropy gradient; low-entropy food energy leaves the organism in the form of degraded heat and other body wastes after providing the energy for the running of the body metabolism and biomass growth through reproduction. Any living organism with a highly ordered and complex structure requires continuous throughput of low-entropy energy and nutrient inputs through food, water, and oxygen to maintain its internal order and low-entropy character. If these life-support supplies are stopped, the body of any organism would degenerate into an increasingly disordered state, ending with its death and subsequently its decomposition.

How Does Entropy Apply to an Economic System and Its Sustainability?

An economic system is also highly ordered and complex, with its organic structure comprising innumerable firms and households. The flow of labour services from households to firms and that of produced goods and services from firms to households describes the interrelationship among the components of the organic structure of an economy. For an economy's metabolic activities—namely, production and consumption—to be carried out repeatedly, the organism of the economic system would require continuous throughput of low-entropy material-cum-energy resources from the ecosystem and the release of high-entropy material-cum-energy wastes to be absorbed by the ecosystems. In case of stoppage of supply of low-entropy resources from nature, the functioning of the economic system would also come to a halt. The human economy is a subsystem of the global ecosystem; its function and growth would thus contribute to the increasing scarcity of low-entropy matter and energy resources for the economic system. This pessimism rests on the presumption that our planet is a finite place, and a materially non-growing system.

Does the Sun's Energy Not Provide Us an Inexhaustible Source of Energy and Resources from Outside?

It is entirely correct that earth does not represent a strictly closed or isolated thermodynamic system since the sun's energy that is received by it is partly absorbed in the earth's biosphere and its terrestrial and atmospheric systems and partly reflected back into outer space. However, there are definite limits to its use in terms of human time scales and pace of use.

Part of the flow of solar energy reaching the biosphere gets transformed into chemically bonded energy through photosynthesis, which further flows through the various plants and animal life forms along the food chain, contributing to the maintenance and growth of their biomass stock. The economic system uses many biotic resources (low entropy) for food as well as non-food uses (such as biomass fuel, agro-based or forestry-based raw materials for industries, base for organic chemicals, and so on). Most of these biotic resources are regenerated and, therefore, renewable in the human time scale.

However, while a share of 30 per cent of solar energy reaching the earth gets reflected back into outer space, it is only a meagre 0.8 per cent of such energy that is converted into chemical bond energy. The balance of solar energy generates heat energy, which is partly utilized in the processes of evaporation and precipitation and in driving the flow of winds, waves, river flows, ocean currents, and so on. The climate system and the flow of water resources, which provide crucial life support to the biosphere, are thus essentially driven by solar energy. The flow of hydro-energy resources and water resources as used for non-energy purposes in the economic system are also derivatives of solar energy flows and renewables. At any given time and place the availability of low-entropy renewable resources—biomass, hydro-potential or wind potential, tidal waves and so on—would, on the one hand, be obtained as transformations of the basic low-entropy energy resources as illustrated earlier, but, on the other hand, would obviously be limited by the limited nature of solar energy flow reaching per unit of the earth's surface area. If the economic system uses these resources at a rate higher than their rates of regeneration by nature, there will be depletion in the stocks of the renewable resources. The harvesting of forest biomass at a rate higher than the rate of regeneration of plant biomass would, for example, cause deforestation. Or, the extraction of ground water at a rate higher than that of its recharging would result in the mining of the aquifer. The fixed rate of flow of solar energy thus tends to limit the rate of use of renewable resources on a sustained basis. It is again the second law of thermodynamics that sets a constraint on the energy potential or the availability of energy services that can be obtained from the use of renewable energy or material resources, whose entropy will go up uni-directionally after their use in the given space and time coordinates.

Apart from regenerating biotic resources, the flow of solar energy also drives the biogeochemical cycles of various nutrient elements in the biosphere. The functioning of our ecosystems indicates how the basic atomic elements of any material resources such as carbon, oxygen, nitrogen, sulphur, phosphorous, and so on, which are essential for life support, are transferred through the food chain from the abiotic environment to living organisms, only to flow back again from the biotic to the abiotic environments through the process of biotic waste disposal. Any biodegradable waste of the economic system gets transformed into resources in the course of such interactive processes between organisms and their abiotic environment through such cycles, which are often interconnected. Through the functioning of ecological laws and the operation of these cycles, nature's resources are regenerated and again made available at lower entropy. For example, photosynthesis fixes CO_2 from the atmosphere, which was possibly released earlier as waste from biomass burning in the economic system, or dead and decomposing plant or animal biomass recreates the top soil of land through decomposition and weathering, processes which are bio-chemically interactive with the sands and rock particles in a given climatic condition. The biogeochemical cycles combined with the low-entropy energy flow facilitate the regeneration of low-entropy resources in the human time scale by converting waste arising from economic processes into chemical compounds with a much lower disorder or entropy in their molecular structures in order to provide valuable services to the ecosystems.

However, if the waste is not biodegradable, it will be degraded and rendered harmless or transformed into new resources only slowly through the weathering process as driven again by the flow of solar energy and induced transformations in the ecosystems. Such processes may entail slow chemical transformations through interaction with the environment over a long period, again involving a fresh flow of low-entropy energy resources. For example, hazardous chemical waste, such as manmade compounds, radioactive waste, and so on may require thousands of years to degrade in the natural environment. The biogeochemical processes that occur on the earth may even be able to regenerate some of the apparently non-renewable resources such as oil, coal, or some mineral-resource compounds at low entropy, but only on a geological time scale involving the elapsing of millions of years from this point.

Cosmology, Entropy, and the Role of Time

One may, however, feel that nature's ability to regenerate low-entropy resources by degrading high-entropy economic waste implies a reversal of the second law of thermodynamics. This impression is incorrect since all these processes of regeneration as indicated earlier involve enormous use of low-entropy solar radiation energy from outer space directly or indirectly. One should remember that the earth is not thermodynamically a closed system and is continuously receiving low-entropy solar radiation energy in the form of electromagnetic waves. Besides, from the cosmological point of view, the solar process of the continuous nuclear fusion, transforming hydrogen into helium and in the process generating radiant (light) energy is itself highly entropic. In the aggregate effect, entropy law is not found to be violated.

The degradation of the waste compounds and regeneration of resources, however, requires time. For any ecosystem, there are upper limits on the time rate of energy flow, the movement of basic chemical elements along the pathways of various nutrient cycles, as well as on the weathering process. There is also a certain indeterminacy in the precise values of these speeds of flows or movements of cycles because of the various degrees of freedom regarding the choice of pathways in the movement of nutrient elements. The rate at which nature can regenerate and supply resources, however, varies from resource to resource and from place to place. The rate at which nature absorbs waste would also vary from one waste compound to another. The existence of an upper limit of the maximum time rate or speed at which nature can absorb waste or supply a given resource by way of regeneration through ecological processes is itself an expression of consequence of entropy law, which affects the time rate of efficiency of the energy of our system. The time rates of demand for eco-services of resource supply and waste absorption through ecological processes is often far exceeded by the time rates of the same as required by the development processes of today's growing economies. This mismatch between the two time rates of regeneration (supply) of low-entropy resources or of degradation (absorption) of high-entropy waste as warranted by ecological processes that are driven by entropy law and the economic developmental process lies at the root of the environmental and resource crisis and of the problem of sustainable development. A resource crisis arises if the rate of regeneration of low-entropy resources falls short of the required flow of resources from the ecosystem to the economic system, rendering the pre-existing growth process unsustainable. If the rate of generation of high-entropy waste, on the other hand, exceeds the rate of absorption of waste by nature per unit of time, the balance of high-entropy waste would be deposited in the ecosystem as pollutant. The stock of the latter would accumulate in the ecosystem and such accumulating stock would adversely affect the primary productivity of the natural economic system, human health, and the regenerative function of nature, all of which characterize economic growth or development.

Can Human Knowledge and Technological Change Not Solve the Problem of Entropy?

One may raise the question of whether the growth of human knowledge and technological progress can reverse the effects of entropy law and delink economic growth and rise of entropy. Technical progress can moderate the rise of entropy as induced by an economic activity carried out at a given level by efficiently using materials and energy resources and reducing the rate of waste generation. However, completely delinking the two would mean that economic growth can be accelerated indefinitely without requiring any additional resources or ecosystem services. This would mean that the requirement of material/energy resource per unit of output of the gross domestic product (GDP) or income would decline over time with indefinite technical progress and tend to zero in the limit. This would imply a complete reversibility of the process of change in the domain of energetics due to the accumulation of technical knowledge, which has been unreal at every stage of human history. In view of the fact that this is unreal even as a limiting case assumption and that resource and environmental crises are very real challenges today, such presumption regarding the total reversibility of the entropic process by the growth of knowledge becomes untenable.

What, however, is real, as observed in history, is that humans have always had to operate within ecological limits—the efficiency with which resources are used to contribute to human well-being—which themselves have been changing over time due to the growth of human knowledge and subsequent technological and institutional changes. Sustainability would thus require such pace, structure, and institutional organization of growth that the scale of economy does not surpass the carrying capacity of the economy, which itself can be augmented by human intervention. We interpret technical change and growth of knowledge as entropy-moderating forces, which also have to be driven by investment in education, research and development (R&D), and by improving the institutional structure, all of which involves use of low-entropy resources.

We also characterize human interventions by way of changes of the knowledge base or operational practices, or by way of observation, monitoring for data collection, and information processing, all of which would contribute to the reduction of the uncertainty in the productivity conditions of an economic system. Such interventions and moves are also to be considered as entropy-reducing ones, involving again, in turn, the use of fresh low-entropy resources. Information is itself a low-entropy resource that would raise the efficiency of the economic system by improving the orderliness of the molecular structure of its material and resource components, its institutional or organizational structures with reference to the predictability of an event, as well as that of economic and energy efficiency. Sustainability of development would thus depend on, among other things, access to the low-entropy resource of information, which would have the effect of reducing uncertainty as well as promoting technological progress.

Is the Concept of Entropy Applicable to Social Disorder and Sustainability?

Finally, the concept of entropy can be applied in the extended field of analysis of the socio-economic sustainability of development. While economic growth is the result of the use of increasing amount of low-entropy energy and material resources, the quality of growth would depend on the equity aspect of growth, its inclusiveness, and inequality in the distribution of the benefit of growth. If the inequality and poverty are prevalent, the people are likely to suffer from inadequate opportunities of human development, access to job opportunities, and the subsistence (poverty) basket of consumption, resulting in a poor quality of life due to hunger, malnutrition, disease, illiteracy, poverty, and destitution. All these would give rise to social tension, crime, violence, and political and economic restlessness. Such socio-economic conditions would lead to social disruption, causing people to suffer from socio-economic disorder, raising the entropy level of the social state and hence leading to disorder. This would adversely affect peace and social cohesiveness in the economy and would affect social productivity in terms of development of human well-being from a given level of production using low-entropy physical energy and resources. This would, therefore, have an adverse impact on the sustainability of the development process. In such a situation, the restoration of social sustainability would warrant policy intervention for moderating the rise of such entropy due to inequality and deprivation. The concept of entropy is thus relevant not only to characterize the sustainability of economic growth but also the environmental equilibrium in terms of balance in the ecosystem such that the risk of environmental collapse is eliminated, on the one hand, and social disruption due to serious inequality in the distribution of the benefit of growth is avoided, on the other.

Issues of Sustainable Development

While the central theme of developmental economics has been the development of the material well-being of people and the sustainability of its process, the subject as it has developed has been broadly concerned with the following three sets of issues.

First, since the improvement of material well-being of society depends on the growth of a country's GDP—the total volume of final goods and services—such development will be related to macroeconomic policies and, hence, points to their importance when it comes to the sustainability of economic growth.

Second, there is an important social aspect of production and distribution of the benefits of development. This, however, follows from the social organization of production, which is carried out by the various stakeholders through their engagement in the production processes, mainly as suppliers of labour, capital infrastructure, and other public good services, the supply of the latter being entrusted with the government. Such engagement of stakeholders also determines the rule of sharing of the social product of the GDP among the different socio-economic classes of a society. These would thus point to the critical importance of the issues of employment, income distribution, and a whole range of social securities, which would characterize the equity of the development process.

Finally, there is a much bigger issue in the context of production and growth in view of the interdependence and interactive relationship between the human economy and our natural ecosystems, as already discussed. As any production process has a bio-physical foundation and involves the entropic use of various eco-services, the issues of sustainable economic growth takes on critical importance due to the finite limit of our ecosystems when it comes to supporting our growing demand of natural resources on the one hand and the eco-services of absorption of wastes on the other.

While the concept of sustainable development has become popular mainly in the context of environmental sustainability of economic processes since the last quarter of the twentieth century, the concept of sustainability has now assumed a much wider applicability and different meanings in the context of each of the three aspects of the development process outlined earlier. The first aspect of development has been concerned with the macroeconomic sustainability of economic growth while the second aspect has dealt with the social and political sustainability of an economic order. The third aspect has focused on environmental sustainability, which is crucial for ensuring sustained flow of eco-services from nature to provide support to the growing economic system in the long run. In the literature of developmental economics, different traditions have grown over time, which have focused on different objectives, contents, instruments, and strategies of development that centre on those alternative aspects of development. However, all such traditions admit that the ultimate concern of development is sustained improvement of the state of human well-being over time, whose benefit should be equitably shared by all segments of society, while simultaneously ensuring that the state of the ecosystem remains in equilibrium. Nevertheless, it is a fact that the propagators of these different traditions have been driven by different conceptual approaches, ideologies, and world views and therefore ended up with different indicators of development and development policies as follows.

Wealth Maximization Approach

The prime focus of macroeconomic sustainability has been the growth of aggregate value of production and accumulation of capital and per capita income, according to the standard literature of neoclassical growth theory. It is, in fact, primarily preoccupied with commodity production, opulence, and financial success and not directly with the distribution of income and wealth or what growth does to the humans through its impact on the natural environment.

The concept of wealth here comprises mainly man-made capital, which includes plants and machinery, and structures. It also encompasses knowledge and know-how created by humans with patent-generating potential (though not all are patented), among others. The dynamic models in such a context have focused on the behaviour of and the interrelationship among the variables representing the macroeconomic fundamentals of an open economy in a globalized world, such as output, income, savings, investment, employment and wages, prices and interest rate, fiscal deficits, balance of payments and financial capital flows, stability of the currency exchange rate, and so on. The concern has, of course, been not only the growth but also the stability of the macroeconomic behaviour. It has therefore focused on the growth of scale of an economy and ended up with per capita national income and savings rate (as share of the GDP or the gross national product [GNP]) as the indicators of level of development and the key drivers of the pace of development. The core concern of macroeconomic sustainability has centred on macroeconomic growth and the stability of output, employment, and prices, along with budgetary and current account balances as part of fundamentals of the determinants of growth and stability.

With reference to the explicit issue of the equity of development, such a wealth-maximizing approach presumes that issues of distribution would be addressed better by societies with higher income and wealth because of their greater ability to mobilize resources by fiscal and other measures for redistribution and financing poverty alleviation through various welfare measures, including spending on social sectors of healthcare, education, child and women's development, and so on.

As environmental protection and its upgradation is again a public service, this school of thought would argue that higher mobilization of public finance resources accompanying higher growth would better facilitate the provision of such environmental service for public good. Besides, with growth in per capita income of a society, the demand for higher environmental services goes up since such services may be considered to be income elastic. This would result in higher environmental standards and environmental regulatory legislation, on the one hand, and a higher willingness to pay for environmental services by the people, on the other. These may also explain the so-called Environmental Kuznets curve hypothesis (EKC) and thereby, the growth-oriented explanation or advocacy of environmental conservation.

Human Development and Capability Approach

The social sustainability of a development process essentially depends on the social acceptability of the pre-existing economic order and on the equity of the development process. The right of the people to have access to a decent life is of critical importance for the social sustainability of the development process. With the high level of deprivation of basic needs in the absence of such freedom, resulting in poverty and destitution, illiteracy, disease, and malnutrition (as it is the reality of many African and Asian countries), the major priority of development would be their alleviations and provision of the basic minimum needs. This is also important for the maintenance of social equilibrium and stability of the social order through the lowering of tension, crime, violence, and terror, which arise out of such deprivation. However, the fundamental and permanent solution to this problem of lack of freedom to access a decent life lies in the development of human capability through attainment of education, health, and earning capabilities. The capabilities are, in fact, the endowments of individuals, including their personal characteristics such as educational and health attainments, which define the set of opportunities or options to which they can have access in their lifetime.

The focus of this approach to development is thus on intra-generational as well as inter-generational equity, the expansion of peoples' capabilities, and on the universalism that makes neglect or discrimination against any particular segment of population unacceptable (Anand and Sen 2000). The conceptual approach has led to the emergence of the capability-cum-human-development approach of development and to the formalization of certain indices of development such as the HDI and the gender-related development index.

Besides, at the macroeconomic level, the major source of long-run growth is the development of human skill and ability to innovate and absorb new technologies. As a result, the focus of this approach has been on the development of human resources and the formation of human capital. Nevertheless, it does not conceive humans merely as members of the human species population who are convertible into human capital by investment in education and health, but as ends in themselves. The value of humans as per the conception of human capital would only be as being instrumental to the process of development. On the other hand, the human development approach views human beings as ends in themselves with intrinsic value.

Finally, it is also expected that with higher education and capability, people will have greater freedom of access to clean air, water, and other household-level living conditions, such as sanitation and congestion. The people of a society are also likely to develop an enlightened preference structure, which shifts in favour of eco-friendly products, ecologically sustainable production processes, and higher environmental standards, which would take care of at least some of the major environmental concerns of development.

Environmental Sustainability Approach

This approach, as already pointed out, focuses on the interactive relationship between nature and economy through material balances and the entropic nature of production processes and emphasizes the requirement of the pattern of inter-temporal resource use to ensure inter-generational equity in the form of non-declining social well-being over generations. It underlines the importance of conservation of the environmental resource base so that the scale of an economy, its composition, and organization do not lead to consequences that tend to violate the carrying capacity of the natural environment and do not generate externalities that would adversely affect the well-being of future generations.

There are two schools of thought in interpreting the nature–economy relationship and the long-run view of a policy approach of sustainability.

- The Environmental Economics Approach
- The Ecological Economics Approach

The Environmental Economics Approach

Environmental and resource economics uses the neoclassical method and approach of analysis of resource allocation and visualizes the environmental resource allocation problem as mainly originating from the scarcity of natural resources, pollution externalities, *ill-defined property rights* on ecosystem resources, and market failure due to the *public good or common property character* of many of the environmental services. This has developed as an extension of applied welfare economics with attempts at internalization of environmental externalities.

The basic assumptions of neoclassical economics with reference to the relationship between the economy and the natural environment is that the ecosystem is a subsystem of the economy as it is merely an *extractive and waste disposal sector*. This branch and school of thought thus visualizes the natural environment as a sector and part of the economy and extends the scope of inter-sectoral allocations of resources by solving for the optimal level of pollution control and regulation along with other inter-sectoral allocation of scarce resources in its general equilibrium setting of analysis. In this task of valuation of environmental service, it becomes inevitable to ascertain the *benefit of pollution control and resource conservation* or, equivalently, the cost of damage on account of the environmental losses in the absence of such regulation.

The thrust of such an analytic approach has therefore been to find out the shadow prices of all kind of environmental resources and to invent market-based instruments as supplemented by other regulatory measures to ensure the Pareto efficiency of all kinds of resource allocations, including environmental ones. The problem of valuation of non-market eco-services has been the most challenging one that researchers have mainly addressed in the field and required some interdisciplinary inputs for meeting the challenges.

Long-run discussions on these issues have been capital-theoretic extensions of the problems of the dynamic resource allocation model, where natural capital is included in the capital base with its distinct dynamics characterized by ecological conditions for estimating the costs of growth. This has essentially been an extension of the neoclassical growth theory, allowing the different degrees of substitutability between natural capital and environmental capital, and defining the notion of social well-being over time (Arrow et al. 2004; Dasgupta 2001; Dasgupta and Mäler 2000; Hartwick 1977; Solow 1986, 1991). The new growth theory also explores the conditions of viability of steady state growth along with maintaining ecosystems in equilibrium, so that there is no decline in the stock of reserves and the carrying capacity.

The Ecological Economics Approach

Ecological economics views the entire problem from a different perspective as compared to that of neoclassical environmental economics. It views the human economy as constituting a subsystem of a larger planetary ecosystem defining the domain of nature and not the other way round, as conceived by the neoclassicals in the context of resource allocation. The total environmental system of the planet is finite, non-growing, and materially closed except for solar energy flow, which, to our planet, is also finite and non-growing per unit of time. With economic growth, the empty world of the pre-Industrial Revolution ecosystem has now become almost a full or a congested world with economic activities and population filling up the eco-space (Daly 1991, 1999).

The human subsystem with such growth is now appropriating almost the entirety of the environmental capital providing eco-services, leaving very limited natural resources and other natural capital services for the other species and for the conservation of biodiversity of the planet. This problem of overuse of natural resources has led to so much growth of the ecological footprint in human economic activities that it has now exceeded the bio-capacity of the planet, resulting in erosion of this bio-capacity. This has led to a rapid loss of biodiversity and the rising trend of the carbon footprint component in the ecological footprint threatening climate change. Ecological economics, therefore, focuses on the limits to scale and estimation of costs of growth in terms of loss of natural resources and environmental capacity and derives the measure of true accumulation of wealth and well-being of the people of a nation after taking care of costs of depletion and degradation of the natural capital and the ecosystem. This leads us to the finding of the opportunity cost of development in terms of loss of ecosystem resources, if not its regenerative capacity. Such cost assessment leads us back to the issue of evaluation of non-traded eco-services in terms of monetization. If we don't use the neoclassical apparatus of such evaluation, we can possibly end up with a final assessment in terms of trade-offs between gains and losses in the two systems of the economy and natural environment expressed in hybrid units. This would, of course, require the use of a multidisciplinary methodology to arrive at these trade-offs in hybrid units. However, the actual policy decision will have to be still resolved and the problem of choice among the options of development and environmental conservation may have to be left to the decision-makers within the political system of a nation.

Interdependences among the Dimensions of Development and Sustainability

As we have seen earlier, there are three aspects of development— economic, social, and environmental. For all three aspects, the issue of sustainability, thus, arises for reasons imputable to entropy law. The scarcity of low-entropy natural resources, the monopolistic or oligopolistic nature of their markets, and the uncertain climate and agrarian production and supplies, often lead to volatile prices of primary commodities. The impact of such price volatility gets propagated through the inter-sectoral linkages across various product and factor markets resulting in uncertainties in prices and business prospects. These, in turn, are likely to adversely affect investment, growth, employment, and market as well as the fiscal stability of a country. Macroeconomic limits to growth and economic instability in a market-driven economic system thus characterizes the unsustainability of the development process as emanating from entropy law. Such an economic state, if leading to prolonged stagnation or increasing instability, is bound to give rise to political and social tensions, which would threaten the sustainability of the political and economic order of a society. The source of social tension is not merely the limited prospect of growth but also its implications in respect of sharing of the limited benefit, say, in terms of pace of poverty alleviation and so on, in developing countries. The social sustainability of the development process has been primarily concerned with the participation of people of all economic and social classes in the development process for ensuring the equitable sharing of the benefit of economic growth.

In view of the long-run social and economic implications of entropy law as imposing ecological limits on economic development, the report to the Club of Rome (Meadows et al. 1972), with the help of a simulation model, tried to project how the limited nature of resources would impose limits to the growth of the global economy. In view of such a prediction, the Bruntland Commission in its report in 1987, titled 'Our Common Future', defined sustainable development as one where the present generation, with the help of technologies and operational practices, uses all available resources of an economy in such a way that at the end of the process, there are enough resources remaining to allow the next generation to have access to the opportunities of attaining at least the same level of social well-being. The focus of the Bruntland Commission was thus on the inter-generational distributional equity and on inter-temporal distribution of social well-being. However, the constraint of resources also creates a problem of intra-generational equity in the distribution of ownership of current resources and in sharing the current benefits of economic growth or development through the use of these resources. It is often a fact that a highly disproportionate quantity of resources are often appropriated by some limited section of the society while the remaining vast majority of the population, particularly in overpopulated African and Asian countries, suffer from huge deprivation. This deprivation can be absolute or relative. In the former case, people are deprived of the subsistence or the poverty-line basket of consumption and as a result, suffer from poverty, hunger, malnutrition, disease, illiteracy, and low human development. However, even if people are not poor and not apparently suffering from deprivation of the subsistence level of consumption there may be relative deprivation, where the relatively poor suffer from inequality arising from externalities of the consumption effect. In either case of deprivation, an economy or society suffers from welfare loss, which happens to be the source of social tension. If the magnitude of such social tension exceeds some threshold level (which varies from society to society depending on social norms of behaviour and culture), social disruption may take place, unfolding itself in the form of violent crimes ranging from homicide, property-related crimes such as dacoity, burglary and robbery, riots, left-wing extremism, among other problems in a country such as India. Often, economic factors get compounded with social factors of discrimination on the basis of religion, caste, and other divisive forces in such countries, which may tend to polarize the people. The interplay of the host of complex factors may thus create problems of social sustainability, which would also have an adverse feedback effect on productivity of resources and economic growth.

In view of the two-way interactive relationship between economy and ecosystem, economic activities or their growth create a pressure on the latter for the flows of resources of various kinds as well as those of waste absorption. These can be translated in terms of respective appropriation of biologically productive land and water area of different types of use, expressed in equivalent cropland with global average productivity. Such a measure, called the ecological footprint of an economy, is the demand for eco-services by an economy in the units of use of such land area. If the measure exceeds the biocapacity of an ecosystem of provision of land area, in terms of the same unit of measure, the excess, called the eco-deficit in the units of land area, is the indicator of stress on the ecosystem. If the ecological stress grows over time, there would be a growing environmental risk of collapse of the functioning of the ecosystem. The carbon footprint amounting to the excess of CO_2 emissions from fossil fuel over and above the absorptive capacity of the global ecosystem, expressed in forest land area that would be required to absorb the excess of unabsorbed CO_2, is a part of the eco-footprint and eco-deficit. The growing eco-deficit has therefore an important implication in respect of growing accumulation of CO_2 along with other greenhouse gases (GHGs) in the atmosphere causing global warming and threatening climate change. The persistence of the eco-deficit also causes loss of biodiversity, which reduces the resilience of the ecosystem in case of any extreme event causing an exogenous shock to it. In the event of such loss of resilience of the state of equilibrium, the ecosystem may become unstable and lose its balance, and it may flip on to a new eco-regime with characteristics that are unfamiliar to the organisms already living in the concerned region of the earth. It is this uncertainty regarding the characteristics of the new eco-regime which is the major factor behind the perception that such changes are going to reduce the well-being of the people of the economy. The same is true about the threat of climate change. The dislocation of an ecosystem from its equilibrium due to the rising ecological deficit and carbon footprint induced by our development processes has led to the threat of climate change in the not too distant future and that of fast depletion of biodiversity and degeneration of human and ecosystem health, which we have already started experiencing. All these, together, characterize the unsustainability of today's economic growth process. The sustainability of economic development in such a comprehensive sense would, in fact, amount to such characterization of the process of economic growth which neither involves any social disruption, nor involves any environmental risk of collapse of the concerned ecosystem.

Welfare State and Social Policy for Sustainability

Each of the above-mentioned three schools of thought on development thus propounds that it can no less fulfil the objective of social and environmental sustainability along with that of growth in a holistic perspective than its competing alternatives. However, the reality is that the ultimate consequence of one line of policy approach is different from the other, depending on the approach and prioritization in the respective policy agendas of each of the approaches as dictated by their prime meaning and context of development. However, an overview of the issues of the three aspects of development as outlined in the preceding sections clearly suggests economic growth as a necessary condition of either of the approaches of sustainability. This, however, requires to be accompanied by a suitable social policy of development to take care of equity and social justice, as well as the environmental sustainability of the development process. State interventions are often imperative to correct any market failure, which is fundamentally responsible for any social and environmental unsustainability. Such social policy is to be visualized as much as inputs into the development process as the conventional inputs required to sustain the growth of economic output. Although the twentieth century saw the emergence, development, and saturation of the welfare state, which was supposed by some (see Flora and Heidenheimer 1981) to have grown to its limits, the socio-economic developments after the turn of the century, as evidenced both by human and other social development reports relating to aspects such as health and education, and climate reports, clearly point to the necessity of retaining the welfare state in the interest of sustainable development, subject, however, to some reforms, which may have to be continued over time, depending on the contemporaneous needs of the age. Let us digress here to review the history of social policy and welfare statism as accompanying economic growth to understand the ratio- nale of their positive role in the future in the interest of sustainable development.

The social investment perspective of development along the lines of welfare statism can be traced back to the early years of the Swedish welfare state in the 1930s, against the backdrop of the Great Depression and a severe fertility crisis in Sweden and the rest of Europe. Prominent social democratic thinkers such as Gunnar and Alva Myrdal concep- tualized social policy ideas that were oriented towards the efficient organization of production and reproduction (More et al. 2012). The social spending from the state exchequer to support such programmes or policies was viewed not as cost, but as investment for future higher returns and welfare accruables as surplus. The decline in the fertility rate leading to the population crisis of this era occurred, according to the Myrdals, due to socio-economic hardships brought about by urban- ization, which raised the individual cost of rearing the children. An additional child was not seen (as it should have been) by the society as an extra labourer—an addition to the productive forces of tomorrow with the potential of contributing towards social productivity—but as an extra cost and hardship to the household. The productive social policy of the Swedish economists therefore considered policies not merely to provide individual security of income and employment through income transfers, but also for the efficient organization of production by imparting skill and capability to the workers through the welfare state programme of education, health, gender, equality, and thus the human capital formation. These included support to female workers, labour-market participation, children's well-being, and social rights. All these aimed to both develop and maintain human capital stock. The interactive relationship between economic growth and social policy has thus been a guiding principle of Swedish social democracy since the 1930s (More et al. 2012). This approach did not see any conflict between equality in distribution and efficiency in production as a serious issue requiring any compromise but as a complementary one, the former being required as a precondition for the optimization of growth—an issue that was again picked up in the 2000s, when social investment became the major orientation of the development process to which we return later.

Keynesianism

Keynesianism, on the other hand, reached the height of prominence in the Great Depression era and continued to dominate the macroeconomic policy scenario till the early 1970s. It is the issue of sustaining high and stable effective demand as well as employment using counter-cyclical fiscal and monetary policies which have been the major concern of both economic and social policies in this era. The maintenance of high real wages in times of recession, reducing income inequalities, and a thrust in public investment in health and education were considered critical to boost economic growth, reduce inequities and inequalities, and promote social rights. The expansion of a welfare state, according to Keynes, can, however, well take place within the political–economic framework of a market economy. According to such thinking, an open market and the organized solidarity of workers in the labour market need not be thought of as opposites but rather as essential ingredients of a socially sustainable process of economic growth. However, in spite of a wide area of commonality in the social policy perspective of economic growth between the early Swedish school led by the Myrdals and that of Keynes, there were subtle differences between the respective approaches of these two strands of thought.

First, the gender aspect of welfare development was not the main focus in Keynes' discourse as it was in the Swedish social policies. With Keynes, social policies were oriented towards families led by a male bread earner and did not cater as much to the issues of the female labour market and female unemployment. Besides, the Keynesian time horizon for social and economic policies was much shorter than that of the Swedish approach. The counter-cyclical Keynesian economic policies were concerned with the 'here and now' time frame (Morel, et al. 2012) and the attendant consequences of such policies were also mainly for the present period. The social policies of the Swedish, on the other hand, had more active elements of initiative as well as investments in human resources whose benefits—economic as well as social—would unfold only over a longer period.

Rise of Neoliberalism

After the oil shock of the 1970s resulting in economic recessions, Keynesian macroeconomics and social policies came under attack by the conventional neoclassical school of thought, which considered the social policies as imposing only costs and not as investments or inputs of development. Wage restraint and high interest rates due to regulations in the face of rising energy costs restrained the growth of profit and resulted in general widespread losses, causing recessions.

It is, in fact, the microeconomic logic of market distortion, especially in the labour market, that provided the basis to explain the recession that was initially triggered by the oil and energy price shock of the 1970s. High unemployment and low growth were considered to be the direct result of high minimum wages, strong job protection, and generous unemployment insurance. The unemployment insurance often had a perverse effect of poor job search even in periods of unemployment. Generous social measures were considered to be the major cause of the difficulty faced in the post-Keynesian era by such neoliberals. This school of thought therefore rejected the Keynesian view that equality and efficiency had no connection of conflict and that there existed no trade-off between social security and economic growth.

Neoliberal economists therefore advocated a paradigm shift in social policies to accompany economic growth. According to them, it is not a demand-side problem, but a supply-side one of high cost due to market rigidities induced by social regulation policies. Their policies therefore focused on budgetary rigour, profitability of investment, wage restraint, monetarism ensuring cheap availability of credit, and market competitiveness for restoring profit and surplus, which would be the source of tomorrow's investment and growth. The welfare state thus becomes an irrelevant institution, since such policies would advocate rolling back of income of social securities. The social actors—the market, community, family—can now find their own way of resolving the redistribution problem through cooperation and sharing, and not through a top-down approach of initiative of redistribution through the social transfer of income. The time horizon of such a supply-side policy of the neoclassicals was, of course, for the long haul and involved short-run sacrifices that were defended in the context of the longer-term benefit of higher growth.

Neoliberal policies could not, however, resolve the socio-economic problems that the capitalists as well as market-based developing countries were facing in the last quarter of the twentieth century. Towards the end of the 1990s, it became obvious that the inequality between the global rich and the poor and also the gap between the rich and the poor at the national level in many of the developing countries were on the rise. The economic polarization within an economy and across economies were on the rise as a consequence of the neoliberal policies of unfettered market-driven capitalism as pursued in many countries till the first decade of the present century, when the process culminated into the financial collapse of 2008 followed by one of the deepest economic crises in the last 100 years.

Return of the Realization of Importance of the Social Investment Perspective of Economic Growth

The social investment perspective of economic growth has assumed again new significance since the aftermath of this latest global economic crisis. It has since then been realized that the consideration of social sustainability of economic growth would not be able to afford the total abandonment of welfare statism. However the new understanding of fundamental changes that were taking place in this era in the realm of technology and society have pointed out that the unemployment and low income had been due to lack of alignment of the changing technology with the level of development of skill and education of workers, and the resulting inadequate absorption of technology in industries, high cost, and low productivity, income and growth. To get out of this situation, new kind of social investment policies along the line of the suggestions of the 1930s Swedish school of thought of the Myrdals were again required.

Social investment in the current age has become important for stimulating growth not primarily because of the demand-side arguments, but because of the necessity of investment in human capital for equipping the labourers with skill and knowledge for the constantly changing knowledge-based economies of the countries. Besides, the need of alignment of work with family and the issue of gender equity, and the associated concern for the female and child rights–related issues require a new direction of social investment, so that this may give support to labour market fluidity and flexible security. While in the Keynesian regime where any employment is good as it provides the benefit of higher family income by the male bread earner, which was supposed to propagate to all the members of the family, the rights issue of female workers and the demand for explicit recognition of the need for certain infrastructural support for the children of working mothers/parents gave new shape to social policies and social investment. Such comprehensive social policies and accompanying investments, which would support human capital formation as well as capability development would, in fact, now be a prerequisite for optimizing economic growth. According to such a view, the efficiency of growth would be consistent with equity of social development.

Given our conceptualization of sustainability of different aspects of development and of supporting social policies and institutions, it is important now to characterize the social policies and identify the composition of its package for ensuring sustainability as conceived in its different dimensions in the preceding sections. These would require not only the inclusiveness of the development process through engagement or employment of people in the development process, but will also have to give due priority to the distributive and quality of life–related issues, which need to be looked into for the assessment of the state of social sustainability. This would include the removal of income as well as of multidimensional poverty by providing the basic needs and amenities of life, the deprivation of which may result in social and political restlessness of a society and in the unsustainability of its pre-existing socio-economic order. This is often corroborated by the high correlation, as observed and analysed in Chapter 3, between the incidences of such criminal events and the alienating factors triggered by inequity in distribution. Too many of such disturbances relating to law and order would threaten to disrupt the social sustainability of an economic order and erode the productivity of the economic system.

Finally, the issue of environmental sustainability of the development process of a human system would warrant investments in energy and resource conservation as well as for abating pollution and environmental protection. These are to be targeted to protect human health as well as an ecosystem's health in terms of its regenerative ability. Most of such measures and the extent of success in achieving them indicate the environmental performance of an economy as captured by the EPI, as, for example, developed jointly by Columbia University and Yale University, and reported from time to time. Social investment orientation of an economy is to thus take due care of such policy issues so as to ensure social sustainability of the growth process as environmental impact mostly works through externalities and causes damage to the society.

Indicators of Social Sustainability
Poverty, Inequality, and Social Tension

Chapter 2 focuses on the indicators of social sustainability. The issue of measuring social sustainability can be approached in two ways: (*i*) basing the indicators of the extent of people's deprivation from basic needs, which thus contribute towards unsustainability, or (*ii*) basing them on the extent of attainment of the development of human capability, which would determine the extent to which people can have access to a decent life and contribute towards social sustainability of the economic system. The latter approach is, in fact, the obverse of the former.

In Chapter 2, we review the issues of income, poverty, and deprivation and trace the relationship between deprivation—in both the absolute and relative sense—and social tension conceived as social welfare loss according to some social welfare function, which underlies any indicator of development. After reviewing the comparative state of inequality-adjusted level of development across developing countries, we have analysed the state of poverty and inequality and estimated the measure of social tension (based on the poverty gap or the Gini coefficient) using India's state-level data to assess the state of social sustainability of the country's economic system.

Indicators of Sustainable Development

The conventional indicator of economic development has been the growth of GDP or the aggregate volume of goods and services produced by an economy. However, the welfare implication of growth is indicated by the accompanying growth of people's employment, both in terms of participation in the growth process as well as to share its benefit. The stability of the macroeconomic aggregate output, prices, fiscal balance, and the extent of indebtedness of an economy are the fundamental determinants of the sustainability of the macroeconomic process of development in the long run. An economic performance indicator of sustainability would thus be dependent positively on the long run rate of growth, and negatively on the deficiencies of performances such as unemployment, inflation, fiscal deficit, and the indebtedness of the economy to the rest of the world. Such an indicator is to be ideally derived in reduced form as a derivative of a core macroeconomic model of development. Since it is often difficult to obtain such a single measure of performance of the economy of a country capturing sustainability, one can alternatively construct a statistical measure to represent the same and intuitively meaningful. This can be the growth rate adjusted for the deficiency in performance in respect of controlling inflation, unemployment, fiscal deficit, and foreign monetary indebtedness. However, it was found by the author that such an economic performance indicator as estimated had little relationship with gross national income (GNI) per capita, growth rate, and any of the other basic macroeconomic variables or any of the social or environmental sustainability indicators from data that represents the cross-section of the country. We, therefore, decided to drop such an economic performance indicator and fall back on the conventional GNI per capita. We have, however, chosen the inequality-adjusted per capita income index to be the true attainment of a country's sustainable economic well-being. In Table 2.1, we present GNI per capita as well as inequality-adjusted per capita income, expressed as their respective scores on a normalized scale. The difference between the cross-section maximum and minimum of the actual from among the selected 54 developing countries is assumed to be unity. This follows the methodology of construction scores of basic constituent factors of the HDI as has been shown in the *Human Development Reports (HDR)*.

It may be noted that China has the best economic achievement in terms of such scale, while India's performance after inequality adjustment is only one-third of China's.

TABLE 2.1 Cross-country Data on Gross National Income Per Capita and Inequality-Adjusted Gross National Income Per Capita on a Normalized Scale (2014)

Countries	GNI Per Capita	Inequality-Adjusted Per Capita
Albania	0.002	0.558
Argentina	0.044	0.560
Armenia	0.001	0.567
Azerbaijan	0.008	0.730
Bangladesh	0.029	0.612
Belarus	0.008	0.357
Benin	0.001	0.685
Bhutan	0.001	0.329
Bolivia	0.004	0.477
Bosnia and Herzegovina	0.002	0.388
Brazil	0.158	0.555
Bulgaria	0.006	0.452
Burkina Faso	0.001	0.618
Burundi	0.001	0.318
Cambodia	0.002	0.264
Cameroon	0.003	0.401
Central African Republic	0.001	0.377
Chile	0.020	0.192
China	1.000	0.516
Congo, Democratic Republic	0.003	0.505
Congo, Republic	0.001	0.410
Costa Rica	0.003	0.155
Ecuador	0.009	0.483
Ethiopia	0.008	0.472
Guatemala	0.006	0.351
Guinea	0.001	0.367
Guinea-Bissau	0.000	0.253
Haiti	0.001	0.244
Honduras	0.001	0.218
India	0.106	0.299
Indonesia	0.140	0.500
Iran, Islamic Republic	0.069	0.559
Kenya	0.007	0.395
Malawi	0.001	0.297
Malaysia	0.001	0.224
Maldives	0.108	0.535
Mexico	0.001	0.500

Moldova	0.002	0.480
Mongolia	0.013	0.588
Morocco	0.002	0.493
Mozambique	0.001	0.250
Namibia	0.019	0.216
Peru	0.045	0.495
Philippines	0.050	0.470
Poland	0.005	0.666
Serbia	0.008	0.618
Slovak Republic	0.003	0.740
Slovenia	0.001	0.755
Tajikistan	0.006	0.409
Uganda	0.003	0.285
Ukraine	0.017	0.593
Uruguay	0.003	0.573
Uzbekistan	0.009	0.478
Zambia	0.003	0.292

Source: World Bank, World Development Indicators (2016) and United Nations Development Programme (UNDP) (2016).

The concept of sustainability, however, has the connotation of characterization of some dynamic process of change. The context or domain of such change may be the natural environment or ecosystem, or the social and economic systems we live in. By sustainability, we mean that the structure and the basic function of the concerned system—whether of the natural ecosystem or of the socio-economic system as evolved or constructed by people—remains unchanged. In other words, sustainability of the dynamic process of change should ensure that the functions of the natural ecosystem to provide eco-services to us or those of the economic system which provides the delivery of human welfare remain unimpaired. In other words, the capacity of the ecosystem to provide eco-services for our life support or that of the productivity of our economic system of production of material goods and services should not be diminished even after the repeated performance of their respective functions. All these have twin implications:

1. There is some value function which we impute to the functioning of the concerned system or subsystem of the nature of the economy, such that the value of the total natural or man-made

stocks making up the aggregate wealth of a nation should not be declining over time.

2. Condition 1 implies that the concerned value judgements in such assessment of national wealth are first of all anthropocentric and secondly, are based on the premise of the existence of instrumental value of all kinds of stocks and their flow in supporting human existence and their level of well-being.

With reference to the second condition, we may, however, recognize the existence value of say, many species or objects of the natural system not for immediate instrumental reasons, but for such subjective reasons of intrinsic value of those constituent elements in the system for existential reasons. However, the valuation of biodiversity, which is critical for the long-run survival of human beings, is again instrumental while the existence value of other species due to religious or philosophical reasons may be considered by people more for existential reasons rather than instrumental ones. In any case, all such values or sustainability have their meaning only in the context of human existence and that of the existence of socio-economic and cultural constructs supporting such existence.

Fundamental Sources of Sustainability

In the context of economic development the issue of sustainability has arisen for the twin reasons of (*i*) concern for sustained economic growth for the betterment of human well-being in a society and (*ii*) resource limitation. Since the First Industrial Revolution, society has invented and produced an endless stream of products and processes, causing continuous creation of new wants, while the potential of resource regeneration and supply along with that of waste absorption of our planet has remained unchanged and finite. However, it is also a fact that the constraints of environmental and natural resources have not led the historical process of growth into stagnation nor ended up with any catastrophic changes. Neither the dismal prediction of Thomas Robert Malthus made in the nineteenth century[1] nor that of the report to the

---

[1] Malthus predicted that as growth of human population would outpace that of food production, an economy would face acute food shortage, hunger, famine, migration, war, disease, and deaths in the long run until it ends up with a new equilibrium of population size and food supply.

Club of Rome in the 1970s (Meadows et al. 1972) based on a simulation model of limits to growth has turned out to be true. While it is true that no new energy or material can be created by man, new human knowledge as created and embodied in the various forms of human skills, physical capital goods, infrastructure, technical know-how, new energy and natural resources, institutions, and norms (social capital) has enabled us to overcome the constraints of environmental and natural resources. It is the R&D activities that create new ideas and different inventions which can potentially serve to preserve the environment to keep the ecosystems in equilibrium. Some of these R&D outputs give ideas for energy and material conservation, others invent new material resources and energy sources, and still some others provide new technologies for abating pollution by investing in some new resource-conserving technology. There can also be the development of ideas and technologies for adaptation to reduce the impact of negative externalities of any kind of pollution or degradation on the aggregative production activities, public safety, and on the wealth of the people at large. However, these inventions or discoveries involve spending on R&D and their outputs would be patented or non-patented ideas or technologies depending on how the intellectual property rights (IPR) are defined on them. The application of all inventions or ideas—old or new—for resource conserving or pollutions-abating technologies may, however, be effected only by follow-up investment in physical capital, infrastructure, or in manuals, documents, software embodying or containing the ideas and discoveries (Jones 2006; Romer 1990, 1993), and other expenditure for the diffusion of such knowledge.

However, in spite of indefinite advance made by people in new research ideas and technologies, the ecological limits due to entropy law would put a ceiling on the attainable welfare reflected in the measures of attainable income and wealth. Any such limitation would also lead to the twin problems of sustaining the macroeconomic rate of growth or of the pace of development on the one hand and of sharing of the benefit of any finite output or growth on the other. The chance of success in overcoming these constraints would depend on the strength of the concerned economy at the macro level, as indicated by the macroeconomic performance indicator, as well as on the social policies accompanying such growth for equitable sharing of its benefits and in conserving natural resources while protecting the health of the ecosystem and the people.

The distributional issue, which arises from the limits on the benefits of the use of resources, depends on the employment and occupational pattern of the distribution of people on one hand, and on the social and institutional norms and regulations and the quality of the governance of the society on the other. The main determinant of the social consequence of the distribution of income and wealth depends on the resultant inequality and inequity, as these are the sources of social tension that can be measured in terms of loss of social welfare. In populous underdeveloped countries, the acuteness of such inequality has been reflected in the measure of poverty—a situation in which a significant share of the population is deprived of income required to meet basic needs. Any problem of income poverty or inequality (in the sense of a high Gini coefficient) of income distribution can, in fact, be shown as resulting in welfare loss, which can be taken as a proxy measure of social tension under some assumption of social welfare function (Kakwani and Son 2016).

The polarization of income distribution and social immobility resulting from any social group not having access to the opportunities of improving their status in terms of better employment and earning due to caste, class, and religious or ethnic identity can further worsen the situation. Such immobility can further aggravate social tension due to welfare loss, again under the reasonable assumption of a social welfare function (Kakwani and Son 2016). Social tension is the driving factor of social crimes of various kinds, including homicide, burglary, and riots originating from the feeling of alienation and a sense of injustice. The social and political unrest culminates in the instability of social and political order and therefore leads to social unsustainability of the economic system or of the development process, giving rise to various socio-political uncertainties. Economic instability, particularly in the form of volatility of income and employment in a dynamic situation of the downward trend of an economic cycle, can further compound an adverse impact on the investment climate of the economy, thus giving rise to further uncertainties and a lower credit rating of investment projects and deceleration of growth. All these would have both economic and social fallouts, which are likely to adversely affect the condition of sustainability.

Poverty, Inequality, and Social Tension

From the viewpoint of deprivation, the distribution of population between poor and non-poor has been, for many developing countries like

India, considered a major determinant or indicator of social sustainability (or unsustainability) of their development process. The poverty line conceptually would represent the monthly per capita expenditure which would be just enough to cover the cost of a basket of goods and services for meeting the basic needs of the people. This has varied from country to country if one goes by the national poverty line as decided by the different countries from time to time. However, the World Bank also provides data on the poverty rate, internationally comparable on the basis of a poverty line in purchasing power parity (PPP) USD 1.90 a day per capita as per 2011 prices or alternatively, PPP USD 3.10 a day on the basis of survey data carried out in some latest base year (as was available in Table 1.2 of the *World Development Indicators: Statistical Tables* published by the World Bank [2016]). For India, the national poverty line was estimated officially on the basis of food security till the time of the Lakdawala Committee of 1989. The consumption pattern was linked to the 1973–74 poverty line consumption baskets of goods and services, although prices were adjusted from time to time depending on the price changes of the components of the poverty line basket of goods and services over time. The poverty line was anchored to the requirement of calorific value of the food component in the consumption basket at the level of 2,400 calories per capita per day in rural areas and 2,100 calories per capita per day in urban areas, which were the appropriately weighted calorie requirements of the people depending on age, sex, and occupational distribution of people. As per such methods, all urban and rural poverty lines in India were respectively INR 33 and INR 27 per capita per day as per 2005–06 prices. However, the Tendulkar Committee subsequently recommended certain changes as follows:

1. The committee advocated a shift away from calorific consumption–based poverty estimation.
2. There was a recommendation to have a uniform poverty basket for rural and urban India.
3. There should be a correction and refinement in the method of price adjustment for temporal and spatial variation in prices over the earlier one. However, poverty lines estimated for rural and urban India differed from each other mainly because of the spatial price variation, in spite of the assumption of the same poverty line basket of real consumption.

4. It was assumed earlier that the state will provide basic educational and health services and therefore, the cost of provision of such services as basic necessities was not considered for the purpose of finding out the private cost of basic needs to decide the poverty line. Unlike the earlier committee, the Tendulkar Committee's recommendation included some of these expenditures in health, education, food, and clothing, among others, in the basic needs basket. The estimate of the income poverty line was obtained by the committee to be INR 33 for urban area and INR 27 for the rural area. The headcount poverty ratio was accordingly found to be 25.7 per cent for rural India and 13.7 per cent for urban India—the all-India ratio being 21.9 per cent for 2011–12.

Subsequently, the Rangarajan Committee further reviewed the poverty line provided by the Tendulkar Committee and the headcount poverty ratio based on the results of the independent household survey data on expenditure. The method now considered food and non-food items such as education, health, and clothing in the subsistence basket of consumption. The additional items that the Rangarajan Committee considered in the consumption basket over the Tendulkar Committee were rent and some non-cereal items that met nutritional requirements. While earlier, food security was anchored only to the calorific value of food, it now also got linked with the broader domain of nutrition: calorie + protein + fat. Such combined consideration reduced some requirement of calories for intake as well. With such revisions, the Rangarajan Committee ended up with a calorific requirement revised downwards to 2,155 for rural areas and 2,090 for urban areas. The estimate of cost of the revised poverty line basket was obtained to be INR 32 per capita per day for rural areas and INR 47 for urban areas. The headcount poverty ratio correspondingly was revised to 30.9 per cent in rural India and 26.4 per cent in urban India in 2011–12—the all-India ratio being 29.5 per cent for the same year. Here arises a problem of choice of optimum diet to meet all the nutrient requirements at least cost, taking due account of the metabolic absorption rate of the different nutrients from food and their respective requirements in the human body, without taking a narrowed-down calorific approach. Besides, we have to take account of cultural factors like food habits and food preferences and their implications in respect of health externalities.

The headcount poverty ratio is, however, not an adequate description of the state of deprivation, particularly the depth and severity of such deprivation, which are critical determinants of social sustainability of our economic development process at the macro level. The poverty gap is a ratio and is measured by the average shortfall of income (consumption) of the poor from the poverty line to the level of poverty lines (those estimated by the Ministry of Statistics and Programme Implementation at the state and national levels). The average of the square of such poverty gaps would yield a measure of severity of poverty of an economy. A measure of social tension may, in fact, be derived from the sense of loss of income suffered due to deprivation by the poor. In that case, if $g(z,x)$ is the sense of loss of an individual with income x, where z the poverty line, the social welfare loss as additive function of the individual losses can be represented by:

$$G = \int_0^z g(z,x) f(x) dx$$

Assuming the total social deprivation to be invariant with respect to a positive transformation, Clark et al. (1981) introduced the idea of equally distributed equivalent poverty gap $\bar{g}$. Equally distributed poverty gap $\bar{g}$ is such that:

$$\bar{g}^\alpha = \int_0^z \frac{(z-x)^\alpha}{n_p} f(x) dx . N$$

$$= \frac{1}{H} \int_0^z (z-x)^\alpha f(x) dx \tag{1}$$

Again total social deprivation:

$$\bar{g} . H = \int_0^z (z-x)^\alpha f(x) dx \tag{2}$$

Again,

$$\text{let } \theta_\alpha = \int_0^z \left(\frac{z-x}{z} \right)^\alpha f(x) dx \tag{3}$$

that is, $\theta_0 = H,$

$\theta_1 = $ Poverty gap ratio,

$\theta_2 = $ Severity ratio of poverty

(2) and (3) imply

Thus $H.\bar{g}^\alpha = (z^\alpha.\theta_\alpha)$

Or,

$$\bar{g} = z\left[\frac{\theta_\alpha}{H}\right]^{\frac{1}{\alpha}}$$

Total social deprivation is thus:

$$\bar{g}.H = Hz\left[\frac{\theta_\alpha}{H}\right]^{\frac{1}{\alpha}}$$

Weighted average of welfare per capita due to poverty $= \mu - Hz\left(\dfrac{\theta_\alpha}{H}\right)^{\frac{1}{\alpha}}$ (Kakwani and Son 2016).

The FGT (Foster, Green, and Thorbecke) class of poverty measure is obtained as follows:

$$P_\alpha = zH\left(\frac{\theta_\alpha}{H}\right)^{\frac{1}{\alpha}}$$

$$= zH^{\left(1-\frac{1}{\alpha}\right)}(\theta_\alpha)^{\frac{1}{\alpha}}$$

For $\alpha = 1$, we get social loss and tension measure as a ratio of income to be:

$$P_1 = \frac{z\theta_1}{\mu_1}$$

Thus social loss or tension per capita is obtained as a proportion of per capita income to be $z\dfrac{\theta_1}{\mu_1}$, which is the poverty line multiplied by the poverty gap as a ratio of per capita income. Again, if μ_1 grows due to economic growth, $\dfrac{\delta P_1}{\delta \mu_1} = -z\dfrac{\theta_1}{\mu_1^2} < 0,$ since $z > 0, \mu_1^2 > 0,$ and θ_1 (poverty gap) > 0 remains unchanged in a situation where inequality of the income distribution or the Lorenz ratio and relative ranking of individuals in terms of earning remain unchanged.

We can further measure the severity of poverty of an economy by the square of the poverty gap ratio—the average of the square of the shortfall of the consumption of poor people from the poverty line. We derive social deprivation and a measure of social tension as:

$$\frac{z\sqrt{H\theta_2}}{\mu}$$

This would imply that social tension on account of severity of poverty would also decline if there is growth which is inequality neutral (Kakwani and Son 2016).

Apart from poverty, the inequality of income distribution can also be a source of social tension. Suppose we have a Gini social welfare function, which presumes that an individual suffers from loss of welfare if his/her income is less than that of some other—due to the externalities arising out of relative income—but suffers no loss if his income is not less than any other. From all possible pair-wise comparisons of individual incomes, one can derive the total welfare derived for each individual and also in aggregate for a given income distribution. Let $U(x, y)$ denote the utility of a given individual with income x, while y is the income of some other individual. For this pair-wise comparison (Kakwani 1988), the utility of the concerned individual is:

$$U(x, y) = x \text{ if } x \geq y, but = x - (y - x) \text{ if } x < y$$

If x is a random variable denoting income of an individual with probability density $f(x)$, his expected welfare in all pair-wise comparison will be obtained as:

$$u(x) = x - \mu\left[1 - F_1(x)\right] + x\left[1 - F(x)\right]$$

where, $F(x)$ is the cumulative probability density function giving the proportion of people with income less than or equal to x and $F_1(x)$ is the proportion of income earned by the people with income less than or equal to x, that is:

$$F_1(x) = \frac{1}{\mu}\int_0^x xf(x)dx$$

The average social welfare can then be shown to be:

$$W_G = \int_0^\infty u(x)f(x)dx = 2\int_0^\infty x\left[1 - F(x)\right]f(x)dx = \mu(1 - G)$$

where G is the Gini coefficient or Lorenz ratio. The Gini index hence yields a measure of social tension and welfare loss caused by the existence of inequality as such, μG being the estimate of the total loss. We can take μG as another index of social loss or tension due to inequality in income distribution (Kakwani and Son 2016).

If growth is to be inequality neutral, the growth of mean income would not affect either the Gini ratio nor the tension index based on such inequality. While growth is likely to reduce poverty, it may, however, still raise inequality and tension arising from it. Similarly, there may be a reduction of inequality but a rise in poverty, in which case inequality-based tension may be reduced but poverty-related tension may rise. Social sustainability would ideally require both inequality and poverty tensions to decline, although there may exist a trade-off between the two types of tensions in many situations.

Empirical Evidence of Poverty, Inequality, and Related Social Tension Measures from Indian State-Level Data

We now examine the relationships between poverty, inequality, and social tensions as evidenced by the Indian state-level cross-section data. We also examine the bi-variate scatter plot of income and each of the two types of estimates of social tension separately, for the different Indian states for finding out if there is any interrelationship between high or low income and high or low social tension. The identity of the state units in terms of relative high or low income and high or low social tension is determined by whether the value of the concerned variable is higher or lower than the average value of it across all the states of the sample. We assume a state to be high (low) income if its per capita income (consumption) exceeds (falls short of) the all-India mean of per capita income (consumption) of all states. Similarly, a state will be characterized as suffering from high or low social tension if its measure of tension exceeds or falls short of the all-India mean of all the states. In Table 2.2, we present data on the headcount ratio, poverty gap, and poverty severity for 2011 for both rural and urban areas, as available in the Planning Commission Databook (2014a) as an illustrative case. Table 2.3 further shows for our sample set of Indian states, the social tension level and social tension index based on the poverty gap following Kakwani's formula. The index is the normalized index value using the difference between the maximum and minimum values as unity in the scale. In other words, the index of tension would be as follows:

TABLE 2.2 Cross-state Data on Poverty Line, Poverty Gap, and Poverty Severity (2011)

States	Per Capita State Consumption Expenditure (at Constant 2004–05 Prices)*		Poverty Line		Poverty Ratio (Per Cent)*		Poverty Gap		Poverty Severity	
	Rural	Urban	Rural	Urban	Rural	Urban	Rural	Urban	Rural	Urban
Andhra Pradesh	603.8	1,091.40	693.8	926.37	10.96	5.81	0.713	0.289	0.51	0.08
Assam	576.7	1,129.60	691.7	870.96	33.89	20.49	0.498	0.350	0.25	0.12
Bihar	445	729.50	655.6	775.33	34.06	31.23	0.427	0.491	0.18	0.24
Gujarat	644.9	1,205.80	725.9	951.41	21.54	10.14	0.509	0.544	0.26	0.30
Haryana	905.2	1,183.50	791.6	975.4	11.64	10.28	0.723	0.743	0.52	0.55
Himachal Pradesh	835.60	1,422.10	707.9	888.31	8.48	4.33	0.507	0.581	0.26	0.34
Karnataka	542.9	1,138.10	629.4	908.03	24.53	15.25	0.336	0.624	0.11	0.39
Kerala	1,031.00	1,353.80	775.3	830.65	9.14	4.97	0.412	0.381	0.17	0.15
Madhya Pradesh	461.10	893.30	631.9	771.75	35.74	21.00	0.689	0.612	0.47	0.37
Maharashtra	596.70	1,228.50	743.8	961.1	24.22	9.12	0.641	0.725	0.41	0.53
Odisha	422.10	789.80	567.1	735.95	35.69	17.29	0.561	0.623	0.31	0.39
Punjab	905.30	1,306.10	830.0	960.78	7.66	9.24	0.446	0.655	0.20	0.43
Rajasthan	598.20	944.60	755.0	845.97	16.05	10.69	0.675	0.432	0.46	0.19
Tamil Nadu	601.60	1,166.30	638.9	800.82	15.83	6.54	0.555	0.412	0.31	0.17
Uttar Pradesh	539.30	879.70	663.7	799.94	11.62	10.48	0.512	0.575	0.26	0.33
West Bengal	575.70	1,159.00	643.2	830.59	22.52	14.66	0.632	0.486	0.40	0.24

Source: Planning Commission (2014a).

Note: *The per capita state consumption expenditure data is based on mixed reference period and poverty ratio as per the Tendulkar Committee methodology.

TABLE 2.3   Cross-state Data on Poverty-Based Tension Measure and Poverty-Based Tension Index (2011)

States	Poverty-Based Social Tension Estimate		Poverty-Based Social Tension Index		Rank (Based on Tension Index)	
	Rural	Urban	Rural	Urban	Rural	Urban
Andhra Pradesh	0.419	0.123	0.945	0.299	14	1
Assam	0.338	0.172	0.762	0.418	7	3
Bihar	0.351	0.411	0.792	1	8	16
Gujarat	0.335	0.266	0.756	0.647	6	9
Haryana	0.376	0.309	0.848	0.751	9	15
Himachal Pradesh	0.234	0.196	0.528	0.476	4	6
Karnataka	0.213	0.233	0.480	0.566	2	7
Kerala	0.128	0.131	0.288	0.318	1	2
Madhya Pradesh	0.402	0.286	0.907	0.695	11	10
Maharashtra	0.41	0.29	0.925	0.705	12	12
Odisha	0.4	0.297	0.902	0.722	10	13
Punjab	0.231	0.3	0.521	0.729	3	14
Rajasthan	0.418	0.234	0.943	0.569	13	8
Tamil Nadu	0.321	0.175	0.724	0.425	5	4
Uttar Pradesh	0.443	0.286	1	0.695	16	10
West Bengal	0.435	0.191	0.981	0.464	15	5

Source: Planning Commission (2014a).

Let x be the tension level of a state; x_{max} and x_{min} are the maximum and minimum values of tension levels across all the states covered in the sample states of India. The tension index of a state is:

$$\frac{\left(x - x_{min}\right)}{\left(x_{max} - x_{min}\right)}$$

Table 2.4 presents the measures of the Gini coefficient and social tension levels, the social tension index and their ranks separately for both rural and urban areas of the Indian states as per NSS data for 2011–12.

It is, however, important for us to ascertain the nature of the relationship between the level of development, which is the GSDP per capita, and the measures of poverty and inequalities. The estimates

TABLE 2.4 Cross-state Data on Gini Coefficient and Gini Coefficient–Based Tension Index (2011)

States	Gini Coefficient		Gini-Based Social Tension Estimate		Gini-Based Social Tension Index		Rank (Based on Index Values)	
	Rural	Urban	Rural	Urban	Rural	Urban	Rural	Urban
Andhra Pradesh	0.278	0.382	167.856	416.915	0.390	0.618	11	10
Assam	0.244	0.324	140.715	365.990	0.327	0.542	7	6
Bihar	0.226	0.332	100.570	242.194	0.233	0.359	1	1
Gujarat	0.253	0.328	163.159	395.502	0.379	0.586	10	9
Haryana	0.301	0.360	272.465	426.06	0.633	0.631	15	11
Himachal Pradesh	0.305	0.399	254.858	567.418	0.592	0.841	13	15
Karnataka	0.235	0.334	127.605	380.125	0.296	0.563	3	7
Kerala	0.417	0.498	429.927	674.192	1	1	16	16
Madhya Pradesh	0.292	0.364	134.612	325.161	0.313	0.482	5	4
Maharashtra	0.268	0.410	159.996	503.685	0.372	0.747	9	14
Odisha	0.262	0.389	110.564	307.232	0.257	0.455	2	3
Punjab	0.288	0.371	260.640	484.563	0.606	0.718	14	13
Rajasthan	0.225	0.378	134.55	357.059	0.312	0.529	4	5
Tamil Nadu	0.264	0.332	158.8224	387.212	0.369	0.574	8	8
Uttar Pradesh	0.356	0.329	191.991	289.421	0.446	0.429	12	2
West Bengal	0.239	0.384	137.592	445.056	0.320	0.660	6	12

Source: Planning Commission (2014a).

of correlation between per capita state income and the poverty- or inequality-related co-variates are presented in Table 2.5. It is important to notice that while growth in state income will reduce poverty and poverty gap–induced tension, it will tend to raise inequality and inequality-induced social tension. Finally, based on data of Tables 2.3 and 2.4, we also found out the correlation between poverty-based social tensions (Kakwani and Son 2016) and inequality-based social tension to be negative but the absolute value to be small, though statistically significant. This is true for both the rural and urban sectors. This implies that social tensions induced by poverty and those based on inequality are almost independent of each other for both the rural and urban areas. Since we would like the social tension of both the types to be reduced by appropriate policies, we would need to adopt a range of measures for both inequality and poverty reduction for rural and urban areas in different states.

Scenario of Comparative Development and Social Tension of Indian States

We also worked out the same set of measures of inequality, poverty, and social tension–related variables, the latter for both poverty- and

TABLE 2.5   Correlation Table between Per Capita Income and Co-variates

Rural Sector	Rank Correlation for Indian States
1. Headcount Ratio	−0.573
2. Poverty-Based Social Tension Index	−0.615
3. Inequality-Based Social Tension Index	0.783
Correlation between Poverty-Induced Social Tension and Inequality-Induced Social Tension	−0.064
Urban Sector	
1. Headcount Ratio	−0.796
2. Poverty-Based Social Tension Index	−0.721
3. Inequality-Based Social Tension Index	0.679
Correlation between Poverty-Induced Social Tension and Inequality-Induced Social Tension	−0.054

Source: Compiled by the author.

inequality-based measures, for Indian states from 2009 to 2014. As already discussed, the data and results are presented in Tables 2.3 and 2.4 for both rural and urban areas. It may be noted that we had to estimate a log normal distribution on the basis of state-wise data on mean consumption, the poverty line, and the poverty ratio in order to find out the poverty gap, assuming, however, log normality of the distribution of pattern of consumption. These, along with the Lorenz ratio, were estimated based on data obtained from Planning Commission sources (Planning Commission 2014a).

In order to find out the pattern of distribution of per capita consumption expenditures as well as inequality-based (based on the Gini welfare function) or poverty-based social tension measures across Indian states, we have presented the concerned data in Tables 2.2, 2.3, and 2.4 for rural and urban areas separately. We also plot this data for all the concerned states for which data was available in scatter diagrams with four quadrants, where the point of intersection of axes represents the mean per capita state consumption expenditure and the mean measure of inequality- or poverty-based social tension levels.

These diagrams show how the individual states are distributed across the following categories in terms of levels of per capita income and social tension for rural and urban areas separately.

1. high income and high social tension (Q1)
2. high income and low social tension (QII)
3. low income and low social tension (QIII)
4. low income and high social tension (QIV)

It is interesting to observe that most of the states in Figures 2.1 and 2.2 are located in the first and the third quadrants both in rural and urban areas, showing how high (or low) income is accompanied by high (or low) social inequality–based social tension due to inequality in income or asset distribution. Similarly, Figures 2.3 and 2.4 show how the states are mostly lying in the second and fourth quadrants, showing that high or low poverty-based social tension moves along with low or high income as determined by the conditions. Figures 2.1 to 2.4 show how the developmental process of Indian states has led to the distribution of the two kinds of social tensions (inequality- and poverty-based) differently in the rural and urban areas. Figures 2.1 to 2.4,

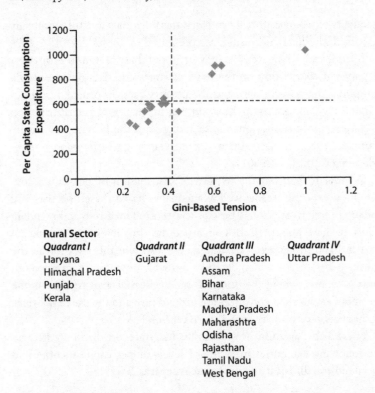

Rural Sector

Quadrant I	*Quadrant II*	*Quadrant III*	*Quadrant IV*
Haryana	Gujarat	Andhra Pradesh	Uttar Pradesh
Himachal Pradesh		Assam	
Punjab		Bihar	
Kerala		Karnataka	
		Madhya Pradesh	
		Maharashtra	
		Odisha	
		Rajasthan	
		Tamil Nadu	
		West Bengal	

Classification of 16 Indian States According to High or Low Income as well as on High or Low Social Tension Based on Gini Coefficient for the Rural Sector

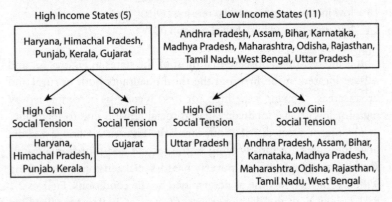

FIGURE 2.1   Gini Coefficient–Induced Social Tension across 16 Major Indian States (Rural Sector)

Source: Author's own representation based on Tables 2.2 and 2.4.

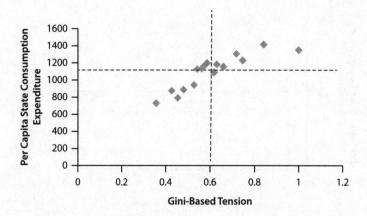

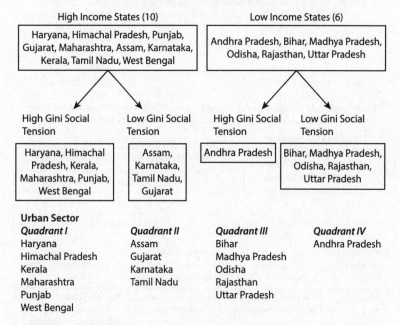

Classification of 16 Indian States According to High or Low Income as well as on High or Low Social Tension Based on Gini Coefficient for the Urban Sector

High Income States (10)	Low Income States (6)
Haryana, Himachal Pradesh, Punjab, Gujarat, Maharashtra, Assam, Karnataka, Kerala, Tamil Nadu, West Bengal	Andhra Pradesh, Bihar, Madhya Pradesh, Odisha, Rajasthan, Uttar Pradesh

High Gini Social Tension	Low Gini Social Tension	High Gini Social Tension	Low Gini Social Tension
Haryana, Himachal Pradesh, Kerala, Maharashtra, Punjab, West Bengal	Assam, Karnataka, Tamil Nadu, Gujarat	Andhra Pradesh	Bihar, Madhya Pradesh, Odisha, Rajasthan, Uttar Pradesh

Urban Sector

Quadrant I	*Quadrant II*	*Quadrant III*	*Quadrant IV*
Haryana	Assam	Bihar	Andhra Pradesh
Himachal Pradesh	Gujarat	Madhya Pradesh	
Kerala	Karnataka	Odisha	
Maharashtra	Tamil Nadu	Rajasthan	
Punjab		Uttar Pradesh	
West Bengal			

FIGURE 2.2   Gini Coefficient–Induced Social Tension across 16 Major Indian States (Urban Sector)

Source: Author's own presentation based on Tables 2.2 and 2.4.

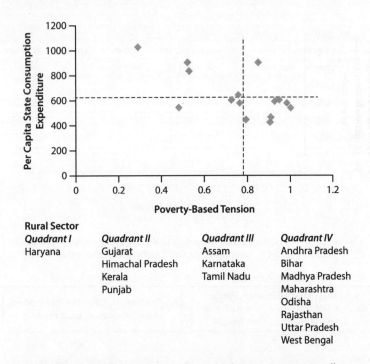

Rural Sector

Quadrant I	*Quadrant II*	*Quadrant III*	*Quadrant IV*
Haryana	Gujarat	Assam	Andhra Pradesh
	Himachal Pradesh	Karnataka	Bihar
	Kerala	Tamil Nadu	Madhya Pradesh
	Punjab		Maharashtra
			Odisha
			Rajasthan
			Uttar Pradesh
			West Bengal

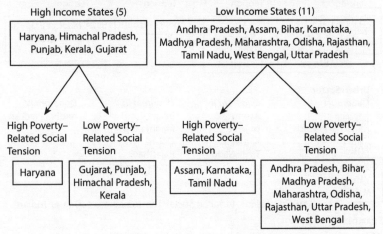

Classification of 16 Indian States According to High or Low Income as well as on High or Low Social Tension Based on Gini Coefficient for the Rural Sector

High Income States (5)

Haryana, Himachal Pradesh, Punjab, Kerala, Gujarat

Low Income States (11)

Andhra Pradesh, Assam, Bihar, Karnataka, Madhya Pradesh, Maharashtra, Odisha, Rajasthan, Tamil Nadu, West Bengal, Uttar Pradesh

High Poverty–Related Social Tension

Haryana

Low Poverty–Related Social Tension

Gujarat, Punjab, Himachal Pradesh, Kerala

High Poverty–Related Social Tension

Assam, Karnataka, Tamil Nadu

Low Poverty–Related Social Tension

Andhra Pradesh, Bihar, Madhya Pradesh, Maharashtra, Odisha, Rajasthan, Uttar Pradesh, West Bengal

FIGURE 2.3   Poverty-Induced Social Tension across 16 Major Indian States (Rural Sector)

Source: Author's own presentation based on Tables 2.2 and 2.3.

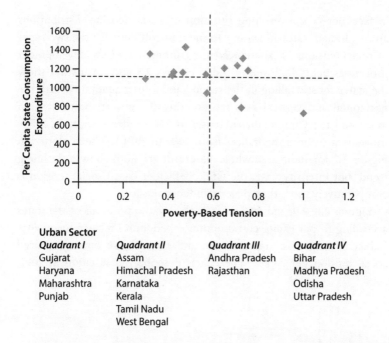

Urban Sector

Quadrant I	*Quadrant II*	*Quadrant III*	*Quadrant IV*
Gujarat	Assam	Andhra Pradesh	Bihar
Haryana	Himachal Pradesh	Rajasthan	Madhya Pradesh
Maharashtra	Karnataka		Odisha
Punjab	Kerala		Uttar Pradesh
	Tamil Nadu		
	West Bengal		

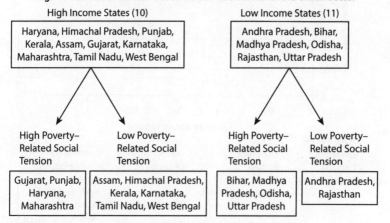

FIGURE 2.4   Poverty-Induced Social Tension across 16 Major Indian States (Urban Sector)

Source: Author's own presentation based on Tables 2.2 and 2.3.

in fact, depict the resulting situation of social tension distributions among Indian states and points to the trade-off between the two types of social tensions as experienced as a culmination of the development process as being followed in India. Figures 2.5 and 2.6 further show the states mostly falling in the second and fourth quadrants, with the horizontal and vertical axes representing the poverty-based tension index and the Gini coefficient–based tension index respectively. The movement of both the indices from 2009 to 2014 has been plotted in Figure 2.7 for India as a whole. Interestingly, both show a declining trend, but intensity-wise, the Gini coefficient–based social tension is comparatively more than poverty-induced tension.

Figures 2.8, 2.9, and 2.10 describe the relative positions of the states according to per capita consumption expenditure, relative inequality-induced social tension per capita, and also relative poverty-induced social tension per capita. The charts describe the situation in 2011,

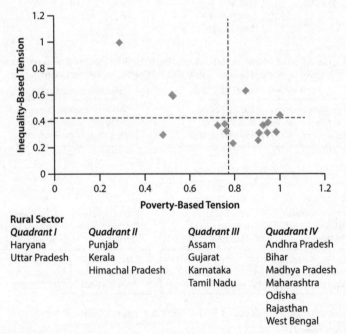

Rural Sector			
Quadrant I	*Quadrant II*	*Quadrant III*	*Quadrant IV*
Haryana	Punjab	Assam	Andhra Pradesh
Uttar Pradesh	Kerala	Gujarat	Bihar
	Himachal Pradesh	Karnataka	Madhya Pradesh
		Tamil Nadu	Maharashtra
			Odisha
			Rajasthan
			West Bengal

FIGURE 2.5   Poverty-Induced Tension vis-à-vis Inequality-Induced Tension across 16 Major Indian States (Rural Sector)
Source: Author's own presentation based on Tables 2.3 and 2.4.

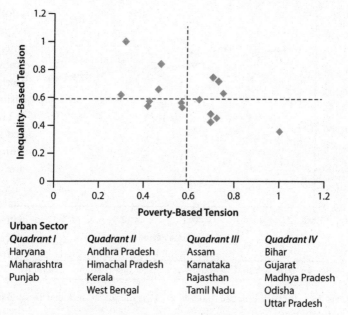

Urban Sector

Quadrant I	Quadrant II	Quadrant III	Quadrant IV
Haryana	Andhra Pradesh	Assam	Bihar
Maharashtra	Himachal Pradesh	Karnataka	Gujarat
Punjab	Kerala	Rajasthan	Madhya Pradesh
	West Bengal	Tamil Nadu	Odisha
			Uttar Pradesh

FIGURE **2.6**   Poverty-Induced Tension vis-à-vis Inequality-Induced Tension across 16 Major Indian States (Urban Sector)
Source: Author's own presentation based on Tables 2.3 and 2.4.

for rural and urban sectors separately. These show that there are five states whose rural per capita consumption expenditure is higher than the all-India rural average, taken as 16 states' average for which the required data were available. Out of these five states, four states (Haryana, Himachal Pradesh, Punjab, Kerala) suffer from relative high inequality-induced social tensions. It is only for Gujarat that the inequality in consumption-induced social tension was found to be less than the all-India average of rural social tension. Among the low rural income-expenditure states, it is only Uttar Pradesh which suffers from higher-than-average inequality-induced social tensions; the remaining 10 states with relative low income suffer from relative social tension due to distributional inequality. On the other hand, as per the distribution of poverty-related social tension across rural sectors of the states, we find that it is only Haryana among the high income-expenditure states which suffers from poverty-induced high social tension, while the remaining relatively high rural-income expenditure states of Himachal Pradesh,

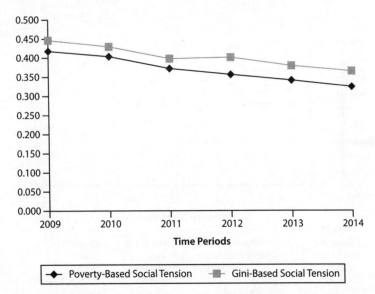

FIGURE 2.7   Poverty-Induced Tension vis-à-vis Inequality-Induced Tension for India (2009–14)

Source: Author's presentation based on the data from Planning Commission (2014a).

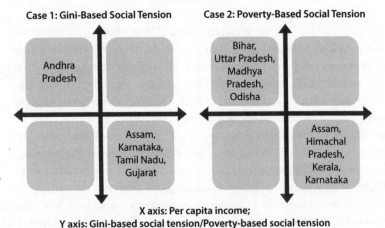

FIGURE 2.8   Comparison between the Per Capita State Domestic Product and Poverty- and Inequality-Based Social Tension across Selected Major Indian States (Urban Sector)

Source: Author's presentation based on Tables 2.2, 2.3, and 2.4.

RURAL SECTOR

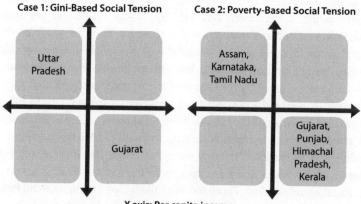

Case 1: Gini-Based Social Tension

- Uttar Pradesh
- Gujarat

Case 2: Poverty-Based Social Tension

- Assam, Karnataka, Tamil Nadu
- Gujarat, Punjab, Himachal Pradesh, Kerala

X axis: Per capita income;
Y axis: Gini-based social tension/Poverty-based social tension

FIGURE 2.9   Comparison between the Per Capita State Domestic Product and Poverty- and Inequality-Based Social Tension across Selected Major Indian States (Rural Sector)
Source: Author's presentation based on Tables 2.2, 2.3, and 2.4.

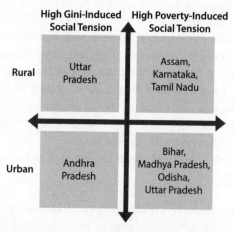

High Gini-Induced Social Tension   **High Poverty-Induced Social Tension**

Rural
- Uttar Pradesh
- Assam, Karnataka, Tamil Nadu

Urban
- Andhra Pradesh
- Bihar, Madhya Pradesh, Odisha, Uttar Pradesh

FIGURE 2.10   Rural–Urban Comparison between Poverty- and Inequality-Based Social Tension across Selected Major Indian States
Source: Author's presentation based on Tables 2.2, 2.3, and 2.4.

Kerala, Punjab, and Gujarat suffer from relatively low poverty-related tension. It is thus Gujarat—the only high rural income–expenditure state—which suffers from relatively low social tension as per both inequality-related and poverty-related tensions. The case study of the rural sector development of Gujarat would possibly further provide policy insight of how to keep both distributional inequality-related social tension (driven by the Gini coefficient) and poverty-related social tension (driven by the poverty depth or poverty gap) low. On the other hand, it is a matter of concern that the rural sector of Uttar Pradesh, a relatively low income-expenditure state, is found to have high inequality-induced social tension. The rural sectors of similar low-income states of Assam, Tamil Nadu, and Karnataka suffer from relatively high poverty-induced social tension. This poses a challenge of finding out the right policy details for mitigating poverty depth–related social tensions in the rural states of such relatively low income-expenditure states.

So far as urban India is concerned, we find that there are 10 states whose per capita consumption expenditure is above the average of 16 states of which data is available. Out of the 10 states, Assam, Karnataka, Gujarat, and Tamil Nadu have relatively high inequality-related social tensions. While urban Gujarat has a low level of inequality-related tension, it suffers from relatively high urban poverty-related social tension. It is worth examining in further detail the factors that could ensure relatively low values of both the types of social tensions to derive policy lessons for both rural and urban areas. On the other hand, it is a matter of concern that urban Andhra Pradesh with comparatively low relative income suffers from relatively high inequality-induced social tension, and hence requires policy initiatives to reduce this. Besides, high poverty-related social tension for the urban sectors of Bihar, Madhya Prdesh, Odisha, and Uttar Pradesh should warrant special attention for developing appropriate policies and strategies of development which can reduce such poverty-related social tension.

To sum up, the tables and charts as presented and referred to earlier clearly show the following:

1. There is, in general, a rising relationship between per capita state-level consumption expenditure in both rural and urban areas of states and the measure of the Gini-driven inequality-induced social tension. The measure of correlation between the two has

been estimated to be 0.929 and 0.884 for rural and urban areas respectively. This is thus true for both rural and urban consumption expenditure and distribution patterns for the given underlying welfare function.

2. There is broadly a negative relationship between per capita state level consumption expenditure (rural or urban) and the measure of poverty-related social tension. The simple correlation value between the two is -0.644 for rural and -0.536 for urban India. The absolute values of such correlation are lower for poverty-related tension than for inequality-induced tension (see Table 2.5).

Figures 2.1 to 2.7 present these results and point to the distribution of the states across four quadrants according to a combination of inequality-related and poverty-related social tension. These are shown for rural and urban areas separately. Since social tensions due to inequalities and the poverty gap change with per capita income or consumption in the states, it is important to analyse the dynamics of social tension as a consequence of growth of per capita consumption. For our cross-sectional state-level data for 2009–14, we obtained the average social tension over all states of the two kinds of social tensions for each year. It may be noted that both the types of tensions have declined gradually over time with economic growth. The level of inequality-based tension is higher than the poverty-based one, as already illustrated in Figure 2.7. It would be, however, important to trace the pathways from economic growth to tension dynamics, which is ultimately responsible for social disruptions through crime.

3

Crime, Inequality, and Poverty

In Chapter 3, we enquire more deeply into the issues of the social sustainability aspect of development by analysing the interrelationship between crime, deprivation, and the resulting social tension in the Indian context. This chapter estimates the relationship of violent crimes such as homicide and property-related crimes—dacoity, burglary, and robbery—with economic inequality or poverty, and social tension induced by either, along with other developmental variables such as the state of education, infrastructural development, urbanization, and so on. We have also covered riots and left-wing extremism in our analysis of Indian crime. We have used panel data and both simple correlation analysis as well as multi-variate regression analysis (the GMM) using panel data in its different dimensions of use and treatment. The analysis of riots also considers the share of minority population, the scheduled caste and scheduled tribe populations, as well as religious polarization as important social explanatory variables.

Violent Crime, Economic Deprivation, and Developmental Factors: An Interrelationship

We have already discussed the concept and alternative measurements of deprivation in terms of inequality and poverty and their important derivative—social tension. In the previous chapter, we also broadly observed and analysed the pattern of social tension arising from poverty and inequality in income distribution in India. However, how do we relate social tension with the social sustainability of development? Sustainable development requires economic growth without social disruption, without risks of ecological collapse, or collapse of the functioning and equilibrium of the ecosystem. Thus, social tension is generated essentially from externalities due to disproportionately high appropriation of resources, wealth, or income by some, leaving very little for those who, in extreme cases, are not able to even earn enough to consume the subsistence level or the poverty line basket of consumption. Even if there is no poverty in the sense of absolute deprivation in a society, there can be an unequal distribution of income due to skewed wage distribution arising from the pattern of distribution of employment opportunities and wage rates faced by workers in the labour market on the one hand, and due to inequality in the distribution of land, natural resources, and capital assets among the people on the other. The resulting inequality in income distribution gives rise to relative deprivation, causing loss of welfare of the relatively poor due to the externalities of the higher income and the consumption patterns of the relatively rich. As we have seen in the preceding chapter, both types of deprivation give rise to loss of social welfare under the two alternative approaches and formulations of the social welfare function. It is this growth of social tension surpassing some threshold level with respect to deprivation and discrimination ends up with social disruption, which unfolds in the forms of crime and violence. We now examine the plausibility and the robustness of such a relationship in the Indian context, using available state-level data on crime and violence along with that of poverty and income distribution. This is important to develop analytical and policy insights into the fundamentals of social sustainability of our development process.

Substantive literature has been developed on the subject of inequality and violent crime. Gary Becker's economic theory of crime (Becker 1974) points to the difference between the potential gains from crime and the associated opportunity cost being the major determinants of crime rate. These net gains are, in turn, determined broadly by the wealth difference between the rich and the poor. The poor take recourse to illegal activities in order to appropriate benefit from the wealth possessed by the rich. The existing income or benefit flow from the asset of the poor obviously represents the opportunity cost of going in for crime, abandoning legitimate means of earning money, although of limited amount. It is also a fact that people belonging to lower economic classes and those living in areas such as slums face higher crime rates than those in other, economically better-off segments of society. This relationship between inequality and crime has also been the subject of sociological analysis. One of the major sociological paradigm centres on the theory of relative deprivation as mentioned earlier. People from the lower socio-economic class suffer as they feel dispossessed compared to the richer sections of the population, especially because the poverty is not due to any major fault of theirs, but because of where they were born or the fact that they live in a society with a highly inequitable distribution of opportunities of access to a higher quality of life because of social prejudices rather than any economic factors. It is often observed that even the public good services—such as police stations or environmental security—are better provided in richer residential areas than in poorer ones. It is this sense of disadvantage and unfairness which breeds frustration and tension. The poor are sometimes desperate to bridge the gap between themselves and the rich by illegal activities if they feel they are doomed to continue in the same state of relative deprivation due to discrimination (see, among others, Andreoni 1995; Becker 1968; Bourguignon 2000; Ehrlich 1996; Fajnzylber, Lederman, and Loayza 2002; Kelly, 2000). These remarks are mostly valid to create an atmosphere of social tension due to absolute deprivation of the subsistence basket of consumption of goods and amenities for the poor, resulting in inequality or poverty of various depths in different segments of society.

To find the links between certain types of violent crimes on one hand and inequality or poverty depth and the associated social tension on the other, we consider the Gini coefficient and its related social tension measure, and alternatively, poverty depth and its associated social tension measure. To investigate the relationship, we have selected violent crimes that fall into the following four categories:

1. Homicide
2. Property-related crimes—dacoity, robbery, and burglary
3. Riots
4. Left-wing extremism

We have worked only with Indian state-level data for 2009–14, for which such data were available. We used the data of the 16 major states and union territories (a total of 16 cross-section units) for our analysis as obtained from the National Crime Records Bureau of the Government of India. We have utilized our panel data (of time series–cross -section data) for all the levels of our analysis as defined later. We have, however, studied riots and left-wing extremism separately from the other crimes—homicide and property-related ones—since the motives and pattern of occurrences of riots and left-wing extremism are different from the others. Riots are chaotic collective action by members of a group against those of another exhibiting the character of herd mentality while murder or property-related crimes are entirely criminal initiatives at an individual level. Riots are, in fact, a form of civil disorder characterized by a group lashing out against other groups or members of authority and involving looting, arson, vandalism, and destruction of public or private property. The insurgency of left-wing extremists is also organized violence by politically motivated groups of a Marxist or Maoist ideology targeting the state power for liberating people of a region (mostly one which is backward and undeveloped) suffering from economic deprivation, whose objective and motivation is also very different from the perpetrators of homicide or property-related crimes.

For comprehensive analysis for robustness, we first found out the bi-variate simple connection between each of the four types of crimes and the different measures of inequality, poverty, and social tension. We considered the Gini coefficient of income (consumption) due to relative deprivation to measure inequality and the poverty ratio along with the poverty gap for absolute deprivation. The social welfare losses per capita associated respectively with the Gini coefficient and the poverty gap are taken as measures of social tensions.

In view of this we have considered both inequality-based social tension (as per Sen's social welfare function) and poverty-based social tension (the Kakwani model of measuring poverty-related social welfare loss) to estimate bi-variate correlations using panel data for the two dimensions as follows.

1. Pooled time series and cross-section data on both crime, and inequality, poverty, and the related social tension measures.

2. First difference of consecutive period for both dependent and independent variables of each state as per our observation (for each state the difference of the value of any period over the previous one and then pooled over all states for estimating the concerned bi-variate correlation). This would yield results that are independent of state-specific factors such as the dominant ethnic or religious identity.

3. State-level averages of each state over all the periods for both independent and dependent variables. (Because of the statistical insignificance of such correlations we have dropped the results from presentations in the tables later and from further analysis.)

For the preceding three cases of analysis based on data dimensions, the pooled time series and cross-section panel data size was 96, that of the first difference for consecutive periods over all the cross-sectional units has been 80, and the number of cross-sectional units for estimating state-level correlations has been 16.

In Table 3.1, we present the description, mean, and standard deviation of the concerned dependent and independent explanatory variables for the sample panel data.

Since a major thrust of our enquiry in the context of the issue of social sustainability is on crime-related sustainability of our development process, it is worth noting the results on direct correlation between any crime and the measures of inequality or poverty and the two types of respective social tension measures related to them.

Tables 3.2 presents the pair-wise correlation values between inequality or poverty or social tensions (both inequality-based and poverty-induced) on the one hand and the incidence of crime of each of our three types on the other, at two of the three levels of use of panel data for Indian states for which correlation estimates were found to be statistically significant. We further work out such pair-wise correlations among the same set of variables, but separately for the variation of the concerned variables over time within any given state, as well as for cross-section variation across states for any given year or period. We also work out a similar correlation for any given year or period as per the cross-sectional variation across states. It is the mean and the median of the correlation value estimates for a state as well as for a period that are presented in Table 3.3 for the different types of violent crimes being considered.

TABLE 3.1 Mean and Standard Deviation for the Variables Used in the Model

Variables	Mean	Standard Deviation
Murder (Number of Incidents)	1,170.03	1,193.34
Dacoity + Robbery + Burglary (Number of Incidents)	4,414.82	5,116.48
Riots (Number of Incidents)	2,435.76	3,109.71
Left-Wing Extremism (Number of Incidents)	40.10	55.188
Log of GSDP Per Capita	4.88	0.69
Gini Coefficient	0.31	0.21
Gini-Based Tension Index	0.54	0.45
Poverty Gap	0.56	0.28
Poverty-Based Tension Index	0.39	0.35
Share of Urban Population (Per Cent)	31.12	14.25
State Literacy Rate (Per Cent)	76.01	7.93
GSDP Per Capita Growth (Per Cent)	4.59	6.18
Police Personnel Employed per 1,000 Population	10.52	1.01
Share of Minority Population (Per Cent)	33.88	28.27
Share of SC and ST Population (Per Cent)	17.01	20.84
Road Density at the State Level Per Sq Km	0.63	0.38

Source: Author's own estimations.

TABLE 3.2 Pair-wise Correlation of the Concerned Variables

	Headcount Ratio	Gini Coefficient	Gini-Based Tension Index	Poverty-Based Tension Index
Murder				
Pooled Levels	0.41	0.23	0.31	0.36
Pooled First Difference	0.44	0.32	0.44	0.48
Dacoity + Robbery + Burglary				
Pooled Levels	30.8	0.28	0.29	0.34
Pooled First Difference	0.23	0.16	0.13	0.19
Riots				
Pooled Levels	0.40	0.42	0.37	0.46
Pooled First Difference	0.39	0.38	0.31	0.35
Left-Wing Extremism				
Pooled Levels	0.38	0.30	0.31	0.35
Pooled First Difference	0.37	0.32	0.31	0.38

Source: Author's own estimations.

TABLE 3.3   Mean and Median of Pair-wise Correlations of the Concerned Variables

	Headcount Ratio		Gini Coefficient		Gini-Based Tension Index		Poverty-Based Tension Index	
Murder								
	Within State	*Within Period*	*Within State*	*Within Period*	*Within State*	*Within Period*	*Within State*	*Within Period*
Mean	0.48	0.46	0.31	0.39	0.29	0.38	0.46	0.44
Median	0.52	0.54	0.44	0.40	0.47	0.45	0.48	0.49
Dacoity + Robbery + Burglary								
Mean	0.49	0.53	0.27	0.34	0.31	0.51	0.41	0.49
Median	0.55	0.60	0.33	0.38	0.39	0.40	0.52	0.56
Riots								
Mean	0.44	0.42	0.33	0.37	0.28	0.26	0.39	0.41
Median	0.46	0.48	0.36	0.39	0.31	0.33	0.41	0.44
Left-Wing Extremism								
Mean	0.39	0.41	0.47	0.49	0.44	0.46	0.49	0.54
Median	0.45	0.45	0.48	0.52	0.46	0.50	0.53	0.58

Source: Author's own estimations.

Table 3.2 presents a pair-wise simple correlation between any of the four types of crimes on the one hand and the Gini index of inequality, inequality-induced social tension, the headcount poverty ratio, and the poverty gap–induced social tension on the other. Since the rural–urban break-up of crime data is not available, to maintain consistency, we have had to take an overall state-level average—the un-weighted simple geometric mean of the urban and rural sector values of both the dependent variables of crime and the independent variables of inequality, poverty, and their associated social tensions for the estimation of our bi-variate correlations. Such a geometric mean will, in fact, indicate the measure of inequality, poverty, or tension for the entire state if the individual rural or urban values of these items are adjusted to get the overall state-level value for their equivalent equalized distribution between the rural and the urban sectors.

We find in Tables 3.2 and 3.3 that among the different possible determining factors in respect of murders, it is the poverty-related social tension index (using the Kakwani formula based on poverty gap) that has the highest simple correlation with expected signs. The simple head-count ratio comes next in order in terms of the magnitude of correlation. In both these cases, the correlation results are stronger for the first difference of the values of the successive periods of both the variables of the panel data. This means that the covariances of the two variables are stronger when the state-specific fixed effects are removed from the observed values of the variables.

So far as the property-related crimes are concerned, it is again the headcount poverty ratio and the poverty gap–related social tension index which have the highest or the second-highest correlation values among the determining factors (see Table 3.2). The property-related crime results show that such high correlations are influenced by both state-specific and any other random factors.

Finally, the incidents of riots are found to have, again, the highest simple correlation of 0.46 with poverty-related social tension using pooled level data (see Table 3.2). This estimate of correlation would, however, drop to 0.42 if we focus on the relationship between Gini coefficient and riots and to 0.37 when it is inequality-induced social tension and riots.

Alternatively, if we focus on the correlation estimates between crime and inequality- or poverty-induced social tension measures within the period across the states or within state across time periods, the following observations are important.

1. The values of correlations within state or within period as presented in Table 3.3 are in general substantially higher than the estimates as presented in Table 3.2 by our initial way of using the panel data in the concerned two dimensions as indicated.
2. For all the four types of crime, the poverty-related measures of social tension have higher simple correlation with crime than relative inequality or inequality-related social tension measures.

However, it is also important to note that the median values of correlation estimates between the variables within state and the same within period methods of analysis are higher than their respective mean values. Thus we may conclude that our first cut of results on the crime and inequality relationship on the basis of simple correlation indicate that poverty and poverty-related social tensions are the most important factors for all violent crimes, including riots and left-wing extremism. However, the 'within state' and 'within period' analysis of the relationship further points to how the strength of such correlations is distributed over the different states and the different periods. The comparative estimates of simple correlation in the context of the 'within state' or 'within period' analysis would further point to the need for explanation of further determining other underlying factors as well which gives rise to the variation of crime over time and space. All these are likely to develop better monitoring and abatement policies of crimes which would require greater attention on the poverty-related tension issues in the Indian context.

Multi-variate Regression Analysis

We have to, however, note that inequality and poverty or the respective measures of tensions are not the only causal factors behind the violent crimes as considered. There are other factors related with economic growth or human development (such as per capita stated, growth rate of GSDP, rate of literacy) that can influence the crime rates and very likely reduce the rate of their occurrence. Urbanization (that is, the percentage of urban population (U) in the total state population) is also a similar influencing factor as the high density of population in urban areas combined with the inferior living conditions of congested slum areas often raise the level of deprivation and suffering from a sense of discrimination in respect of the supply of public goods, including urban civic amenities. Again, the high density of population in state can impact the crime rate in two ways: (i) it increases the supply of potential victims who do not know the criminal and (ii) it reduces the chance of being caught (Glasser and Sacerdote 1999; Kelly 2000). Finally, the availability of better supply of public goods—such as internal police security—would also have a definite impact on the crime rate. It also influences the risk of such criminal activity in the perception of the perpetrator of the crime.

The total number of events of a crime of a given type (homicide, property-related ones, and so on) is, in fact, a result of:

1. the size of the population (N);
2. factors conditioning the crime environment;

3. factors determining the share of population predisposed towards committing crime; and

4. the perceived level of risk of a particular crime, which is not the same for all situations of crime opportunities.

With reference to the second point, the circumstances for committing a possible crime arise if a potential victim comes across other people who are unknown to him and the potential perpetrator perceives the crime as not involving too much risk. High population density raises the supply of potential victims and reduces the chance of a criminal being caught; it would, in fact, raise the expected number of opportunities or situations of committing crimes by its perpetrators. Let ∂ be the rate at which such opportunities arise per capita of criminally predisposed population, ∂ depending on population density and social interaction.

As we have already discussed, it is mainly inequality, poverty, and socio-economic discrimination (inequality or poverty related) that give rise to social tension variables (vector X), which are the major determinants of the share of population predisposed towards committing crime (Q), or the malefactor for the population.

However, the Q factor would also be influenced, favourably moderated, or reduced, by the level of economic development of a state economy—per capita GDP (y), GDP growth rate (g), rate of literacy of the state (l). The rate of urbanization (u) (which is the share of the urban population in the total population) is expected to have a moderating effect, provided that urbanization is equitable in terms of distribution of benefit of urban public good services.

There are some opportunities that are considered to involve not too high a risk as per the perception of the potential criminals: Let π be the fraction of such potential situations or opportunities of such moderate risk that make it worth committing a crime. Such π will be determined by the density of the population (d) as well as the scale of police activity or internal security service available (p). The p may be measured either in terms of size of police personnel or of the financial budget or expenditure for police or internal security.

The number of occurrences of the event of any type of crime is a discrete random variable and its average rate of occurrence (λ) is fixed for a defined period. Again, the chance of occurrence of the event at any point of time is independent of when last the event had occurred. Since all these conditions are mostly satisfied by these variables of crime rate per period, we assume the probability density function of the number of occurrences of a crime in a large number of trial experiments of the crime event, to be a Poisson density function:

$$P(x=k) = \frac{e^{-\lambda}\lambda^{k}}{k!}$$

Its mean and variance would both be λ.

For any of the individual crimes, if λ is the expected or average number of occurrences per period, then $\lambda = Q(N, \theta, \delta, \pi)$. In light of the earlier discussion, since θ, ∂, and π are, in turn, dependent on x, d, p, e, y, l, g, and u, we have set up an econometric model of a double-log linear relationship between each type of crime and such explanatory variables. We have normalized the measures of some of the variables and/or changed the units of measurement in the interest of better presentation or interpretability of results. For example, we normalized all the relevant variables in per capita terms, or say variables such as the size of the police force in terms of number per 1,000 of population, and so on.

Again, given the nature of the dependent and independent variables, the multiple regression models would often involve endogeneity problems due to dependence of some of the explanatory dependent variable itself on the error term or dependent variables. In view of this, we have run the GMM to estimate most of the relationships, which would essentially search for some instrumental variables as proxy for the explanatory variables suffering from the problem of endogeneity. These instrumental variables have to be uncorrelated with the error term and provide the best fit (maximum likelihood–based estimator) relationship. Instrumental variables are often chosen to be the lagged values of the concerned variables suffering from the endogeneity problem.

We have estimated a set of multi-variate GMM models of regression to explain the different types of crimes in terms of socio-economic factors expressed mostly at the macro state level in India in order to develop a policy for a sustainable society by reducing the crime rate.

These models can be classified and grouped as follows: For a given crime variable, there would be a selected set of alternative causal variables to serve as regressor variables. In our context, the regressor variables would be of two kinds: (*i*) social tension variables related to either inequality or poverty that are the sources of social unsustainability, and (*ii*) other socio-economic co-variables simultaneously influencing crime rate. For the models together, these socio-economic co-variates used are listed in the generalized model specification as described below.

Let Z_i be the *i*th regressed crime variable, X_J be the *j*th inequality/poverty or social tension–related variables, Y_K be the *k*th socio-economic co-variates; influencing the crime variables, the proposed models are the following double-log linear ones:

$$\log z_i = \alpha_i + \sum_j \beta_{ij} \log x_j + \sum_k \gamma_{ik} \log y_k + \in$$

where I = Murder, property-related crimes, riots, and left-wing extremism

j = Gini coefficient (inequality) index, social tension index (Gini coefficient–based or Sen's social welfare function–based poverty ratio, poverty gap–related social tension index (Kakwani 2016)

K = GSDP per capita or consumption, GSDP growth rate, state literacy rate (per cent), share of urban population (per cent) in the state, size of police personnel per 1,000 population, road density of the state, share of minority population (per cent), share of SC/ST population, religious polarization index at the state level.

The models have been estimated for the different combinations of the independent variables that were considered relevant or important for investigating the causal factors of the concerned crime. Besides, while estimating the models, all the variables—dependent as well as independent—were once taken at the original absolute levels and once again at the level of first difference between the values of the successive periods in the panel data. We discuss later the results of the models for estimating the elasticity of the different crimes as presented in Tables 3.4a to 3.9b.

TABLE 3.4A   Model for Elasticity Estimate of Homicides with Respect to Causal Factors of Inequality along with Socio-economic Ones

Regression Specification	Double Log at Levels (Including Observed and Unobserved State-Specific Effects)	Double Log at First Difference (Removing the Unobserved State-Specific Effects)	Double Log at Levels (Including Observed and Unobserved State-Specific Effects)	Double Log at First Difference (Removing the Unobserved State-Specific Effects)
Independent Variables	Coefficients			
1. Inequality Variables				
(a) Gini Coefficient	0.887*	0.548*	—	—
(b) Gini-Based Social Tension	—	—	0.493*	0.880*
2. Other Socio-economic Variables				
(a) GSDP Per Capita	−0.214*	−0.136*	−0.319*	−0.250*
(b) GSDP Per Capita Growth Rate	−0.150*	−0.585*	−0.118*	−0.329*
(c) State Literacy Rate	−2.997*	−3.441*	−2.383*	−2.971*
(d) Urbanization	−0.155*	−0.150*	−0.151	−0.365*
(e) Size of Police Force	−1.187*	−1.284*	−1.158*	−1.101*
3. Intercept	6.952*	6.918*	7.052*	13.312*
4. Number of States	29	29	29	29
5. Number of Time Periods	6	6	6	6
6. Sargan Test (p Value)	0.51*	0.48*	0.46*	0.37*

Source: Author's own estimations.

Note: *Represents significant at the 95 per cent level.

TABLE 3.4B   Model for Elasticity Estimate of Homicides with Respect to Causal Factors of Poverty along with Socio-economic Ones

Regression Specification	Double Log at Levels (Including Observed and Unobserved State-Specific Effects)	Double Log at First Difference (Removing the Unobserved State-Specific Effects)	Double Log at Levels (Including Observed and Unobserved State-Specific Effects)	Double Log at First Difference (Removing the Unobserved State-Specific Effects)
Independent Variables	Coefficients			
1. Poverty Variables				
(a) Poverty Gap	1.038*	1.185*	—	—
(b) Poverty-Based Social Tension	—	—	1.012*	1.618*
2. Other Socio-economic Variables				
(a) GSDP Per Capita	−0.298*	−0.783*	−0.258*	0.001
(b) GSDP Per Capita Growth Rate	−0.281*	−0.999*	−0.322*	−1.015*
(c) State Literacy Rate	−3.074*	−3.557*	−5.395*	−4.957*
(d) Urbanization	−0.037	0.052	0.205	−0.062
(e) Size of Police Force	−1.251*	−1.263*	−1.175*	−1.220*
3. Intercept	3.827*	4.530*	14.240*	10.823*
4. Number of States	16	16	16	16
5. Number of Time Periods	6	6	6	6
6. Sargan Test (p value)	0.54*	0.52*	0.67*	0.59*

Source: Author's own estimations.

Note: *Represents significant at the 95 per cent level.

Results: Murder

The results of GMM regressions on this particular crime are presented in Tables 3.4a and 3.4b, which have been obtained using panel data for the period 2009–14 for all the major states and union territories for which data was available. The regressions were estimated for both dependent and independent variables at the level values, as well as at their first-difference level where the state-specific fixed effects of unobserved variables were removed from the data. Although the values of unobserved variables may be correlated with the pure error term, the GMM, which involves use of instrumental variables, ensures consistency of the estimates in both cases. For the regression models with homicide as the dependant variable, we find that the Gini coefficient or the social tension index based on the Gini welfare function and alternatively, the poverty gap or social tension based on it (Kakwani 1988), are also significant in explaining homicide. However, the elasticity measure of homicide with respect to these variables shows that homicide is more elastic with respect to poverty gap–based social tension (or poverty gap) in the range of 1.012 to 1.618 than those of inequality or inequality-induced social tension measures in the range of 0.493 to 0.887. This implies that the depth of poverty (inequality of the distribution of income among poor) matters in at least the partial determination of the homicide rate. So far as the other socio-economic variables are concerned, variations in all of them—except urbanization—have a significant effect with expected positive or negative sign of relationship. The per capita state income (or the level of a state's development) does not have significant effect on this crime rate when we consider the equation of the relationship or impact on homicide at the first difference level by eliminating the state-specific effect and when the social tension due to the poverty gap is considered as a co-variable along with other determinants. What is particularly worth noting is that the homicide rate is highly elastic with respect to a state's literacy rate and size of the police personnel in all the model versions. Economic growth is also found to have a statistically significant impact in reducing the homicide rate.

However, it is difficult to explain the greater importance or impact of absolute deprivation vis-à-vis relative deprivation in the incidence of this crime in India. Poorer states with deeper poverty are likely to have a higher homicide rate. However, it is difficult to conclude anything further from panel data that does not have any urban-rural break-up in the crime aspect of the statistics, although we have segregated income distribution of poverty data for rural and urban areas. Besides, one cannot make out the reason for homicide without making some of the case analyses to find out the real motive behind such a crime. It may so happen that the murder has occurred as a follow-up of other incidents, such as property dispute, rape, or other personal reasons which may not have anything with poverty or inequality.

Property-Related Violent Crime

In explaining property-related crimes of dacoity, burglary, or theft, we find Gini inequality measures to have a much greater impact—with higher elasticity estimates varying in the range of 0.435 to 2.193—than poverty-related measures whose elasticity of impact is in the range of 0.823 to 1.347, as shown in Tables 3.10a and 3.10b, where all coefficients of impact are significant with expected expected positive or negative sign of relationship. The higher elasticity value of impact on the crime in the concerned model can probably be explained in terms of sociological factors of higher wealth and consumption of the rich generating externalities such as a sense of wrongful deprivation and discrimination among the poor, inducing them into such crimes. All other socioeconomic variables have a mostly significant impact on the crime rate with the expected positive or negative sign of relationship, except in the case of urbanization, when it is the Gini tension index which is the considered co-variate along with these. Again, the GSDP per capita as well as urbanization become insignificant as explanatory factors when the poverty-related social tension index is considered as a co-variate in the model along with these.

Riots

So far as riots are concerned, the nature of the incidence of such a violent crime is different from homicide or property-related crimes. It is not the suffering of any individual perpetrator due to absolute or relative deprivation which is the root cause of such crime. Such violent incidences take the form of violent clashes between different groups of people in the society, each having a different identity in respect of religion, ethnicity, language, or culture. The proclivity of such groups

TABLE 3.5A   Model for Elasticity Estimate of Property-Related Crimes with Respect to Causal Factors of Inequality along with Socio-economic Ones

Regression Specification	Double Log at Levels (Including Observed and Unobserved State-Specific Effects)	Double Log at First Difference (Removing the Unobserved State-Specific Effects)	Double Log at Levels (Including Observed and Unobserved State-Specific Effects)	Double Log at First Difference (Removing the Unobserved State-Specific Effects)
Independent Variables	Coefficients			
1. Poverty Variables				
(a) Poverty Gap	0.435*	1.425*	—	—
(b) Poverty-Based Social Tension	—	—	2.193*	2.038*
2. Other Socio-economic Variables				
(a) GSDP Per Capita	−0.391*	−0.382*	−0.475*	−0.299*
(b) GSDP Per Capita Growth Rate	−0.135*	−0.686*	−0.115*	−0.122*
(c) State Literacy Rate	−2.364*	−2.316*	−1.622*	−2.266*
(d) Urbanization	0.342*	0.389*	−0.059	0.473*
(e) Size of Police Force	−0.945*	−0.986*	−1.213*	−1.366*
3. Intercept	7.471	6.397	−4.761	−11.527*
4. Number of States	29	29	29	29
5. Number of Time Periods	6	6	6	6
6. Sargan Test (p Value)	0.55*	0.49*	0.57*	0.46*

Source: Author's own estimations.

Note: *Represents significant at the 95 per cent level.

TABLE 3.5B Model for Elasticity Estimate of Property-Related Crimes with Respect to Causal Factors of Poverty along with Socio-economic Ones

Regression Specification	Double Log at Levels (Including Observed and Unobserved State-Specific Effects)	Double Log at First Difference (Removing the Unobserved State-Specific Effects)	Double Log at Levels (Including Observed and Unobserved State-Specific Effects)	Double Log at First Difference (Removing the Unobserved State-Specific Effects)
Independent Variables	Coefficients			
1. Poverty Variables				
(a) Poverty Gap	0.823*	1.065*	—	—
(b) Poverty-Based Social Tension	—	—	1.097*	1.347*
2. Other Socio-economic Variables				
(a) GSDP Per Capita	−0.512*	−0.461*	−0.388*	−0.321
(b) Per Capita GSDP Growth Rate	−0.296*	−0.202*	−0.104*	−0.336*
(c) State Literacy Rate	−1.713*	−1.788*	−3.489*	−2.732*
(d) Urbanization	0.268*	0.362*	0.394*	0.397
(e) Size of Police Force	−1.079*	−1.062*	−1.016*	−1.022*
3. Intercept	0.144	−0.314	7.086	3.280*
4. Number of States	16	16	16	16
5. Number of Time Periods	6	6	6	6
6. Sargan Test (p Value)	0.51*	0.47*	0.57*	0.52*

Source: Author's own estimations.

Note: *Represents significant at the 95 per cent level.

or communities to commit such a violent crime may be caused by economic deprivation commonly suffered by most of the members of the group, in respect of differing objectives of their respective self-fulfilment, or group-level self-interest.

An issue may arise here if religious, caste-wise, linguistic, or ethnic fragmentation due to pluralism in a vast country like India would be responsible for violent conflicts, which may take the form of riots. However, pluralism as such need not lead to a situation of violent conflicts and clashes among different communities that have coexisted peacefully over several centuries in India, leading to the evolution of a cultural and socio-economic formation that has shown broad resilience to many exogenous shocks or temporal disturbances. However, pluralism does not ensure that there will *never* be any violent confrontations in a polarizing situation of class or sectional interests. It is, in fact, the polarization of different groups—due to heterogeneity in their attributes or characteristics leading to differences in their preferences of socio-economic outcomes or agendas of development—that may lead to tension or conflict.

According to Jaon-Maria Estaben and Debraj Ray (1994), the population of a country can be thought of as being grouped according to a vector of characteristics or attributes into groups that may be called 'clusters'. In a polarizing situation, members within each such cluster according to the grouping are very similar but members across clusters are dissimilar in terms of their attributes. The choice of attributes for such groupings should be relevant in the context that can capture the basis of the conflict among groups because of divergent and conflicting interests for their respective development, resulting in violent conflicts such as riots, civil wars, revolutions, and so on. For polarization to occur, clusters should meet the following criteria.

1. There should be a high degree of homogeneity among members within each group or cluster.
2. There needs to be a high degree of heterogeneity among members across clusters.
3. There should be only a small number of significantly sized clusters and groups with an insignificant size (outliers) should carry little weight in the distribution of population across groups or clusters.

If there are m number of such groups in a society with population N, a fragmentation index often commonly chosen (following the Herfindahl index of diversity) is:

$$F = 1 - \sum_{i=1}^{m} \left(\frac{n_i}{N} \right)^2$$

where, n_i is the size of the ith group. While this index conveys the extent of information regarding the diversity or fragmentation of the society, it does not convey any information regarding the polarization of the people in terms of potential of conflict due to divergence of their interests. On the other hand, the RQ Index (Montalvo and Reynal-Querol 2003) as given later conveys the information regarding the polarization of the people as classified into groups according to their attributes or agendas of interest.

$$RQ = 1 - \sum_{i=1}^{m} \left(\frac{0.5 - \pi_i}{0.5} \right)^2 \pi_i$$

where,

$$\pi_i = \frac{n_i}{N}$$

This formula can be justified as a polarization index in terms of a rent-seeking model as outlined in the Appendix 3A.

Table 3.6 shows the religious polarization index values for all major Indian states in 2010–14. The basic assumption behind the table has been that the Indian population across the states mainly consists of five religious groups: Hindus, Muslims, Christians, Sikhs, and others. It should be noted that states such as Assam, Uttar Pradesh, Kerala, West Bengal, and Punjab have very high values of the polarization index, while Himachal Pradesh, Odisha, and Maharashtra have a low polarization index. Punjab and Himachal Pradesh have the highest and least religious polarization respectively.

We have, however, estimated GMM regression models for estimating the determining role of the different factors for riots. We first use only the inequality- and poverty-related variables reflecting deprivation and social tension arising from them, as well as the proportion of the minority communities and the SC/ST sections in the total state

TABLE 3.6 Values of Polarization Index for 16 Major Indian States

States	2010	2011	2012	2013	2014
Andhra Pradesh	0.382	0.395	0.392	0.395	0.396
Assam	0.801	0.895	0.892	0.883	0.888
Bihar	0.558	0.568	0.569	0.570	0.571
Gujarat	0.380	0.393	0.394	0.395	0.396
Haryana	0.390	0.411	0.413	0.413	0.411
Himachal Pradesh	0.179	0.178	0.177	0.177	0.169
Karnataka	0.569	0.511	0.510	0.509	0.509
Kerala	0.855	0.860	0.860	0.861	0.861
Madhya Pradesh	0.316	0.318	0.319	0.319	0.319
Maharashtra	0.568	0.582	0.583	0.585	0.585
Odisha	0.221	0.229	0.229	0.230	0.234
Punjab	0.920	0.929	0.925	0.925	0.925
Rajasthan	0.407	0.391	0.389	0.387	0.386
Tamil Nadu	0.399	0.408	0.409	0.410	0.411
Uttar Pradesh	0.616	0.635	0.637	0.638	0.641
West Bengal	0.770	0.800	0.803	0.806	0.810

Source: Author's own estimations based on data from National Crime Records Bureau Database.

population, as indicators of social divisiveness and other developmental co-variates as explanatory factors of riots. These models do not consider the polarization index as a determining factor for riots. The results are presented in Table 3.7a. We next estimate a model without variables such as the proportion of religious minorities and the SC/ST classes in the population and replaced them with the religious polarization index. We estimated the model with polarization as the explanatory factor, first with economic inequality- or poverty-based social tension as co-variates and then without such deprivation-related tension as a co-variate. The results of these models are presented in Tables 3.7b and 3.7c. However, other socio-economic developmental variables such as state literacy, per capita state income, among others, have been considered as co-variates in all these model versions.

The models quite expectedly show that it is social tensions due to both poverty and inequality that have a statistically significant impact on the number of riotous incidents, although the elasticity value of the number of riots is of higher value with respect to poverty-induced social

TABLE 3.7A   Model for Elasticity Estimate of Riots with Respect to Causal Factors of Poverty along with Socio-economic Ones

Regression Specification Independent Variables	Double Log at Levels (Including Observed and Unobserved State-Specific Effects)	Double Log at First Difference Level (Removing the Unobserved State Specific Effects)
1. (a) Inequality-Induced Social Tension	0.407*	—
(b) Poverty-Induced Social Tension	—	0.871*
2. **Other Socio-economic Variables**		
(a) GSDP Per Capita	−0.644*	−0.627*
(b) GSDP Per Capita Growth Rate	−0.653*	−0.166*
(c) State Literacy Rate	−3.088*	−1.621*
(d) Urbanization	−0.426*	−0.333*
(e) Size of Police Force	−0.670*	−0.800*
(f) Minority Population Share	0.714*	0.450*
(g) SC/ST Population Share	0.925*	0.706*
3. **Intercept**	−14.616	−13.155
4. **Number of states**	29	16
5. **Number of Time Periods**	6	6
6. **Sargan Test (*p* Value)**	0.41*	0.49*

Source: Author's own estimations.

Note: *Represents significant at the 95 per cent level.

tension than the inequality-induced one (see Tables 3.7a, 3.7b, and 3.7c). It is, however, important to note that all the other development-related variables have a significant impact on riots with expected sign (that is, negative). The variables representing the share of the minority or SC/ST populations have, on the other hand, a significant impact with a positive sign. This implies that the policy of promoting social cohesion and the protection of minority and Dalits are important for peace and cohesion.

Poverty- or inequality-based social tension as well as religious polarization in India has a significant impact on the number of riots but the partial impact of inequality-related tension is comparatively of a lower magnitude (see Tables 3.7b and 3.7c) when compared with

TABLE 3.7B Model for Elasticity Estimate of Riots with Respect to Causal Factors of Poverty-Related Tension and Inequality-Related Tension in the Presence of Polarization along with Socio-economic Ones

Regression Specification	Double Log at Levels (Including Observed and Unobserved State-Specific Effects) with Inequality-Related Social Tension	Double Log at First Difference (Removing the Unobserved State-Specific Effects) with Inequality-Related Social Tension	Double Log at Levels (Including Observed and Unobserved State-Specific Effects) with Poverty-Related Social Tension	Double Log at First Difference (Removing the Unobserved State-Specific Effects) with Poverty-Related Social Tension
Independent Variables	Coefficients			
1. Poverty Variables				
(a) Inequality-Based Social Tension	0.510*	0.827*	—	—
(b) Poverty-Based Social Tension	—	—	1.113*	1.235*
(c) Polarization Index	0.759	0.901*	1.224*	1.351*
2. Other Socio-economic Variables				
(a) GSDP Per Capita	−0.453*	−0.528*	−0.418*	−0.468*
(b) GSDP Per Capita Growth Rate	−0.316*	−0.189*	−0.141*	−0.318*
(c) State Literacy Rate	−1.411*	−1.510*	−2.967*	−2.399*
(d) Urbanization	0.321	0.116	0.401	0.212
(e) Size of Police Force	−0.995*	−1.034*	−1.021*	−1.005*
3. Intercept	0.712	−0.423	8.191	4.890*
4. Number of States	16	16	16	16
5. Number of Time Periods	6	6	6	6
6. Sargan Test (*p* Value)	0.50*	0.44*	0.55*	0.50*

Source: Author's own estimations.

Note: *Represents significant at the 95 per cent level.

TABLE 3.7C   Model for Elasticity Estimate of Riots with Respect to Causal Factors of Polarization along with Socio-economic Ones

Regression Specification	Double Log at Levels (Including Observed and Unobserved State-Specific Effects)	Double Log at First Difference (Removing the Unobserved State-Specific Effects)
Independent Variables		
Polarization Index	1.451*	1.399*
Other Socio-economic Variables		
(a) GSDP Per Capita	−0.512*	−0.481*
(b) GSDP Per Capita Growth Rate	−0.391*	−0.297*
(c) State Literacy Rate	−1.919*	−1.888*
(d) Urbanization	0.491	0.681
(e) Size of Police Force	−1.591*	−1.002*
3. **Intercept**	0.214	−0.467
4. **Number of states**	16	16
5. **Number of Time Periods**	6	6
6. **Sargan Test (*p* Value)**	0.51*	0.52*

Source: Author's own estimations.

Note: *Represents significant at the 95 per cent level.

that of the impact of poverty-induced social tension with polarization. Polarization, in fact, becomes insignificant as an explanatory variable when it is considered as a co-variate with inequality-induced social tension. On the other hand, polarization is found to be a significant causal factor with an elasticity impact greater than unity in both the cases of treatment of the panel data inclusive of observed and unobserved effects and in the case of use of data after the removal of only the unobserved effects. As in the case of models for other crimes, the socio-economic developmental co-variates have a significant impact on riots with the expected sign (positive abating effects). However, polarization has a significantly high elasticity value of impact on riots when no deprivation-related social tension variable is not considered as co-variate.

Left-Wing Extremism

Extremist activities constitute a source of violence and crime in India in certain regions like Kashmir, parts of the Northeastern states, as well as states such as Jharkhand, Bihar, Chhattisgarh, Madhya Pradesh, Odisha, and West Bengal. The form of violence has mostly been insurgency, terror attacks by poor people mobilized by the political leaders, who are driven by their political and economic ideology and agenda. The terror attacks in the Kashmir Valley are mostly driven by political factors and issues of dispute between the Indian state on the one hand and the Pakistani state, Pakistan-supported terror groups, or local Kashmiri political-economic entities on the other. The insurgency problem of the Northeast can again be attributed to complex regional, ethnic, and political issues along with the long neglect of development in the region. However, the violent insurgency in parts of the eastern, central, and southern states has been driven by mainly left-wing extremist (Maoists or Naxalite) groups. These states and regions are endowed with natural resources of forests and minerals, but are characterized by poor development, poverty, and highly inequitable or unequal distribution of assets and income. Most of the poor

TABLE 3.8 Number of Incidents of Violence Causing Deaths Due to Left-Wing Extremism (2011–14)

States	Incidents in 2011	Incidents in 2012	Incidents in 2013	Incidents in 2014
Andhra Pradesh	54	67	28	18
Bihar	316	166	177	163
Chhattisgarh	465	370	355	328
Jharkhand	517	480	387	384
Madhya Pradesh	8	11	1	3
Maharashtra	109	134	71	70
Odisha	192	171	101	103
Uttar Pradesh	1	2	0	0
West Bengal	92	6	1	0
TOTAL	**1,760**	**1,415**	**1,136**	**1,091**

Source: State-wise details of left-wing-extremist violence from 2011–18, Ministry of Home Affairs, Government of India.

people from rural areas, often the adivasis (ST) of these states, are dispossessed of their natural resources because of the exploitation or aggression on these poor by the rich landlords or contractors and traders of the natural resources. Left-wing extremists therefore organize the poor exploited people of such states and regions and mobilize them to launch attacks on their exploiters—the landlords, moneylenders, and the police, who are taken as agents of the state protecting the interest of the exploiters.

It may further be noted that the regions (districts), which are affected by poverty and inequality in income distribution also suffer from lack of infrastructural support, particularly road connectivity. The latter facilitates terror attacks in the form of insurgency. The maps of forest cover, distribution of poverty, and that of low level of road density overlap each other in such regions.

However, the incidences of such left-wing extremism is also contingent on the most fundamental determinants of human development—education and economic growth—which are likely to reduce such crime rates. The development of internal security infrastructure (the size of the police force for example) in the state would also help abate the incidences of such crimes.

In order to examine the significance of the impact of the above-mentioned factors on the incidences of this kind of violence, we set up the following two econometric models:

MODEL A (RESULTS IN TABLE 3.9A) Dependent variable: Number of incidents of violence causing death due to left-wing extremism.

Independent variables: Inequality Gini coefficient–related social tension measures, road density, literacy rate, growth rate of per capita GSDP, size of police force per 1,000 population.

MODEL B (RESULTS REPORTED IN TABLE 3.9B) Dependent variables: Number of incidents of violence due to left-wing extremism causing death.

Independent variables: Poverty gap–related social tension measures, road density, literacy rate, growth rate of GSDP per capita, size of police force per 1,000 population.

We have estimated these models with panel data formed out of basic data on crimes or violence due to left-wing extremism, road density, and other developmental factors as obtained from the Crime Bureau

TABLE 3.9A   Model for Elasticity Estimate of Number of Incidents of Violence Causing Death Due to Left-Wing Extremism with Respect to Causal Factors of Gini-Based Social Tension along with Socio-economic Ones

Regression Specification	Double Log at Levels (Including Observed and Unobserved State-Specific Effects)	Double Log at First Difference (Removing the Unobserved State-Specific Effects)
Independent Variables	Coefficients	
1. Inequality Variables		
Gini-Based Social Tension	0.8177*	0.2326
2. Other Socio-economic Variables		
(a) Road Density Per Sq Km	−1.9838*	−2.7499*
(b) GSDP Per Capita Growth Rate	−1.0447*	−0.0720*
(c) State Literacy Rate	−5.0536*	−4.8034*
(d) Size of Police Force	−0.1742*	−0.1597*
3. Intercept	58.422	20.626
4. Number of States	11	11
5. Number of Time Periods	4	4
6. Sargan Test (*p* Value)	0.34*	0.38*

Source: Author's own estimations.

Note: *Represents significant at the 95 per cent level.

of Statistics, Road Research Wing of the Ministry of Transport and Highways and former Planning Commission and the Central Statistics Office (see Table 3.8). In all the versions of the model, we have used the double-log GMM regression method for estimation. We have estimated each of the two models at the level values of the dependent and independent log variables as well as at their first difference values. The inequality- or poverty-related social tension measures as independent variables have a significant impact on such violence. However, infrastructural variables such as road development and internal security infrastructure in terms of road density per sq km and number of police personnel per 1,000 population tend to reduce such impact on the dependent variable of violent incidents as expected, while the human development factors like the level of literacy in the state also have a significant moderating

TABLE 3.9B   Model for Elasticity Estimate of Number of Incidents of Violence Causing Death Due to Left-Wing Extremism with Respect to Causal Factors of Poverty-Based Social Tension along with Socio-economic Ones

Regression Specification	Double Log at Levels (Including Observed and Unobserved State-Specific Effects)	Double Log at First Difference (Removing the Unobserved State-Specific Effects)
Independent Variables	Coefficients	
1. Poverty Variables		
Poverty-Based Social Tension	0.5517*	0.0389
2. Other Socio-economic Variables		
(a) Road Density Per Sq Km	−1.3482*	−3.5070*
(b) GSDp Per Capita Growth Rate	−0.7138*	−1.1822*
(c) State Literacy Rate	−7.9944*	−8.9701*
(d) Size of Police Force	−3.0367*	−2.8185*
3. Intercept	55.7522	69.2350
4. Number of States	11	11
5. Number of Time Periods	4	4
6. Sargan Test (p value)	0.49*	0.54*

Source: Author's own estimations.

Note: *Represents significant at the 95 per cent level.

effect on such events through its impact on the overall level of development of that state. However, we observe that the results at the first difference level show the impact of social tension related with inequality or poverty as insignificant, possibly due to a small sample problem on account of data limitations. We have therefore to use the results of Tables 3.9a and 3.9b based on level values of the variates for framing policies and other analytic purposes.

The policy implications of the results as presented in Tables 3.9a and 3.9b point out clearly that both inequality- and poverty-related social tensions have a significant impact with high positive elasticity on left-wing extremism. The inequality-related tension measure has, however, a relatively higher impact in terms of its absolute elasticity value in comparison to that of poverty-related social tension. All the other developmental variables, including security-related infrastructural connectivity, are found to reduce such violent activities. However, two points need to be noted here:

1. The relative disparity in income and asset, not just poverty, has a high role in accelerating violence of the kind being discussed.
2. Education or literacy is the most important developmental instruments in abating such acts of violence driven by political economic factors.

While economic growth plays a definite positive role in abating such violence, developmental policies require some definite direction of growth to not only remove absolute deprivation or poverty but also reduce the absolute gap between the rich and the poor, and particularly have a role to play in reducing the levels of inequality among the poor. Besides, development strategies should give high priority to literacy, education, and human development if they are to have a sustainable impact in reducing violence by left-wing extremists and promoting peace in India.

All the results for the different crimes discussed earlier imply the importance of growth with job creation so that both income and employment grow simultaneously with required redistributive and poverty-alleviation effects. This points to the important role that programmes such as the Mahatma Gandhi National Rural Employment Guarantee Act (MGNREGA) can play to achieve such objectives that are fundamental for social sustainability. A targeted poverty-alleviation programme would also be helpful in intensifying the process of making development socially more sustainable by reducing crime. The focus on education, especially the literacy rate, needs to be prioritized for attaining a crime-free sustainable society. It is also important to focus on reinforcing the infrastructure for internal security, including the size of the police force and the budgetary spending for strengthening the infrastructure to effectively contain crime in a vast country with inter-linkages and connectivity among its often densely populated states and regions. Finally, social harmony among castes and religious groups is of crucial importance in reducing the incidents of riots in India over and above other development programmes in general.

Appendix 3A: Polarization Index

Let us consider a society composed of N individuals distributed into m groups with m different issues of interests or agendas (for example, supply of different public goods). Let π_i be the proportion of individuals in group i. The society would choose an outcome over the m possible issues of interests, which concerns the ith group. We define u_{ij} as the utility derived by group i from the jth issue. Let this utility function be of the pure contest type:

$$u_{ii} > u_{ij} = 0 \text{ for all } i, j \text{ with } i \neq j$$

Let us further suppose that each group spends effort or resources to alter the outcome of the society in its favour by lobbying and spending resources for the purpose. Let x_i be the amount of expenditure on resources by group i. The total resources spent for lobbying by the society would be:

$$R = \sum_{i=1}^{m} \pi_i x_i$$

R can therefore be interpreted as the intensity of social conflict due to the divergence among the interest of the different groups. Let $c(x)$ be the cost of spending resources of amount x by each individual irrespective of the group identity. Let us assume the following:

$$c(x) = \frac{1}{2} x^2$$

In this rent-seeking RQ model, the basic element of the contest success function is defined by the probability of success, p_i for the issue i, the value of which would depend on resources spent by each group in favour of outcome i. We assume here R is positive.

Then,

$$p_i = \frac{\pi_i x_i}{\sum_{i=1}^{m} \pi_i x_i} = \frac{\pi_i x_i}{R}$$

It may be noted that in such contest function, an equi-proportionate change in spending of resources by all groups would leave the winning probability of each group unchanged. Each member of group i would spend resources in a manner so as to maximize the expected utility function, taking into account that he or she does not care about the non-preferred outcomes and the contest success function, giving the probability p is of the ratio form as given earlier.

The ith group maximizes

$$\sum_{i=1}^{m} p_i u_{ij} - c(x_i) = \sum_{i=1}^{m} p_i u_{ij} - \frac{1}{2} x_i^2 = p_i u_{ii} - \frac{1}{2} x_i^2$$

subject to $p_i = \dfrac{\pi_i x_i}{R}$

In the pure contest case, $u_{ij} = 0$ *for all* $j \neq i$ and for at least one j, x_j is positive for some j, $j \neq i$

The first order condition would yield,

$$\pi^2_i (u_{ii} - p_i u_{ii}) = \pi_i x_i R$$

Therefore,

$$R^2 = \sum_{i=1}^{m} \pi^2_i \left(u_{ii} - p_i u_{ii} \right)$$

From here one can derive by algebraic manipulations the value of R^2 by choosing the numeraire of u_{ii}, that is, of the marginal utility of a member of the ith group for the choice of the ith outcome to be some constant, say k; in this case, say $k = 4$.
This yields

$$R^2 = POL_i = 1 - \sum_{i=1}^{m} \left(\frac{0.5 - \pi_i}{0.5} \right)^2 \pi_i$$

The above can be interpreted as polarization or the intensity of the conflict index for the concerned economy or society.

4

Human Development, Environmental Sustainability, and Index of Overall Development

In Chapter 4 we introduce the issue of multidimensional poverty and review its method of measurement and estimation. We next review the notion of a human development indicator as the obverse of such multidimensional deprivation in terms of attainment of human capability. We also take up the issues and indicators of environmental sustainability. Two types of measures have also been developed to capture environmental unsustainability or sustainability (as its obverse indicator) in the chapter. We have reviewed the concept of the ecological footprint, which is a measure of stress, caused by human demands on the ecosystem in terms of appropriation of land of primary productivity expressed in some normalized standard unit. It shows the dominance of the component of the carbon footprint in the total ecological footprint, explaining the relative importance of climate change. We have also reviewed the environmental performance indicator as an obverse of the footprint measure, which indicates the extent of performance of environmental conservation and protection in terms of abatement of damage to the ecosystem, which is driven by human policy initiatives by different countries.

We finally try to develop an OSDI based on the three components of sustainability. The OSDI has been finally chosen to be a geometric mean of these three indicators of development—economic, social, and environmental. We give our estimates of OSDI for most of the countries, their rank as per this index, and the difference between OSDI and the per capita income–based conventional indicator (without any inequality adjustment).

Multidimensional Poverty

Income poverty focuses only on the inadequacy of income for meeting the basic needs of an economy. Income is only the purchasing power at the disposal of an individual to buy commodities and services to meet the basic needs as defined by the poverty line basket of consumption. However, income is not the only deprivation from which people suffer so far as their well-being in the comprehensive sense is concerned. The way the national poverty line is defined for different countries, it is anchored to a subsistence need and does not cover all the basics that are required for human health, education, sanitation, amenities, access to mobility and information, and so on, which are all essential to build the capability required for human development. It is therefore important to focus further on the dimensionalities of the basic needs and examine if a family is able to command the minimum requirement in each of the dimensions. Multidimensional deprivation would better human life in all kinds of different ways (Sen, 2000; Anand and Sen, 1997) deeply affecting human capability. The development of a multidimensional poverty index (MPI) has therefore been considered to be of importance to capture the extent and acuteness of human deprivations. The dimensions that have been considered for such index development have been education, health, and living standards (or conditions) for ascertaining the extent of deprivations and poverty in a multidimensional sense. The UNDP has presented a methodology of construction of a MPI in its *HDR* 2014, which follows the methodologies of Sabina Alkire and Maria Emma Santos (2010), Alkire et al. (2014), and others. The method considers several indicators in each dimension with their respective threshold values for deciding whether a family can be considered as deprived or not. These benchmarks of threshold values of indicators are as follows:

Education (Two Indicators)

1. School attainment: No member of the household has completed six years of schooling.
2. School attendance: At least one of the school-age children (up to grade 8) is not enrolled in school.

Health (Two Indicators)

1. At least one adult or child of the household is malnourished as per the body mass index for adults and by height-for-age index for any child under five years of age as per the World Health Organization (WHO) criterion.
2. At least one child has died in the family in the five years prior to the survey.

Standard of Living (Six Indicators)

1. Electricity: The household has no access to electricity.
2. Drinking water: The household has no access to safe drinking water, with nearest source of drinking water more than a 30-minute walk away.
3. There is no access to improved sanitation as per the MDG or if it is improved, it is shared.
4. Cooking fuel: The household primarily uses dirty biomass-based fuel such as fuel wood, charcoal, or dung cake for cooking.
5. If the house where the family lives has a floor made of dirt, sand, dung, and so on.
6. If the household does not own any asset which allows access to mobility or information relating to livelihood (such as the radio, TV, telephone, and motorbike or any other vehicle).

All the dimensions of poverty—education, health, and living conditions—are of equal weight, 33.3 per cent, and each indicator within a dimension is given the same weightage as per the *HDR* (2014). Thus, each of the indicators of education and health has weights of 1/6 or 16.7 per cent and each indicator of the standard of living (six in number as enlisted above) has been assigned a weightage of 1/18 or 5.6 per cent in the overall deprivation index. The score of deprivation is calculated at the household level by adding the deprivation score, where the maximum value can be 100 for all dimensions taken together. A family would, however, be defined as multidimensionally poor if the total deprivation score exceeds 33.3 per cent of such deprivation. If the score is more than or equal to 20 per cent or less than 33.3 per cent, then the family is near multidimensionally poor. However, a family having a score of such deprivation less than 20 per cent would be considered to not be multidimensionally poor. On the other hand, if the score of such a family is found to be exceeding 50 per cent, it will be considered as severely multidimensionally poor. The share of population of such a multidimensionally poor family in the total population is called the headcount multidimensional poverty ratio.

One can also find out the intensity of multidimensional poverty which is the ratio of the (*a*) weighted deprivation score of multidimensionally poor families using the family size as the weight to (*b*) the total size of population of multidimensionally poor families.

Thus, let s_i be the score of deprivation of *i*th family and *q* the number of multidimensionally poor people, that is, the number of such poor families weighted by family sizes as added up. In other words, if the number of families, for each of which s_i exceeds 33.3 per cent and *n* is the size of the total population of the economy, then;

$$H \text{ (headcount multidimensional poverty ratio)} = \frac{q}{n} \text{ and}$$

$$A \text{ (intensity of such poverty)} = \frac{\sum_{i \in m \, poor} s_i}{q}$$

Finally, we define the MPI to be calculated as $H \times A$.

If s_{ij} is the score of deprivation of the *i*th family in terms of *j*th dimension, then the share of the *j*th dimension in such multidimensional MPI is:

$$\lambda_j = \frac{\frac{\sum_i s_{ij}}{n}}{\text{MPI}}.$$

This ratio is an important indicator with important policy implications in the context of decisions that need to be taken for the removal of multidimensional poverty.

Given the earlier conceptual definition, the UNDP worked out the multidimensional poverty–related results as presented in the *HDR* (2014). Table 4.1 presents this result for a selection of countries, mostly the South Asian nations, China, and two Sub-Saharan African countries—Nigeria and the Democratic Republic of Congo. The table shows that the head-count multidimensional poverty ratio as well as its intensity are quite high in India, particularly in comparison to China. The MPI is, in fact, lower in Pakistan and Bangladesh than what has been observed for India. It is, of course, clear from Table 4.1a that multidimensional poverty is higher in sub-Saharan Africa than in India. However, it is interesting to note that in the Himalayan countries of Nepal and Bhutan, the index of multidi-mensional poverty is relatively low. It is a matter of concern that both India and Pakistan suffer from severe multidimensional poverty of 27.8 and 26.5 per cent respectively in term of headcount multidimensional poverty ratio. These are indicative of social unsustainability.

Human Development Indicator

The obverse of the issue of human poverty is human development; poverty in any dimension results in the lack of access to certain types of opportunities because of the concerned type of deprivation. A short-run answer to such a problem, particularly for income poverty, has been the introduction of various poverty-alleviation schemes under MGNREGA, which guarantees some minimum employment and income to enable people to get out of poverty. The government takes up targets and mis-sions for drinking water, electrification of rural areas with a lifeline tariff, slum removal, improved sanitation, and so on. These are concerned with addressing some of the dimensionality of multidimensional poverty. From an overall perspective, poverty in multidimensional form con-tributes to waste of human resources. From the viewpoint of long-run sustainability of human well-being, it is not only important to eradicate poverty, but to develop human capability so that human resources are not wasted and may not only be converted into human capital through better provision of educational and health services, but also make life fulfilling and worth living for the individuals themselves.

As is well known, the HDI is based on attainment across the dimen-sions of health, education, and standard of living, each having equal weight in developing the aggregate indicator. The health indicator, in

TABLE 4.1A Multidimensional Poverty for Selected Developing Countries

Country	Consumption Poverty		Multidimensional Poverty		MPI Index	Near Multidimensional Poverty	Population in Severe Poverty	Share of Education	Share of Health	Share of Living Standard (Amenities)
	A National Poverty Line	B PPP USD 1.25 poverty line	Headcount	Intensity		Headcount				
India	21.9	32.68	55.3	51.1	0.282	18.2	27.8	22.7	32.5	44.8
Pakistan	22.3	21.4	45.6	52.0	0.237	14.9	26.5	36.2	32.3	31.6
Bangladesh	31.51	43.25	49.5	47.28	0.237	18.8	21.0	28.4	26.6	44.9
Bhutan	1.66	12.0	27.2	43.5	0.128	18.0	8.8	40.3	26.3	33.4
Nepal	25.2	24.82	41.4	47.4	0.197	18.1	18.6	27.3	28.2	44.5
Afghanistan	36.0		58.8	49.9	0.293	16.0	29.8	45.6	19.2	35.2
China		11.8	6.0	43.4	0.026	19.0	1.3	21.0	44.4	34.6
Nigeria	46.0	67.98	43.3	55.2	0.239	17.0	25.7	26.9	32.6	40.4
Congo Republic	71.3	87.72	74.4	53.7	0.3999	15.5	46.2	18.5	25.5	55.9

Source: UNDP (2014).

turn, is based on the life expectancy of people of an economy while the education index is based on mean years of schooling as well as expected years of schooling (both having equal weightage). A decent standard of living, on the other hand, is based on GNI per capita, which provides a family with finance to access other necessities and amenities.

In order to avoid the problem of aggregation of attainment over the different dimensions, the UNDP's *HDR* methodology measures the attainment of each dimension in terms of the ratio of the difference between the actual value and the minimum attained value across the countries, to the difference between maximum and minimum values as observed across the countries. (This assumes that a higher numerical value of an indicator is a better one. Otherwise, we have to take the similarly normalized value of the difference between the maximum and the actual values to be the indicator of achievement.) In any case, maximum or minimum values would be the goalpost value, the aspirational natural value, or zero, where the lower value represents better attainment. In the case of per capita income, the minimum value may be taken as the subsistence consumption minimum or minimum income from non-market production. The aggregation of three indices is, however, done by taking the geometric mean of the scores of attainment as ratios. The average of the two compound educational indicators is taken as the simple un-weighted arithmetic mean of the two. The final index value as computed over time will thus focus on relative achievement vis-à-vis other countries, which are following their respective paths of growth or development.

We have already noted the suitability of the inequality-adjusted GNI per capita as an indicator of the economic dimension of sustainable development in Chapter 2. However, the consideration of per capita income as a component of the HDI, on the other hand, constitutes a conceptual mix-up of human capability development and that of the conventional measure of the standard of living and level of development. It is therefore not surprising that the HDI and the per capita income are often found to be highly correlated. If capability is to be the basis of long-run social sustainability of development, its indicator should not be based on the outcome of capability—income—as it would amount to begging the question. Since it is undeniable that education and health constitute the fundamental basis of capability and of getting access to a decent life, it is appropriate to choose the normalized value

TABLE 4.1B   Non-income Human Development Index for Selected Developing Countries (2013)

Country	Non-income Human Development Index
India	0.580
Pakistan	0.516
Bangladesh	0.590
Bhutan	0.559
Nepal	0.580
Afghanistan	0.479
China	0.612
Nigeria	0.460
Congo Republic	0.552

Source: UNDP (2014).

of the non-income component of the HDI (for the selected countries as shown in Table 4.1b) as the indicator of capability development and of long-run social sustainability.

Environmental Sustainability: Ecological Footprint, Resource Conservation, and Environmental Protection

So far as environmental sustainability is concerned, we may again view the issue of choice of indicators from two viewpoints:

1. Impact of environmental stress caused by human economic activities in a given period.
2. Performance in respect of environmental protection and resource conservation for upgrading and maintaining human health and ecosystem vitality.

While the first indicator focuses on the overuse of regenerative biocapacity of the ecosystem, the second one represents the environmental performance of the economic system through policy interventions to ensure the sustenance of human health and the regenerative ability of the ecosystem. While one indicator is the obverse reflection of the other, the two together describe the state of attainment of environmental quality from two different aspects.

Concept and Measurement of Ecological Footprint

How can we describe or measure the pressure of human activities on the biosphere and monitor the sustainability of human society and its development process. Human activities create the pressure in the form of demand for natural resources and eco-services expressed in units of land use of various types, the normalized aggregate of which is called the ecological footprint. Given the pattern of land use, there exists a potential regenerative capacity or bio-capacity. It represents the total biologically productive area—in terms of crop land, pasture, forest, fisheries, and other so on—that is available to meet the human needs of food, fibre, timber, absorption of CO_2 wastes, and other necessities.

In case the demand for bio-capacity to meet human needs exceeds the availability, it would lead either to over-harvesting of the biomass resulting in the depletion of the stock of standing biomass in the areas of land, including water bodies, or to the overuse of the concerned land area by temporarily raising the primary productivities per unit of land area per unit of time which is not sustainable. The consequences of such demand for bio-capacity exceeding its availability has been twofold: (*i*) depletion of the biotic resource stocks and ending up with the loss of biodiversity and (*ii*) erosion of the regenerative ability of the biosphere to support the human population.

Measurement of Ecological Footprint

The calculation of the ecological footprint as per the global ecological footprint network[1] involves the calculation of the requirement of biologically productive land and water areas for human use by way of direct use for primary productivity of land or by way of its diversion of from bio-productive use to other ones. This, in turn, assumes certain norms of footprint intensity of human consumption of food, fibre, fuels, timber, and housing or construction and infrastructure. These norms of footprint intensity would, in turn, depend on the technology and the practice of resource management prevailing in the country or region of the concerned economy and the biological primary productivity

---

[1] The Global Footprint Network, 'Our Work', available at: www.footprintnetwork.org/our-work/ecological-footprint/ (accessed 12 December 2019).

of land, which varies across different types of land uses, such as crop land, forest, pastures, ocean, fisheries, and so on varying across space and time. The ecological footprint for any particular type of end use of land for any biomass product of any region has been based on the world average yield of the concerned primary biomass product per unit of land (or water) area and thus expressed in units of global hectares for that end use per capita of the concerned country.

There is, however, a second scaling factor used in normalization of such land requirement over the different types of uses of land, which are varying in suitability in terms of their potential photosynthetic or primary productivity. Each type of land use is assigned a suitability index depending on its relative efficiency in primary photosynthetic productivity. Finally, equivalent factors are derived on the basis of the global average distribution of land use and its suitability index (as given later) as a ratio of the suitability index of the concerned type of land use to the global average suitability index. The equivalent factors are given in Table 4.2.

Suitability Indices:

1. Very suitable (VS) Crop Land: 0.9
2. Suitable (S) Forest Land: 0.7
3. Moderately Suitable (MdS): 0.5
4. Marginally Suitable (MrS): 0.3
5. Not Suitable (NS): 0.1

As the global land use pattern changes from time to time, the average suitability indices and the equivalent factors also change over time.

TABLE 4.2   Equivalent Factors for the Different Types of Land Use (2005)

Area Type	Equivalent Factor
Primary Crop Land	2.64
Forest and Grazing Land	1.33
Marine Area	0.50
Inland Water	0.40
Build-up Land Area	2.64

Source: World Wide Fund International, *Living Planet Report*, 2006, available at: https://www.panda.org>livin_planet_report_timeline>lpr_2006 (accessed 9 December 2019).

The ecological footprints are thus expressed in normalized units of land requirement of average global primary or photosynthetic productivity (see Sengupta, 2013 for further details).

However, we would like to point out what the carbon footprint should precisely mean in the context of the ecological footprint. On the demand side of land requirement for ecological services for human consumption, the single most important source has been the absorption of CO_2 arising from the use of fossil fuel. The CO_2 creates maximum pressure on the planetary ecosystem for absorbing the wastes of human economy. In terms of bio-productive land requirement, however, it is the area of forest land that would be additionally required for the absorption of the unabsorbed CO_2 emissions over and above what has been absorbed by the planetary ecosystem through some amount of recycling by the vegetal or forest area and by way of absorption by the ocean.

In the ecological footprint account for the selected individual countries and the world as a whole as presented in Table 4.3, it is seen that the carbon footprint has the greatest share, above 50 per cent, for most of the countries and the world as a whole. The human appropriation of the earth's primary productivity resources has thus far exceeded its bio-capacity in terms of how much more land or the country would be required to maintain ecological balance, taking due cognizance of the role of entropy law in the functioning of the economic system. It is important to note that the world requires another additional 1.5 times the surface of the earth to maintain the demand–supply balance of the ecosystem. China and India similarly require another additional 0.93

TABLE 4.3 Ecological Footprint and Carbon Footprint in Hectares Per Capita (2011)

Countries	Population (in Billions)	Ecological Footprint	Carbon Footprint	Bio-capacity	Ecological Deficit
World	6.998	2.65	1.46	1.72	−0.9
India	1.221	0.6	0.4	0.5	−0.4
China	1.399	2.5	1.5	0.9	−1.6
USA	0.315	6.8	4.5	3.7	−3.1

Source: The Global Footprint Network, available at: http://www.footprintnetwork.org/en/index.php/GFN/(accessed 9 December 2019).

and 0.25 of our earth to meet all the demand of eco-services of the respective economies (see Figures 4.1, 4.2, 4.3, and 4.4).

Again, in an open economy, with the export and import of goods and services to or from the concerned country, the estimation of the ecological footprint embedded in such traded goods and services requires to be correctly assigned to the consuming country, which requires adjustments

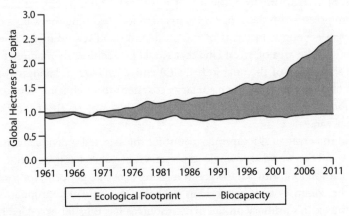

FIGURE 4.1   China's Ecological Footprint
Source: Available at: http://www.footprintnetwork.org/en/index.php/GFN/ (accessed 9 December 2019).

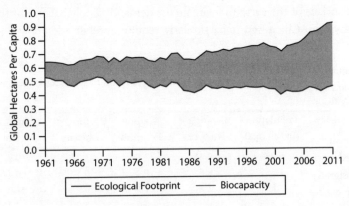

FIGURE 4.2   India's Ecological Footprint
Source: Available at: http://www.footprintnetwork.org/en/index.php/GFN/ (accessed 9 December 2019).

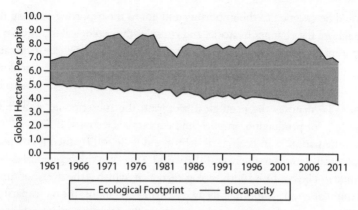

FIGURE 4.3   United States of America's Ecological Footprint
Source: Available at: http://www.footprintnetwork.org/en/index.php/GFN/ (accessed 9 December 2019).

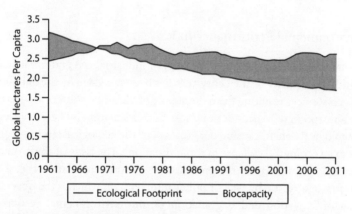

FIGURE 4.4   World's Ecological Footprint
Source: Available at: http://www.footprintnetwork.org/en/index.php/GFN/ (accessed 9 December 2019).

for such trade flows. In order to arrive at the ecological footprint as embedded in the final goods and services delivered, it is important to correctly assign the footprint as calculated and tallied at the point of primary harvest or waste absorption (through carbon recycling) by land uses of various types, to the different final end-user country of the goods and services. The ecological footprint of imports of a country should be assigned to that country itself, while the ecological footprint of exports of a country should be assigned to the importing and not to the exporting country. If we ignore the changes in stocks and consider the ecological footprint of apparent consumption (EF_c) which is production + import − export, then,

$$EF_c = EF_p + EF_m - EF_x$$

where EF denotes the ecological footprint, the subscripts p, m, and x standing for production, import, and exports respectively. If $EF_c > EF_p$, then the nation is an ecological debtor and if $EF_c < EF_p$, then it is a net ecological creditor to the rest of the world. However, this ecological debt should not be confused with ecological deficit, which is the overshooting of the ecological footprint, if its own demand overshoots the bio-capacity of the concerned country and not merely the footprint of its exports. Ecological deficit of a country is, in fact, likely to be larger than ecological debt in view of substantive overshooting of the ecological footprint over bio-capacity, particularly for overpopulated, poor developing countries.

Environmental Performance Index

In many regions of the overpopulated or industrialized and urbanized world, the capacity of the ecosystem has been exceeded by the demand for eco-services resulting from the supply of natural resources as well as the absorption of wastes or pollution. Such a situation is likely to result in ecological deficit, causing degradation of the ecological landscape, if not in an ecological collapse in some situations. The issue of the protection and upgradation of the pre-existing environmental landscape of a country or a region by way of policy intervention, which is the obverse issue of depletion and degradation of the environmental resource stock, has therefore become critical for environmental sustainability. A big challenge in this respect arises due to uncertainty and knowledge gap, particularly in view of the non-linearity and complexity of the ecosystem's behaviour in the concerned domain and the possible existence of thresholds, which, if exceeded, may lead to serious implications for the ecosystem and economy. The Yale Centre for Environmental Law and Policy (YCELP) and the Centre for International Earth Science Information Network (CIESIN) at the Columbia University have jointly researched on these issues and devised a set of performance indicators which have been very useful tools for policy- and decision-makers. These indicators have enabled them to navigate the uncertain information landscape and arrive at the identification of critical spots and areas of environmental policy concern and finally devise policies for intervention on those focused issues. Environmental performance indicators are those variables whose values are set against some targets for assessing the extent of the efficacy of policy initiatives. The architecture of the EPI would be described by the range of environmental variables capturing the dimensionality of sources of the environmental sustainability problem and their weightages in the aggregative process.

The current architecture of the EPI as it has developed till date focuses on two kinds of adverse impacts arising from externalities: (*i*) The health problems of people resulting from a polluted environment and (*ii*) the loss of vitality of the ecosystem due to the adverse impact of externalities. These two types of indicators have been given 40 per cent and 60 per cent weightage in the aggregate of the final index, for assessing the overall role of these two types of interventions in the overall impact of environmental protection or conservation. The state of environmental health for humans has been assumed to be determined by three indicator variables:

1. Child health (mortality)
2. Air quality (indoor household air pollution) as well as outdoor air pollution (concentration of suspended particles) due to excessive PM 2.5
3. Access to safe water and sanitation

For the vitality of the ecosystem, the developer of EPI index identified the indicators of performance to be (with differential weightage):

1. Wastewater treatment
2. Agricultural subsidies
3. Pesticide regulation
4. Change in forest cover
5. Fishing stock and overexploitation of coastal fishing, putting pressure on the continental shelf
6. Protection of areas of biodiversity and habitat conservation
7. Trend in carbon intensity—change in the intensity per unit of GDP as well as that of power generation

In respect of biodiversity conservation, the value of the indicator is based on the area of terrestrial protection (national and global levels), marine protected area, and areas of critical habitat protection. For climate change and CO_2 emissions, the indicator's values are based on the estimates of itsemissions per capita, its intensity of GDP, its intensity of electrical energy, and the shares of renewables in power generation. Table 4.4 shows both the dimensions and the indicators along with the respective weightage diagram.

TABLE 4.4   Dimensions and Indicators along with Their Weights in the Environmental Performance Index

Objective (Per Cent)	Issue Category (Per Cent)	Indicators (Per Cent)
Environmental Health (50)	Health Impacts (33)	Environmental Risk Exposure (100)
	Air Quality (33)	Household Air Quality (30)
		Air Pollution—Average Exposure to PM2.5 (30)
		Air Pollution—Average Exposure to PM2.5 (30)
		Air Pollution—Exceeding PM2.5 (30)
		Air Pollution—Average Exposure to Nitrogen Dioxide (10)
	Water and Sanitation (33)	Unsafe Sanitation (50)
		Drinking Water Quality (50)
Ecosystem Vitality (50)	Water Resources (25)	Wastewater Treatment (100)
	Agriculture (10)	Nitrogen Use Efficiency (75)
		Nitrogen Balance (25)
	Forests (10)	Change in Forest Cover (100)
	Fisheries (5)	Fish stocks (100)
	Biodiversity and Habitat (25)	Terrestrial Protected Areas (National Biome Weights) (20)
		Terrestrial Protected Areas (Global Biome Weights) (20)
		Marine Protected Areas (20)
		Species protection (National) (20)
		Species Protection (Global) (20)
	Climate and Energy (25)	Trend in carbon intensity (75)
		Trend in CO_2 emissions per kwh (25)

Source: World Wide Fund International, *Living Planet Report*, 2006, available at: https://www.panda.org>livin_planet_report_timeline>lpr_2006 (accessed 9 December 2019).

TABLE 4.5   Ecological Footprint Index, Environmental Performance Index, Carbon Dioxide Per Capita, and Environmental Index of Various Countries

Countries	EPI	EFI	Environmental Index	CO_2 Per Capita (tonnes)
Afghanistan	0.22	0.966	0.591	0.3
Bangladesh	0.67	0.965	0.815	0.4
Bhutan	0.53	0.722	0.626	0.7
China	0.62	0.845	0.734	6.2
Congo (Democratic Republic)	0.29	0.780	0.533	0.0
India	0.37	0.934	0.652	1.7
Nepal	0.69	0.518	0.604	0.1
Nigeria	0.80	0.480	0.639	0.5
USA	67.52	0.553	34.036	17.6

Source: Author's own estimations based on UNDP (2014); World Bank Database, World Development Indicators (2016); World Wide Fund International, *Living Planet Report*, 2006, available at: https://www.panda.org>livin_planet_report_timeline>lpr_2006 (accessed 9 December 2019).

So far as the method of the construction and estimation of EPI is concerned, it is a country-level relative performance of the concerned country vis-à-vis others in their respective development paths. It follows the methodology of the HDI in determining the relative position of any country depending on its score in a normalized scale from 0 to 1, the score reflecting the progress of improvement of a indicator's value as attained in the given concerned year (represented by the actual value of concerned variables) from the minimum (maximum) value across all countries or a natural zero, depending on weather a higher (or a lower) value of the variable is desired.

Table 4.5 presents the cross-section country-wise EPI scores, EFI scores, the CO_2_PC and environmental index for a selected number of countries, reflecting the relative environmental performance quite similar to that of the HDIs.

Overall Development Index

After defining the indices of sustainability of the three dimensions of developmental sustainability, we now propose to define an OSDI, which takes account of the attainment of an economy in all the three aspects of sustainability of progress—economic, social, and environmental. The OSDI aggregates all the three components with equal weight as we presume that they are equally important in defining or characterizing overall development. For the economic performance index, we choose the inequality-adjusted per capita income index, while for social sustainability, we take the non-income component of the HDI, in order to avoid double-counting the income component and thereby overemphasizing it. So far as the environmental sustainability indicator is concerned, we have considered both the EFI and EPI, by taking an un-weighted arithmetic mean of the two indices—the environmental footprint being an indicator of the stress on the ecosystem caused by economic activity and the EPI being the policy-driven indicator of attainment of environmental protection of the economy. Both these two indices are important in assessing the sustainability of the ecosystem of the concerned country. Each of these three indices are score values normalized between zero and one as in the case of construction of the HDI. The OSDI is defined to be the un-weighted geometric mean of these three indices. We can alternatively, also propose a sustainable development index which will be the simple geometric mean of the non-income HDI and the environmental sustainability index, without incorporating per capita income attainment. This index becomes relevant if one is interested in tracing the relationship between the sustainable development index and the economic performance index, to make an idea of trade-off between the conventional economic development measure and the purely social and environmental sustainability achievement. We present country-wise OSDI and social sustainability index (SSI) values along with their respective components and the ranking of the countries as per such indicators in Table 4.6. In addition, Table 4.7 presents some of the correlation values to appreciate the strength of interrelations among some of these component indices.

The results in Table 4.7 show that the OSDI, the Income Index, and the SSI are highly correlated with each other. It may even be noted that the SSI (which does not contain any income element and the SSI which is entirely determined by EFI, EPI, and the Non-income HDI) and income index have a linear correlation of 0.89. The table also shows rank correlations among these variates. These inter-correlations imply that income and economic growth are also the main drivers of human capability development and that environmental conservation and upgradation

TABLE 4.6   Cross-country Overall Development Index and Social
Sustainability Index: Estimates and Rankings of Various Countries

Countries	OSDI	Rank OSDI	SSI	Rank SSI
Afghanistan	0.503	115	0.515	113
Albania	0.702	56	0.688	52
Angola	0.571	101	0.621	83
Armenia	0.718	49	0.695	48
Australia	0.733	40	0.637	73
Austria	0.787	23	0.751	26
Azerbaijan	0.733	39	0.730	34
Bahamas	0.668	68	0.619	85
Bangladesh	0.576	99	0.569	100
Belarus	0.737	37	0.710	41
Belgium	0.743	34	0.686	53
Benin	0.460	124	0.441	128
Bhutan	0.602	94	0.624	79
Bolivia (Plurinational State of)	0.646	76	0.621	82
Bosnia and Herzegovina	0.667	69	0.627	75
Botswana	0.665	70	0.673	61
Brazil	0.659	71	0.622	81
Bulgaria	0.776	26	0.771	14
Burkina Faso	0.476	120	0.536	109
Burundi	0.430	130	0.425	130
Cambodia	0.591	96	0.573	99
Cameroon	0.436	126	0.403	135
Canada	0.854	4	0.833	4
Cape Verde	0.645	79	0.647	69
Central African Republic	0.409	136	0.422	131
Chad	0.415	134	0.452	125
Chile	0.787	22	0.766	17
Colombia	0.719	47	0.725	36
Congo	0.605	90	0.634	74
Congo (Democratic Republic)	0.410	135	0.407	134
Costa Rica	0.760	31	0.752	24
Côte d'Ivoire	0.491	118	0.525	111
Croatia	0.788	21	0.771	15
Cyprus	0.775	27	0.743	30
Czech Republic	0.789	20	0.749	28
Denmark	0.815	11	0.778	13

(Cont'd)

TABLE 4.6   (Cont'd)

Countries	OSDI	Rank OSDI	SSI	Rank SSI
Dominican Republic	0.698	60	0.699	45
Ecuador	0.723	44	0.725	37
Egypt	0.698	59	0.712	40
El Salvador	0.656	73	0.650	67
Estonia	0.852	5	0.853	3
Ethiopia	0.421	131	0.402	136
Fiji	0.719	48	0.696	46
Finland	0.839	8	0.823	7
France	0.778	25	0.731	33
Gabon	0.628	86	0.627	77
Georgia	0.714	50	0.673	60
Germany	0.895	1	0.888	2
Ghana	0.518	110	0.484	119
Greece	0.830	10	0.814	9
Guatemala	0.624	88	0.624	78
Guinea	0.436	127	0.453	123
Guinea-Bissau	0.469	121	0.499	115
Guyana	0.641	81	0.639	72
Haiti	0.467	123	0.453	124
Honduras	0.645	78	0.645	70
Hungary	0.810	12	0.804	11
Iceland	0.850	6	0.821	8
India	0.604	92	0.616	87
Indonesia	0.683	65	0.681	56
Iran (Islamic Republic)	0.723	46	0.708	42
Iraq	0.644	80	0.669	62
Ireland	0.803	17	0.751	25
Israel	0.766	30	0.706	43
Italy	0.793	19	0.757	22
Jamaica	0.708	53	0.692	49
Japan	0.807	14	0.769	16
Jordan	0.732	41	0.718	38
Kazakhstan	0.646	77	0.604	91
Kenya	0.575	100	0.575	98
Kiribati	0.558	103	0.508	114
Kyrgyzstan	0.615	89	0.579	97
Lao People's Democratic Republic	0.604	91	0.623	80

Latvia	0.698	58	0.649	68
Lebanon	0.706	54	0.679	57
Lesotho	0.520	109	0.542	107
Liberia	0.432	129	0.411	133
Lithuania	0.736	38	0.690	50
Luxembourg	0.894	2	0.920	1
Madagascar	0.515	112	0.494	117
Malawi	0.437	125	0.414	132
Malta	0.779	24	0.759	20
Mauritania	0.511	113	0.531	110
Mauritius	0.755	33	0.748	29
Moldova (Republic)	0.630	84	0.598	94
Mongolia	0.692	61	0.683	54
Montenegro	0.769	28	0.750	27
Morocco	0.646	75	0.668	63
Mozambique	0.435	128	0.445	127
Namibia	0.657	72	0.689	51
Nepal	0.499	116	0.462	121
The Netherlands	0.804	16	0.753	23
Nicaragua	0.631	83	0.627	76
Niger	0.419	132	0.464	120
Nigeria	0.497	117	0.516	112
Norway	0.862	3	0.831	5
Pakistan	0.549	105	0.566	101
Paraguay	0.672	66	0.664	65
Peru	0.654	74	0.611	89
The Philippines	0.627	87	0.603	92
Poland	0.685	64	0.616	86
Portugal	0.807	15	0.800	12
Romania	0.768	29	0.758	21
Russian Federation	0.689	62	0.656	66
Rwanda	0.515	111	0.490	118
Senegal	0.533	108	0.552	104
Serbia	0.703	55	0.676	58
Sierra Leone	0.417	133	0.458	122
Slovakia	0.723	45	0.676	59
Slovenia	0.803	18	0.762	19
Solomon Islands	0.467	122	0.433	129
Spain	0.839	7	0.824	6
Sri Lanka	0.687	63	0.642	71
Suriname	0.671	67	0.666	64

(Cont'd)

TABLE 4.6   (*Cont'd*)

Countries	OSDI	Rank OSDI	SSI	Rank SSI
Swaziland	0.565	102	0.603	93
Sweden	0.758	32	0.700	44
Switzerland	0.836	9	0.805	10
Tajikistan	0.584	98	0.541	108
Tanzania (United Republic)	0.550	104	0.565	102
Thailand	0.724	43	0.730	35
The former Yugoslav Republic of Macedonia	0.709	52	0.695	47
Timor-Leste	0.585	97	0.584	95
Togo	0.510	114	0.497	116
Trinidad and Tobago	0.739	36	0.742	31
Turkey	0.742	35	0.740	32
Uganda	0.478	119	0.451	126
Ukraine	0.711	51	0.682	55
United Kingdom	0.701	57	0.621	84
United States of America	0.808	13	0.766	18
Uruguay	0.629	85	0.560	103
Uzbekistan	0.596	95	0.552	105
Venezuela (Bolivarian Republic)	0.728	42	0.714	39
Vietnam	0.632	82	0.616	88
Yemen	0.544	107	0.583	96
Zambia	0.602	93	0.609	90
Zimbabwe	0.547	106	0.543	106

Source: Author's own estimations.

TABLE 4.7   Correlation Values between Different Indices

Correlation between OSDI and SSI Scores	Rank Correlation between OSDI and SSI
0.975907606	0.973717857
Correlation between OSDI and Income Scores	Rank Correlation between OSDI and Income Index
0.932452169	0.926919641
Correlation between SSI and Income Scores	Rank Correlation between SSI and Income Index
0.890249732	0.871785083

Source: Author's own estimations.

need to be financed by public spending. A higher income of a country with higher government and private spending is better able to accelerate achievements in these dimensions of development. However, it is also a fact that such correlations cannot guarantee elimination of either income deprivation for meeting the subsistence basket of consumption or multidimensional poverty, particularly, malnutrition, disease, lack of sanitation, housing, universal access to clean energy, children's and women's healthcare and quality school education. We get two important lessons from these observations:

1. Growth of national income and its stability is a necessary condition of sustainable development.
2. This needs to be supplemented by social investment policies which would direct the development spending of the government to be targeted to ensure the elimination of deprivation in the society and universal social access to the benefits of growth for the people.

This again brings us back to the issue of the relevance of the social policy of development and of the institution of a welfare state in the context of sustainable development.

Interdependence among Stages of Economic Development, Human Development, and the Natural Environment

Chapter 5 points to the interactive nature of the different aspects of sustainability of development. It investigates the interrelationships between the different components of the OSDI using cross-country data with the help of a simple econometric model using a quadratic single equation. The chapter makes deeper analysis of the dynamic links between human development, the natural environment, and economic growth using simultaneous equation econometric models (mostly of the two-stage least square [TSLS] type) and global cross-country data of different time periods. The models and analysis in this chapter are based on the data of all the concerned variables presented in Chapter 4.

Relationship among Different Components of Overall Development Index

This chapter is devoted to tracing the interrelationships among the different components of the OSDI. We have already chosen the inequality-adjusted per capita income (as indicated in Chapter 4) as the indicator of economic sustainability of development. On the other hand, we have chosen the non-income HDI as the SSI and the un-weighted mean of EFI and EPI indices as the environmental sustainability indicator of development. The entire analysis of this chapter is based on the cross-country data from various sources. We first analyse the plotting of bi-variate data in a two-dimensional plane, taking two variables relating to any two dimensions of sustainability of development at a time and making a simple curve fitting (see Figures 5.1–5.11). As we found that a quadratic equation is likely to be a good fit in most of the cases, we fitted such a curve by estimating a quadratic single equation regression model to each set of bivariate data. Since such regression models would often involve endogeneity or the simultaneity problem of causation between the two variables regarding their determinism, we shall next address the issue of linkage among economic growth, human development, and environmental sustainability in terms of the solution of appropriate simultaneous equation models of econometric estimation.

In this investigation of the interrelationship between economic growth, human development, and the state of natural environment, we begin by analysing the cross-sectional data of the countries as covered in the *HDR* of 2014. We first find two-way interactive quadratic relations between the GNI per capita in PPP USD (without any normalization) and non-income human development as follows (see Figures 5.1 and 5.2):

$$y(GNI\ per\ capita) = 14347x^2 - 9897x + 19214$$

where x = non-income HDI, with $R^2 = 0.819$ at p- value (0.00)

$$y(non\text{-}income\ HDI) = (-3E - 10)x^2 + (3E - 0.5)x + 0.307;$$

where x is GNI per capita in PPP USD units with $R^2 = 0.812$ at p-value 0.00.

The comparative value of R^2 of the above two relations suggests that the explanatory power of the two variates of determining each other's values is equally strong, involving the endogeneity problem. There exist, in fact, two-way causal chains between economic growth and human development (for details, see Ranis and Stewart 2005). Economic growth and the consequent higher mobilization of financial resources by the government and higher investment for social infrastructure of education and health, among others, would explain

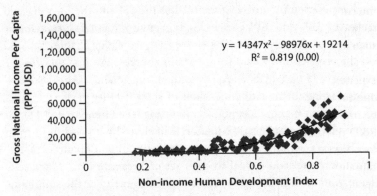

FIGURE 5.1   Stage of Economic Development as Depending on Attainment of Non-income Human Development
Source: Author's estimates based on *HDI* (2014).

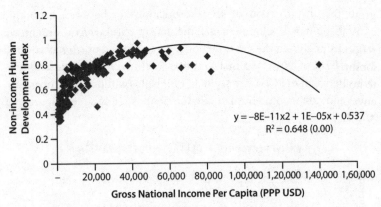

FIGURE 5.2   Attainment of Non-income Human Development as Depending on Stage of Economic Development
Source: Author's estimates based on *HDI* (2014).

such relationships. However, the efficiency of such investment and the strength of such causal chains would depend on several critical allocation ratios: (*i*) The share of GDP spent on public investment for social sectors, (*ii*) the share of human development sectors, such as education, healthcare, family welfare, amenities, safe water and sanitation, and so on, in the total social sector investment, and (*iii*) both the composition of spending on human development sectors, and the technology and institutional arrangement for delivery accompanying such investment.

The rise in human development, as found from the cross-country experience, shows an accompanying rise in the level of GNI per capita due to growth on account of greater labour productivity, which can be imputed to higher educational attainment, skill, innovation, better R&D performance, better provision of healthcare, and other such factors. Further on in this chapter, we will discuss the two-way chains of causality between economic growth and human development in more detail and show how their dynamics of interaction reinforce the positive correlation between the two. We will also estimate a TSLS model, which can provide reliable estimates of parameters, taking care of simultaneity of equations and endogeneity. The results of the dynamic convergence of growth (per capita income) and human development also reflect how the latter is important for the sustenance of economic growth and development in the long run.

With reference to the relationship between economic growth as reflected in the rise in GNI per capita and variation in the ecological footprint, we find in Figure 5.3 a concave, moderately rising relationship to hold between the two. Since the ecological footprint is a measure of environmental stress, we find the observation to be consistent with the

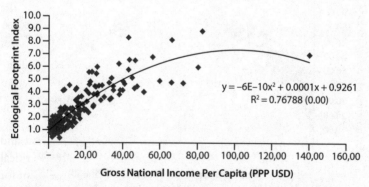

$$y = -6E-10x^2 + 0.0001x + 0.9261$$
$$R^2 = 0.76788 \ (0.00)$$

FIGURE 5.3   Ecological Footprint Index as Depending on Gross National Income Per Capita

Source: Author's estimates based on *HDI* (2014).

Kuznet's curve hypothesis as applied to the environment. The relationship is equivalent to,

$$y(EFI) = (-6E - 10)x^2 + (0.0001)x + 0.9261; \quad x = GNI \; per \; capita$$

with the highly statistically significant measure of R^2 with a value 0.76788.

The ef_i measure reaches its maximum around PPP USD 8,000. It may also be noted that the EPI, based on environmental resource conservation and pollution abatement measures for the protection of human health and the health of the ecosystem, has similar rising concave relationship with respect to per capita income. We have estimated it as the following quadratic equation with $R^2 = 0.7204$ at a high level of statistical significance and showing the peaking value of ep_i again being attained around the same GNI per capita in PPP USD 8,000 (see Figure 5.4).

$$y(EPI) = (-9E - 0.9)x^2 + 0.001x + 33.79 \text{ with } R^2 = 0.724 \; (p\text{-value } 0.00)$$

Human development and environmental sustainability are, on the other hand, also likely to have a growing interactive relationship, as in the case of economic growth and human development. As the level of human skill and knowledge increases along with a rise in the use of

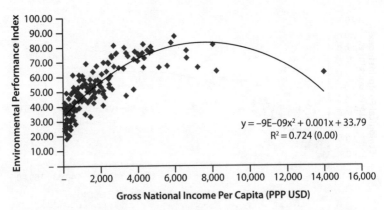

FIGURE 5.4   Environmental Performance Indicator as Depending on Gross National Income Per Capita

Source: Author's estimates based on *HDI* (2014).

innovative technology by the people—which should be the outcome of higher attainment of human capability—they will enable a society to conserve ecological resources, abate pollution, and use resources more efficiently, contributing to both the lowering of the ecological footprint and attaining a better performance in environmental protection of the health of the people and the ecosystem. The efficiency of such an interactive effect of human development and the environment would, however, depend on the strength of people's environmental preferences, or their demand for a better-quality environment, because of higher environmental education and consciousness, which should follow human development.

Since ep_i results are policy-driven, the outcome of the environmental performance would be sensitive to government policies and budgetary allocations of public as well as private entities. With reference to the relationship between human development and the EPI, it is important to notice that the scatter diagrams in Figures 5.5 and 5.6 show a very clear positive rising convex relationship of the environmental indices—both the EFI and EPI—with the non-income HDI. The estimated equations are found to be,

$$y(EFI) = 11.56x^2 - 6.638x + 2.096$$

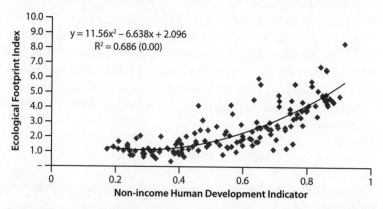

FIGURE 5.5 Ecological Footprint Index as Depending on Non-income Human Development Indicator

Source: Author's estimates based on *HDI* (2014).

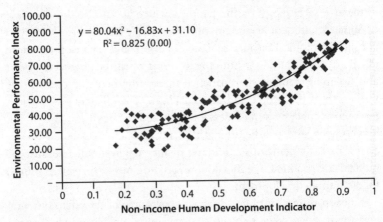

FIGURE 5.6   Environmental Performance Index as Depending on Non-income
Human Development Indicator
Source: Author's estimates based on *HDI* (2014).

where x = non-income HDI; with $R^2 = 0.686$ at p-value (0.00) indicating
a high level of statistical significance.

$$y(EPI) = 80.04x^2 - 16.83x + 31.10;$$

where x = non-income HDI with $R^2 = 0.825$ at p-value (0.00)

With economic growth or a rise in human development, we, however, find growth in the EFI and the EPI at the same time. This is not
surprising, because with economic growth or a rise in the HDI, we
find in the bivariate data, a positive rising trend of both EFI and of
EPI. However, the scatter plot of EPI and EFI shows that normalized
EFI index would rise with the EFI in the course of development (see
Figure 5.7). The quadratic equation best suited to the data has been
estimated to be,

$$Y(EPI) = -1.117x^2 + 14.82 + 22.35$$

where x = EFI with $R^2 = 0.602$, at p-value 0.00, indicating a high level of
significance.

However, we may further ask if the environmental state, as indicated
by the EFI or the EPI, could have a significant impact on the state of
development, as represented by GNI per capita, or on the non-income

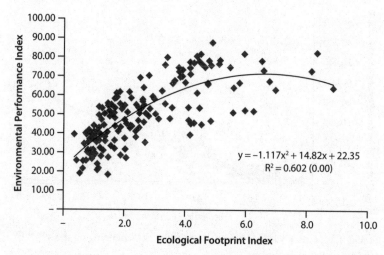

FIGURE 5.7   Environmental Performance Index as Depending on Ecological Footprint Index
Source: Author's estimates based on *HDI* (2014).

HDI. From the scatter diagrams in Figures 5.8 and 5.9, we find that there exists a non-linear (quadratic) relationship, indicating a positive relationship of GNI per capita with the EFI as well as separately with the EPI, both of which have a positive determining influence. Greater per capita resource use (footprint) or better protection of environmental health by way of attaining a higher EPI value would contribute towards higher availability of resource throughput in the production process in the former case, and higher productivity of resources in the latter situation of better health of humans and the ecosystem. Figures 5.8 and 5.9 show these positive rising relationships, which are statistically significant as given later.

$$y(GNI\ per\ capita) = 326.2x^2 + 6651x + 4015, x = EFI$$

with $R^2 = 0.676$ at a very high level of statistical significance where x is EFI. And

$$y(GNI\ per\ capita) = 11.26x^2 - 327.4x + 2089, x = EPI$$

with $R^2 = 0.544$, at less than a 1 per cent level of significance where x is EPI.

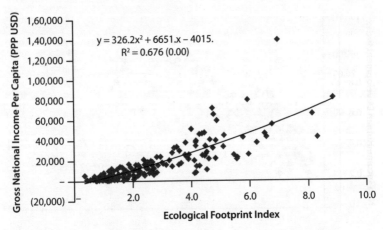

FIGURE 5.8   Gross National Income Per Capita as Depending on the Ecological Footprint Index
Source: Author's estimates based on *HDI* (2014).

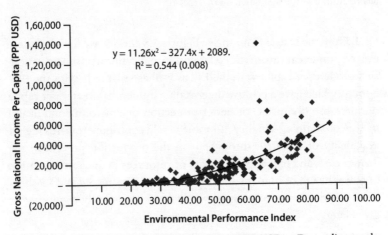

FIGURE 5.9   Gross National Income Per Capita PPP USD as Depending on the Environmental Performance Index
Source: Author's estimates based on *HDI* (2014).

Similarly, Figures 5.10 and 5.11 show the effects of the higher values of EPI or *EFI* on the attainment level of a country's non-income HDI. While variation in EPI has some significant impact on our indicator of non-income human development, the variation in EFI

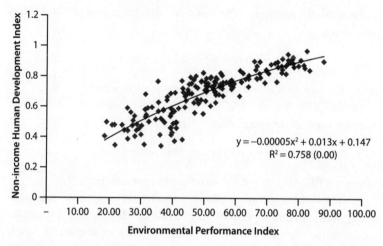

FIGURE **5.10**   Non-income Human Development Indicator as Depending on
the Environmental Performance Index
Source: Author's estimates based on *HDI* (2014).

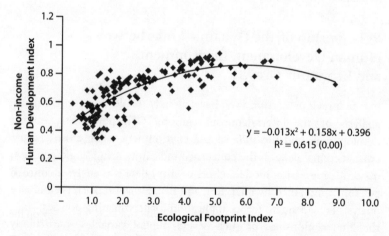

FIGURE **5.11**   Non-income Human Development Indicator as Depending on
the Ecological Footprint Index
Source: Author's estimates based on *HDI* (2014).

across the cross-country data has also been found to have a statistically significant impact on the same, but the strength of the EFI's impact on non-income human development is comparatively lower than that of the EPI. The impact of the latter on raising non-income human development on the basis of the cross-country data was obtained as:

$$y = -0.00005x^2 + 0.013x + 0.147,$$

where x is EPI with $R^2 = 0.758$ significant at p-value (0.00).

Similarly, the impact of EFI on raising non-income human development on the basis of cross-country data was obtained as:

$$y = -0.013x^2 + 0.158x + 0.396,$$

where x is EFI with $R^2 = 0.615$ significant at p-value (0.00).

In the following section, we further analyse the issue of such linkages among the different aspects of sustainable development in a dynamic model framework for tracing the pathways towards sustainable development covering the sets of linkage between economic growth and human development, human development and environmental development, and finally, between economic growth and environmental sustainability with the help of econometric models.

Relationship of the Dynamic Links between Human Development, Environment, and Economic Growth

In the previous section, we have already made some preliminary analysis of the interrelationship among GNI per capita, human development, and the state of the environment using cross-country, cross-sectional data on the concerned indicators using single equation quadratic regression models. Cross-country data was analysed for GNI per capita, non-income HDI, EFI, and EPI. However, such preliminary analysis is inadequate for its application for formulating policies, since the interrelationships of such developmental variables—particularly their inter-linkages—are much more complex, involving problems of multidimensional causation and those of endogeneity in explaining interrelated behaviours. Besides, like the analysis of the earlier section as based on cross-sectional data, it could only reflect how interrelated variables would change contingent upon some given change in one of the supposed exogenous casual variables. This assumes that a country passes through the different stages of growth along with various aspects of development in the same way as experienced by the countries which are situated at different stages of development in a given time period. And, it is also presumed that such results contingent upon some change in some causal factors will be insensitive with respect to the timing of the contingent change and its relation across time periods. There is thus no analysis of truly dynamic linkages among the concerned variables of growth and those of social and economic sustainability in the preceding analysis. We would now like to trace the dynamic linkages in at least in some limited way by analysing the data of actual (historical) change over real time as experienced by a selected set of countries and therefore, the estimating and testing significance of the dynamic relationship among the concerned variables of any typical country which is representative of the sample of countries selected.

However, the relationship and pathways of development with reference to the interactions among the different aspects of development are quite complex if the objective of development is sustained growth in income without any social disruption and without any disturbance in the equilibrium of the ecosystem. G. Ranis and F. Stewart (2005) and T. Suri, M.A. Boozer, G. Ranis, and F. Stewart (2011) have developed empirical economic models to estimate the relationship between human development and economic growth, which points to the two-way interactive relationship. Here, however, we focus on the following connections or links between economic growth (growth of GDP/GNP per capita) and sustained improvement in human development. Economic growth provides the critical income resources to households that they would allocate for expenditure so as to meet the basic minimum needs of food, healthcare, amenities of clean water and sanitation, education, and other such essential requirements so that people can get out of poverty and develop better earning capabilities with the accessibility to a greater spectrum of opportunities.

However, spending by a household, particularly on health and education—given its purchasing power in most situations in developing countries would be far from adequate, for the purpose of development of such basic needs—would require to be supplemented substantially by public spending on these. The allocation ratios of public expenditure on health and education would, in fact, be important determinants for human capability and capacity build-up.

However, the effectiveness of the impact of income growth on human capability development would be affected by the prevailing inequality in the distribution of income or the poverty ratio during a specific period. High poverty and inequality due to highly skewed distribution of benefit of income and growth are adverse factors in the realization of the full potential of human development. In such a situation, public spending on redistribution schemes and poverty alleviation can play complementary roles to spending on health and education infrastructure in uplifting the people for capacity development with wider coverage.

There exists the other important arm of linkage between human development and economic growth. As human capability develops, people have greater access to the labour market and opportunities of diverse types of occupation. Besides, with higher education and better health, a higher rate of human capital formation contributes to the growth of labour productivity and thereby to the rate of growth. Apart from expanding the human capital base, the higher level of education enables workers and managers to make better or more appropriate choices when it comes to technology, technological innovations, and local adaptation to the changing environmental and social conditions through the process of their learning by doing. Both R&D activities and wider diffusion of their successful outcomes are facilitated when people are endowed with better health, higher education, and greater scientific knowledge, and greater awareness of the socio-ecological landscape.

All this positive development at the micro level can contribute to higher economic growth at the macro level, provided there are some macro-level policy initiatives such as higher rate of investment, promotion of exports, and higher inflow of foreign capital. Human development raises the potential of growth as each skilled labourer can contribute towards it through higher productivity. However, the realization of the potential into actual change in the intended direction would depend on how many job opportunities are going to be created to translate higher human capability into higher per capita output. Higher and wider education can, in fact, end up creating greater educated unemployment if the macro policies end up with jobless growth. Countries like India have undergone demographic transitions that have seen growth in the share of the population of the working age group over time; this constitutes an important force to push growth ahead, provided the growing workers' population can develop the required skills as per the demand patterns of the labour market. All these are necessary conditions for the realization of what is called the demographic dividend of countries like India. The extent of translation of potential of development of human capabilities into actual realization would depend on the rate of investment and expansion of both home and foreign markets. While the development of the home market would depend on the growth and spending patterns of the government and households, the development of the export market has often been dependent on the trade and export policy of the government.

I would like to point out again that distributive factors and the state of poverty are likely to affect the process of the progress of human development, influencing economic growth. A higher poverty ratio or higher Gini coefficients are likely to adversely affect the impact of human development on economic growth, conditional upon the given values of other variables such as the macroeconomic rate of investment and oppenness of the economy. The basic reason behind such adverse effects is the fact that poverty and economic inequality stand in the way of everyone getting equal or universal access to better opportunities and higher incomes. Social inequalities are fundamentally rooted in economic disparities, which also emanate from social constraints, causing deprivation on grounds of caste, religious and ethnic identities, and other such aspects.

Economic Growth, Human Development, and the Environmental Conservation-cum-Protection Model of Inter-linkages

We can, therefore, set up a model of dynamic linkages of economy–environment–human development as follows. This would be an extended version of integrating the environment–economy linkage in addition to the economic growth–human development linkage. This would again be represented as a simultaneous equation system estimated over the time horizon 1990–2016 with 1990 as the base year,[1] which may be presented as follows:

[1] The data set on cross-country data considered for the purpose of estimation has been, in general, for the period 1990–2016. However, for the EPI, the basic data was available for certain years such as 2006, and either 2012 or 2016. As a result, the estimates of change in EPI have been recorded here for some country during the period 2006–12 and for some others 2006–16.

1. Dependent variable: growth in GNI per capita over the time horizon.
   Independent variables: (*i*) the non-income HDI in the base year, (*ii*) improvement in non-income HDI over the time horizon, (*iii*) GDP/GNI per capita in the base year, (*iv*) average Gini coefficient over the time horizon, (*v*) average headcount poverty ratio over the time horizon, (*vi*) domestic investment as share of GDP, (*vii*) exports as share of GDP, and (*viii*) average EPI the time horizon (see Table 5.1).
2. Dependent variable: growth of non-income HDI over the time horizon.
   Independent variables: (*i*) GDP/GNI per capita in the base year, (*ii*) growth of GDP/GNI per capita over the time horizon, (*iii*) non-income HDI in the base year, (*iv*) average Gini coefficient

TABLE 5.1   Results on Growth of Gross National Income Per Capita

Variables	Coefficient	Standard Error	z Value	$p > \lvert z \rvert$ Value
D (Developing)	0.846	0.027	31.3	0.00
Base Non-income HDI	0.219	0.019	11.6	0.00
D × Base Non-income HDI	0.191	0.033	5.79	0.00
Non-income HDI Growth	1.026	0.041	25.1	0.00
D × Non-income HDI growth	0.994	0.061	16.5	0.00
Base GNI Per Capita	2.781	0.182	15.4	0.00
D × Base GNI Per Capita	1.991	0.322	6.22	0.00
Gini Coefficient (Average)	−0.153	0.045	−3.4	0.00
D × Gini Coefficient (average)	−0.255	0.102	−2.5	0.00
Poverty Ratio (Average)	−0.551	0.234	−2.4	0.00
D × Poverty Ratio (Average)	−0.710	0.042	−17.8	0.00
Investment as a Ratio of GDP	1.621	0.461	3.52	0.00
D × Investment as a Ratio of GDP	0.944	0.312	3.03	0.00
Exports as Ratio of GDP	3.910	1.131	2.98	0.00
D × Exports as Ratio of GDP	4.201	1.262	3.33	0.00
Improvement in Environmental Performance	1.261	0.297	4.24	0.00
D × Improvement in Environmental Performance	2.988	0.983	3.05	0.00
Constant	5.711	1.211	4.71	0.00

Source: Author's own estimations.

TABLE 5.2   Results on Growth of Non-income Human Development Indicator

Variables	Coefficient	Standard Error	z Value	$p > |z|$ Value
D (Developing)	0.334	0.091	3.71	0.00
Base GNI Per Capita	2.221	0.994	2.24	0.02
D × Base GNI Per Capita	0.991	0.322	3.07	0.00
GNI Per Capita Growth	0.851	0.251	3.40	0.00
D × GNI Per Capita Growth	0.653	0.041	15.9	0.00
Base Non-income HDI	0.548	0.012	45.6	0.00
D × Base Non-income HDI	0.421	0.011	38.3	0.00
Gini Coefficient (Average)	−0.79	0.145	−5.45	0.00
D × Gini Coefficient (Average)	−0.293	0.011	−29.3	0.00
Poverty Ratio (Average)	−0.922	0.066	−15.4	0.00
D × Poverty Ratio (Average)	−0.467	0.032	−14.6	0.00
Expenditure on Education to GDP Ratio	0.354	0.090	3.93	0.00
D × Expenditure on Education Ratio of GDP	0.733	0.195	3.84	0.00
Expenditure on Health Ratio of GDP	0.176	0.071	2.51	0.00
D × Expenditure on Health Ratio of GDP	0.595	0.121	4.91	0.00
Improvement in Environmental Performance	2.998	1.024	2.93	0.00
D × Improvement in Environmental Performance	2.071	1.046	1.98	0.04
Constant	1.550	0.291	5.33	0.00

Source: Author's own estimations.

over the time horizon, (*v*) average poverty ratio over the time horizon, (*vi*) average public expenditure on health as a share of GDP, (*vii*) average public expenditure on education as a ratio of GDP, and (*viii*) average EPI over the period for which data are available (see Table 5.2).

3. Dependent variable: growth of CO_2 per capita.
   Independent variables: rate of change of non-income HDI, growth of GNI per capita, change in EPI, and share of renewable energy in the total energy use (see Table 5.3).

TABLE 5.3   Results on Growth of Carbon Dioxide Per Capita

Variables	Coefficient	Standard Error	z value	$p > \|z\|$ value
D (Developing)	0.412	0.089	4.61	0.00
Base GNI Per Capita	2.922	1.220	2.39	0.00
D × Base GNI Per Capita	2.651	0.912	2.91	0.00
GNI Per Capita Growth	1.120	0.030	37.4	0.00
D × GNI Per Capita Growth	0.999	0.221	4.52	0.00
Average Environmental Performance Index	−0.664	0.033	−20.1	0.00
D × Average Environmental Performance Index	−0.383	0.034	−12.6	0.00
Average Share of Renewable Energy in Final Energy Consumption	−0.902	0.046	−19.6	0.00
D × Average Share of Renewable Energy in Final Energy Consumption	−0.371	0.029	−12.8	0.00
Constant	0.199	1.867	0.107	0.91

Source: Author's own estimations.

4. Dependent variable: rate of change of forest area (as a percentage of total land area).

   Independent variables: change in forest area, growth of GNI per capita, rate of change of non-income HDI, change in EPI, and share of urban population (see Table 5.4).

5. Dependent variables: EPI.

   Independent variables: GNI per capita and level of non-income HDI (see Table 5.5).

The results of models on growth, human development, and environmental sustainability are presented from Tables 5.1 to 5.6. They present the regression coefficients of the equations of the two models along with their *p*-values indicating their levels of significance.

The results of the first model on the dynamic linkage between economic growth and human development are presented in Table 5.1. The estimated coefficients of the TSLS model clearly shows that the progress of non-income human development and its initial level for the time horizon of 1990 to 2015 have a significant impact on the growth of GNI per capita for both developed and developing

TABLE 5.4   Results on Rate of Change in Forest Area

Variables	Coefficient	Standard Error	z Value	$p > |z|$ Value
D (Developing)	0.344	0.020	17.2	0.00
Base GNI Per Capita	−2.910	0.991	−2.94	0.00
D × Base GNI Per Capita	−2.618	1.033	−2.53	0.00
GNI Per Capita Growth	−0.159	0.054	−54.2	0.00
D × GNI Per Capita Growth	−0.999	0.330	−9.01	0.00
Average Environmental Performance Index	0.814	0.081	10.17	0.00
D × Average Environmental Performance Index	0.399	0.019	21.0	0.00
Average Share of Urban Population	−0.377	0.041	−9.15	0.00
D × Average Share of Urban Population	−0.545	0.189	−2.88	0.00
Constant	3.817	0.892	4.28	0.00

Source: Author's own estimations.

TABLE 5.5   Results on Change in the Environmental Performance Index

Variables	Coefficient	Standard Error	z Value	$p > |z|$ Value
D (Developing)	0.553	0.089	6.21	0.00
Base GNI Per Capita	2.911	1.131	2.57	0.00
D × Base GNI Per Capita	0.173	0.046	3.69	0.00
GNI Per Capita Growth	2.722	0.353	7.71	0.00
D × GNI Per Capita Growth	0.449	0.065	6.91	0.00
Constant	4.680	1.034	4.54	0.00

Source: Author's own estimations.

countries. However, the initial level of GNI per capita in the base year, that is, in 1990, has no statistically significant effect on the GNI per capita growth over the time horizon. While the exogenous variables of rate of investment as share of GDP and that of exports in GDP would raise the extent of growth that is estimated for the time horizon, the average level of inequality (the Gini coefficient) or poverty ratio would depress the growth achievement as expected over the same time horizon, all the concerned coefficients of equation being statistically significant.

The impact of economic growth on the improvement of non-income HDI is exactly similar to the obverse impact. Both the initial level of GNI per capita and extent of its growth during the planning horizon have a significant positive impact on the improvement of non-income HDI over the chosen time horizon. The initial level of the non-income HDI, however, has no significant impact on the extent of its improvement over the time horizon. However, the policy variables of allocation of public expenditures in social sectors as a share of GDP have significant impact on the progress in human development as expected. On the other hand, a rise in inequality and in the poverty ratio would have opposite depressing impact on non-income human development of both developed and developing countries from our sample.

It is, therefore, important to note that growth of per capita GNI and rise in human capability development have a positive linkage both ways. They can thus play a complementary role in ensuring the sustainability of these two aspects of development—each one reinforcing the other. The choice of the policy package should thus combine macroeconomic growth–promoting strategies such as a higher rate of investment and the development of export market with a higher rate of public spending in the social sectors of health and education. Neglect of either of these kinds of policies in favour of the other for any reason of resource constraint may lead to lopsided development and may be counterproductive in the long run for the sustainability of the development process.

Besides, the result of Table 5.1 also tells us that there is no necessary conflict between higher growth and lower inequality. The negative sign of the Gini coefficients of inequality in the model with the dependent variable as the GNI per capita ensures that any rise in inequality, *ceteris paribus* (other things being equal), would necessarily lead to lower growth in GNI. The rise in inequality is also regressive for the progress of human development under a similar *ceteris paribus* condition when we consider the progress in human development as the dependent variable. It is, however, not a surprising result, on the other hand, that reduction in poverty would separately be both growth promoting and promoting the pace of human development. Any policy on redistribution of income or wealth as well as on poverty alleviation would be helpful for the sustainability of both economic growth and human development by accelerating their respective paces.

Table 5.2 presents the results of TSLS model, showing the dynamic linkage between the growth of GNI per capita and the growth of non-income HDI. Before we interpret the results, let us clarify that the average growth of the variable GNI per capita over the time horizon has been taken to be the semi log growth rate as fitted to the basic data of income per capita over the time span 1990–2016 for a combination of 70 countries, both developed and developing covered separately. Similarly, we have taken the average of the semi log growth rate of the non-income HDI score to be the one as estimated on the basis of the basic data over the same time horizon as that of the growth of income per capita for any country. Other variables have been either the value of a variable in the base year for a country or its average value for the concerned time period as determined from secondary sources or calculated as the geometric mean of the observed values over the individual years of the time horizon. The TSLS method has, in fact, used this cross-sectional data of the average growth rates or mean of other variate values as observed over the time horizon for the various countries separately.

Tables 5.3 to 5.5 show that coefficients of any of the TSLS regression models as finally estimated and whose results have been presented have all been significant and appear in the equations mostly with the expected positive or negative sign of relationship. We have used a dummy to distinguish between the estimates of coefficients for developing countries as distinct from the developed ones, because of the possible basic structural differences in the behavioural pattern of the variables between the two groups of countries.

Table 5.6 shows the coefficients of the relevant variables as estimated for developed and developing countries separately. It may be noted here that the values of coefficients of the GNI per capita growth rate to estimate the partial effects of its variation on the growth rate of human development are found to be substantively higher for the developing countries compared to those for the developed ones. Similarly, the coefficients of average growth rate of non-income HDI to indicate its partial impact of variation on the per capital GNI growth

TABLE 5.6 Projected Growth of Gross National Income Per Capita and Non-income Human Development on the Basis of the Linkage Model

Year	GNI Per Capita Growth (Semi Log)— Developed	GNI Per Capita Growth (Semi Log)— Developing	Non-income HDI (Semi Log) —Developed	Non-income HDI (Semi Log) —Developing
1990	1.29	2.42	0.73	0.55
2000	1.44	2.07	0.85	0.57
2010	1.13	1.96	0.89	0.64
2015	1.33	2.29	0.89	0.68

Source: Author's own estimations.

rate are obtained to be higher for developing countries as compared to the developed ones.

We thus find that both economic growth and growth of non-income human development reinforce each other, and the strength of this linkage is higher for developing countries than the developed ones. Besides, the coefficients of the inequality or poverty ratio variables show their partial negative impact on both income growth and the rate of growth or progress of non-income human development indicator. However, the order of this negative impact is again higher for the developing countries.

For the actual observed values of all the independent or exogenous variables, we estimated the rate of growth of GNI per capita as well as that of non-income human development indicator for the developed and developing countries on the decadal dates of 1990, 2000, 2010, and 2015 using the results of the TSLS model. It is important to notice that the growth rate of per capita income has been systematically higher for developing countries when compared to the developed ones, while the order is opposite for a similar comparison in the case of levels of growth rate of the non-income component of human development. So far as the time trend of such growth rate is concerned, this has fluctuated in the case of growth rate of income per capita while it has risen secularly for the growth rate of the value of non-income human development indicator over time, although the gradient of the rise has been higher for developing countries. These results for the years covered correspond to the historical experiences of economic fluctuations (see Table 5.6 onwards and Figure 5.12 onwards).

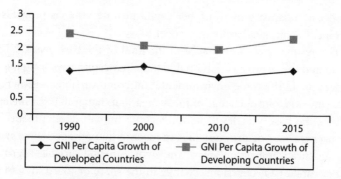

FIGURE 5.12   Estimated Growth of Gross National Income Per Capita across Developed and Developing Countries
Source: Based on Table 5.6.

While none of the results as obtained for the estimated model of linkage appear to be surprising, the policy implications are nevertheless of particular significance in respect of developing countries. Since income growth and progress of human development (particularly health and education) are complementary, the policies need to take a balanced approach in deciding the development strategy of these countries. Both macro-level investment and trade policies, as well as public spending on social sectors are important for accelerating growth and translating it into determinants of capabilities of human development. It is, however, difficult to infer from our data, set on a limited time horizon, which of the linkage of interdependences between human development and economic growth are more fundamental or influential. While the behaviour of the rate of growth of non-income human development is more stable than that of the growth rate of per capita income, it is well known that the effect of human capability change on the latter takes a longer time than the growth process to impact human development. It requires panel data for a much longer time horizon to find out if high economic growth would necessarily lead to human development irrespective of policies specifically targeting non-income human development, or if non-income human development is a more basic and fundamental factor in sustaining economic growth over time. One has to analyse the histories of the growth and the development process to arrive at more robust conclusion. Having said that, we discuss later how, given our data set, the ordering of the countries changes in respect of relative growth of per capita income vis-à-vis progress of non-income human development over time.

The results now show that both the level of the base year GNI per capita and the growth of national income per capita have a significant impact on all the three environmental outcome variables—growth of CO_2 emission, rate of change of forest area, and change in EPI. However, neither the base year level of non-income human development, nor the average rate of progress in non-income human development has any significant impact on any of the environmental variables—growth of per capita CO_2 emissions, change in the share of forest area in the total land area, and the variable of improvement in environmental performance.

However, we have found that the EPI reduces the growth of CO_2 emissions per capita as well as raises the share of forest area and thus favourably tend to conserve the environmental resources as expected. It is also significant as a causal variable in favourably impacting both the growth of GNI per capita as well as progress in non-income human development. Besides, the exogenous variables of the share of renewable energy in the total final energy consumption and the share of urban population have a significant impact on CO_2 emissions per capita and the share of forest area as expected.

Thus we observe that economic growth in terms of growth of per capita national income is important for both human development as well as for environmental conservation and protection. Since the EPI (as per its definition and construction) is a policy-driven exogenous variable, it is the most effective in impacting environmental sustainability as expected. For environmental sustainability, both growth policy and direct environmental policies relating to protecting human health and the health of the ecosystems would be of prime importance. The linkage or pathway from human development to qualitative environmental changes being complex and remote, the impact works out in a longer time horizon. It is therefore not surprising that the model shows that the impact of environmental factors on the progress in non-income human development is not significant. Human development can have an impact on the environment only via its impact on the growth of income and its financial capability in affording policies of environmental and energy conservation as well as resource substitutions, which often turn out to be costly.

What is important for us is to note is the interdependence of the growth, non-income human development, and environmental sustainability in the light of the results observed from the five-equation extended TSLS econometric model. The relative significances of the different linkages and the immediacy of the impact relationship are important when it comes to prioritizing alternative policy options for ensuring sustainable development in a comprehensive sense. In this context we have found the estimated growth rate or rate of change of all the five major outcome variables— growth of per capita income, annual average rate of progress of non-income human development, rate of changes in per capita CO_2 emissions, the share of forest area, and that of environmental performance—as per the results of the estimates of the coefficients of the TSLS models for the years 1990, 2000, 2010, and 2015, as presented in Tables 5.6–5.8. Figures 5.12–5.16 show the dynamics of movement of the concerned growth rates or rates of change for the above-mentioned years.

TABLE 5.7 Estimated Growth of Carbon Dioxide Per Capita and Forest Area across Developed and Developing Countries

Year	Growth of CO_2 Per Capita (Developed)	Growth of CO_2 Per Capita (Developing)	Forest Area (Developed)	Forest Area (Developing)
1990	11.21	2.20	35.6	28.9
2000	16.12	3.10	33.4	30.6
2010	9.80	11.41	33.9	27.8
2015	10.11	8.21	31.1	26.4

Source: Author's own estimations.

TABLE 5.8 Estimated Growth of Environmental Performance Index across Developed and Developing Countries

Year	EPI (Developed)	EPI (Developing)
2002	72.1	65.5
2010	82.3	71.2
2014	83.3	74.6

Source: Author's own estimations.

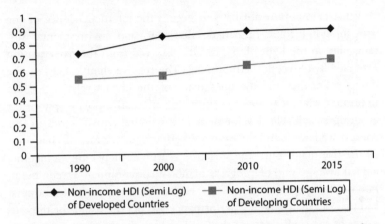

FIGURE 5.13   Estimated Growth of Non-income Human Development Index across Developed and Developing Countries
Source: Based on Table 5.6.

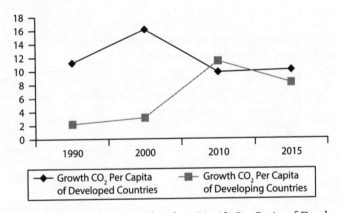

FIGURE 5.14   Estimated Growth of Carbon Dioxide Per Capita of Developed and Developing Countries
Source: Based on Table 5.7.

In order to get more insight into the character of the relative process of change and the dynamics of the structure of rates of growth as generated by the above-estimated model, we further present some more observations based on the results submitted in the following tables and

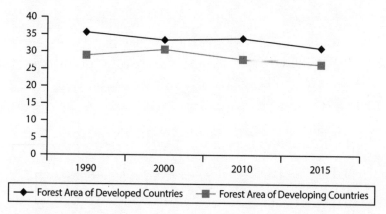

FIGURE **5.15**   Estimated Growth of Forest Area across Developed and Developing Countries
Source: Based on Table 5.7.

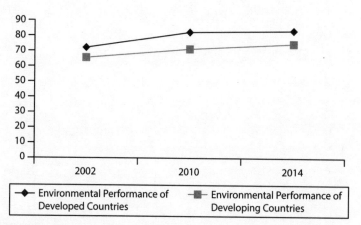

FIGURE **5.16**   Estimated Growth of Environmental Performance Indicator in Developed and Developing Countries
Source: Based on Table 5.8.

charts. These tables present bivariate data on growth rates on the combination of two out of five growth variables at a time and show their attained combined values in 1990 and 2015 for the analysis of change in the structure of the economy, which would have important implications on development sustainability.

PART II

THIRD INDUSTRIAL REVOLUTION AND SUSTAINABLE DEVELOPMENT OF INDIA'S POWER SECTOR

We have modified our environment so radically that we must modify ourselves in order to exist in this new environment.

—Norbert Weiner
(*The Human Use of Human Beings: Cybernetics and Society*)

Energy, Sustainability, and Third Industrial Revolution

While in the chapters in Part I, I have discussed at length the conceptual issues of the different dimensions of sustainability, in Part II, I focus on the same issues as arising in the context of the power and energy sector development in India. Chapter 6 describes the country's energy scenario, including its carbon footprint, against the background of a macroeconomic setting of growth with cross-country comparison. It focuses on the issues of energy security, energy poverty, and distribution, as well as the carbon footprint and fuel choice for power generation with reference to controlling climate change. In this context the chapter points to the difference in perspectives of developed and developing countries in respect of the relationship between inclusive economic growth and climate control and argues for possible complementarities in policies for the two. Finally, it outlines the roles of new renewables in describing the new power and energy landscape of the economy in the era of the Third Industrial Revolution.

Issues of Sustainable Development of the Indian Energy and Power Sector

While reviewing the concept of sustainable development in the preceding chapters, we observed the importance of the different dimensions of sustainability—economic, social, and environmental—to ensure that a sustained process of economic growth is socially and environmentally non-disruptive. While economic sustainability requires the growth process to be cost-effective (that is, minimize the real source cost of production) to generate the surplus and savings of a society to be reinvested for growth, social sustainability would require the process to be socially inclusive as well, so as to generate adequate gainful employment, permitting people's participation in the development process, and thereby ensuring equitable distribution of the benefit of growth among the people. Environmental sustainability, on the other hand, requires the conservation of natural resources and the control of waste generation arising from the entropic process of conversion of resources into products so that there is no environmental risk of collapse of the ecosystems. The latter is of critical importance from the point of view of controlling the negative externalities of economic production on both human health and health of the ecosystems (that is, their regenerative capacity) in the different regions of our planet. These requirements of multidimensional sustainability would have obvious implications in respect of the energy policy for sustainable development of the energy sector of developing economies, including India.

We therefore focus in this chapter on energy poverty and security of the Indian people for the social sustainability of our development process, as well as on the major challenge of environmental sustainability as posed by the threat of climate change arising from the use of fossil fuel and the intrinsic entropic nature of any energy use. As already pointed out in the Preface, it is mainly the use of energy, for which the impact of entropy law is most serious, that deserves special importance in any discussion on the issues of energy policy concerning the role of entropy law in the sustainability of economic processes.

Energy is the most crucial infrastructural sector in determining the pace of economic growth, as well as the impact of stress created by an economy on the ecosystem as measured by the carbon footprint component of the ecological footprint. In the specific context of India's energy policy, the sustainability of economic growth and the social sustainability of the development process would require the following:

1. There needs to be energy security at the macro level so that there is always adequate supply of energy in primary or final forms (such as

in the transformed form of electricity or refined petroleum products) to fuel the process of economic growth. This implies that there should be wide access to and use of electricity (the cleanest source of energy) and petroleum fuel for both production and transportation of goods and people.

2. The distribution of income or purchasing power of the households and fuel prices has to be such that households have universal access to clean cooking fuel (LPG) and lighting fuel (electricity). Social sustainability should require that there is no energy poverty in terms of lifeline supply of electricity for lighting and gas or petroleum fuel like kerosene as defining the poverty benchmarks.

3. The energy use and conversion of primary energy (fuels) into final forms should be as efficient and clean as possible. This is important both from the viewpoints of economic efficiency and environmental sustainability. The carbon footprint, which is entirely due to fossil fuel use, constitutes the single largest component of the ecological footprint at an economy-wide level. This highlights the importance of both energy conservation and the choice of clean fuel, particularly in the electricity industry, by way of substitution of fossil fuel by renewables in power generation. This leads to policy issues relating to the drawing up of the roadmap of the Third Industrial Revolution, which is to be driven by the widespread decentralized development of new renewables-based electricity and road transportation based either on electricity or hydrogen-cum-fuel cells.

While the considerations of (1) and (2) are likely to raise the use of fossil fuel, those of (3) are targeted to reduce it. Before we enter into a more detailed discussion on the role of renewables in the Third Industrial Revolution in the following chapter, we will quickly review the state of India's energy efficiency, energy poverty, and energy dependence on the rest of the world. The state of sustainability of energy production and use in India, in fact, depends on both the consideration of energy security as well as the cleanliness of fuel.

Economic Growth and Energy Scenario of India

Since the introduction of economic reforms in 1990, the Indian economy grew at an annual average rate of 6 per cent till 2000, followed by a period of accelerated growth of 7.5 per cent during the period from 2000 to 2016. Against this average growth rate of 6.56 per cent in the entire period of 1990 to 2016, the energy use of all kinds of fuel together grew at an annual average rate of 4.1 per cent during the period from 1990 to 2013. This yields an estimate of GDP elasticity of energy use of 0.625 in India, which is lower than the world average value of 0.734 of such elasticity, but higher than those of China and USA. In view of the value being lower than unity, the overall energy intensity of GDP has been declining over this period, although the per capita energy use of India was only 607 oil equivalent kg (kgoe) in 2013, which has been less than one-third of the global per capita energy use value of 1893 kgoe. India is, in fact, a relatively energy-poor country. See Table 6.1 for the comparative estimates of per capita energy consumption and growth of energy use vis-à-vis GDP growth across major economies of China, USA, India, and the world.

So far as the composition of primary energy supply is concerned, Table 6.1 shows fossils fuels to be having a high share of 72.3 per cent and the combustible renewables and waste (which are mostly highly polluting with health-damaging effect on humans) as having 24.5 per cent, which is higher than the world average in 2013 (See Table 6.1). So far as the final energy use is concerned, the cleanest fuel is electricity. India's energy poverty is highlighted more by the fact of low per capita electricity production and use, which was 995 kilowatt hour (kwh)

TABLE 6.1   Primary Energy Use

Countries	Per Capita Primary Energy Use (All Fuels) in 2013 (in kgoe)	Annual Average Growth Rate of Energy Use from 1990 to 2013 (Per Cent)	Rate of Growth of GDP from 1990 to 2016 (Per Cent)	Share of Fossil Fuel (Per Cent)	Share of Renewables, Combustible Biomass, and Waste (Per Cent)
India	607	4.1	6.56	72.3	24.5
China	2,214	6.1	10.1	88.1	7.2
USA	6,902	0.6	2.4	82.9	4.7
World	1,893	2.1	2.83	81.1	10.2

Source: World Bank, World Development Indicators 2015, 2017.

in 2014, which is less than one-third of the world average, one-fourth of China's, and less than 7.5 per cent of the USA's (see Table 6.2). In the same year, only 79.2 per cent of India's population had access to electricity while it was 85.3 per cent at the global level, and 100 per cent for the people of USA and China. Besides, an issue of major concern has been that most of the CO_2 emissions in the energy sector take place from fuel combustion in the electricity and transport sectors, both of which are heavily dependent on fossil fuel in India. Table 6.2 provides the fuel-wise comparative composition of gross generation of power in India for 2014 as compared to those of China, USA, and the world. It may be noted that the share of fossil fuel–based power generation has been as high as 81.8 per cent for India in 2014, while those of hydro, nuclear, and new renewables (that is, wind, solar, and so on) in percentage terms have been 10.2, 2.8, and 5.2, respectively in the same year. Table 6.2 shows that India's power generation has been more dependent on fossil fuels and less sustainable compared to other large economies such as China, USA, and even the global average.

One of the major problems facing India regarding energy security is its high dependence on imports for energy supply. Net imports of energy in India had a share of 34 per cent of total energy use in India in 2013–14, which has grown over time from a relative low level of 8 per cent in 1990 (see Table 6.4). The shares of import in the total apparent consumption of coal, oil, and natural gas had risen over time in the period since 1990 and reached a level of 22.7 per cent, 78.5 per cent, and 27.3 per cent, respectively in 2013–14 due to the growth of demand

TABLE 6.2 Electricity Production

Countries	Per Capita Gross Generation in 2014 (kwh)	Share of Fossil Fuel in Gross Generation in 2014 (Per Cent)	Share of Renewables in Electricity in 2014 (Per Cent)*	Share of Nuclear Energy in 2014 (Per Cent)
India	996	81.8	15.4	2.8
China	4,154	74.8	22.6	2.3
USA	13,548	67.5	13.0	19.2
World	3,287.5	66.4	22.3	10.6

Source: World Bank, World Development Indicators 2015, 2017.
Note: *Storage hydro power and new renewables.

outpacing their respective supplies from domestic sources. The import prices of all the three fossil fuels had also grown in nominal USD and INR terms as well as in real INR terms in the two-decade period from 1989–90 to 2010–11. While the growth of net imports of all fossil fuels together in oil-equivalent terms has been 8.79 per cent per annum over the period under reference (its share in the total apparent consumption of energy increasing at the rate of 3.25 per cent per annum), the unit price of the fossil fuel in oil equivalent unit increased in nominal USD and INR terms at the rates of 15.05 per cent and 19.92 per cent respectively. This led to a situation of growth of the net import bill of India at an unsustainably high rate of 19.2 per cent per annum, leading to an almost 55 times increase in 2010–11 over the base of 1990–91 (see Sengupta 2015).

However, the international price of oil crashed in 2014–15 and the share of the import bill of oil as well as of net energy (that is, including share of coal, coke, and so on) has since then declined to the levels of 12 per cent and 16 per cent respectively of the total export earnings on merchandise and service accounts together as observed in 2015–16 and 2016–17 (see RBI website). The price volatility of energy as experienced in recent years in the global market does not necessarily lead to any predictable condition of stable low prices in the coming years, but adds to the uncertainty regarding prices induced specially by the imperfectly competitive nature of the oil market. Price volatility of a large energy-importing country such as India gives rise to the conditions of such uncertainties which result in both energy insecurity and macroeconomic unsustainability of development as may arise from its pressure on the balance of payments situation due to its deficit and its fluctuations. This becomes an added reason for India's special thrust on switching to new renewable energy resources to replace fossil fuels. Besides, this also underlines the policy importance of the strength of the macroeconomic fundamentals of the Indian economy to develop resilience to energy-price volatility and high import dependence.

For an energy-deficient economy, energy efficiency is of critical importance for both energy security and sustainability. In respect of energy efficiency, it is, however, interesting to note that India has performed better than China and the world at the macro level in terms of productivity of energy use (2011 PPP USD per unit of kgoe use of energy) as well as CO_2 kg per unit of 2011 PPP USD GDP in 2014. However, this

TABLE **6.3**   Energy Efficiency and Carbon Emission

Countries	Net Energy Import Per Cent of Use, 2014	GDP Per Unit of Energy, 2014 (2011 PPP USD per kgoe of energy)	Carbon Intensity (kg per Oil Equivalent Tonne of Energy Use), 2014	CO_2 Emissions Per Capita, 2014	CO_2 Emissions Per 2011 PPP USD of GDP, 2014
India	34	8.5	2.7	1.7	0.3
China	15	5.7	3.4	7.5	0.6
USA	9	7.5	2.4	16.5	0.3
World	—	7.9	2.6	5.0	0.3

Source: World Bank, World Development Indicators 2015, 2017.

data, as presented in Table 6.3, should not be necessarily interpreted to represent higher efficiency of energy use in real thermodynamic sense. These, along with India's low per capita CO_2 emissions compared to the global average or to those of China or USA, are more a reflection of the income and energy poverty of the Indian people, which is a result of their low access to modern fossil fuel–based final energy supply, rather than energy efficiency. The penetration of the use of electricity or other modern forms of final energy has in fact been far from complete because of their high capital costs, as the concerned technologies are often knowledge intensive. The high correlation between CO_2 emissions per capita and per capita income in cross-country data as observed in Chapter 5 can clarify the issue. See Table 6.3 in this context for the comparative data on such energy and CO_2 efficiency in production as well as CO_2 emissions per capita.

Energy Poverty and Social Sustainability

From the viewpoint of socially sustainable development of energy supply, it is, however, more important to focus on micro household-level data regarding access people have to electricity and clean cooking fuel rather than macro-level data on energy or the CO_2 intensity of GDP. What would be important for environmental sustainability, on the other hand, would be, among others, the share of electricity

TABLE 6.4   Sustainable Energy and Access to Clean Energy

Countries	Per Capita Primary Energy Use (All Fuels), 2013 (in kgoe)	Renewable Electricity Share (Per Cent), 2014	Access to Electricity (Per Cent Share of Population), 2014		
			(Rural)	(Urban)	(Overall)
India	34.2	15.4	70.00	98.3	79.2
China	57.2	22.6	100	100	100
USA	100	13.0	100	100	100
World	57.4	22.3	73.00	96.4	85.3

Source: World Bank, World Development Indicators 2015, 2017.

generated using renewable resources, particularly the new renewables such as wind, solar, and micro-hydel or biomass. Table 6.4 shows that India's attainment of values of these indicators falls substantially short of the achievements of China and the global level due to its higher energy poverty. An analysis of the 66th Round National Sample Survey Office (NSSO) data on household consumption for the year 2011–12 shows that rural Indian households uses biomass, LPG, and kerosene as main cooking fuels while electricity and kerosene are used mainly for lighting. The NSSO survey data also shows the number and share of households who report separately for cooking and lighting the names of the principal fuels they use. We consider a household to be cooking-energy poor for the following analysis if biomass is its principal fuel used for cooking. The other households have been considered as non-poor. Again, any household which declares electricity to be its primary lighting fuel would be considered as non-poor and the other households would be treated as poor (see Tables 6.5 and 6.6). The households' consumption data of the 68th Round of NSSO for 2011–12 shows the cooking poverty ratio to be 79 per cent in rural India and 19 per cent in urban India as per such definition. Similarly, it was found that in rural area the lighting poverty ratio is 30 per cent while the same is only 5 per cent in urban areas (see Tables 6.5 and 6.6). Such a definition of energy poverty does not consider any benchmark of lighting or cooking fuel requirements in quantitative terms to define poverty line and accordingly derive the poverty ratio. The diverse range of fuels with a wide range of variation in their efficiency in delivering energy for lighting

Table 6.5 Rural Household Energy Poverty

Decile Class of MPCE	Cumulative Share of Population up to the Decile Class	Share of Total Population Falling in Decile Class and Primary Cooking Fuel as Biomass	Cumulative Share of Population up to the Decile Class (for Preceding Column)	Share of Total Population Falling in Decile Class and Primary Cooking Fuel as LPG	Cumulative Share of Population up to the Decile Class (for Preceding Column)	Share of Total Population Falling in Decile Class and Principal Fuel for Lighting as Electricity	Cumulative Share of Population up to the Decile Class (for Preceding Column)
1	10	0.092	0.092	0.000	0.000	0.045	0.045
2	20	0.089	0.181	0.001	0.002	0.051	0.096
3	30	0.088	0.269	0.003	0.004	0.056	0.151
4	40	0.089	0.359	0.004	0.008	0.065	0.216
5	50	0.084	0.442	0.006	0.014	0.068	0.284
6	60	0.082	0.525	0.009	0.023	0.073	0.357
7	70	0.079	0.604	0.014	0.038	0.080	0.437
8	80	0.075	0.679	0.018	0.056	0.085	0.522
9	90	0.066	0.744	0.029	0.085	0.087	0.609
10	100	0.046	0.790	0.045	0.130	0.093	0.703

Source: Author's own estimations based on NSSO data of 68th Round NSS Report of the Ministry of Statistics and Programme Implementation (MOSPI), Government of India.

Notes: Households with biomass as principal fuel for cooking are classified as poor for cooking energy.

Households with fuel other than electricity as principal fuel for lighting are classified as poor for lighting energy.

Poverty ratio for cooking energy (rural) is 0.79.

Poverty ratio for lighting energy (rural) is 0.3.

TABLE 6.6 Urban Household Energy Poverty

Decile Class of MPCE	Cumulative Share of Population up to the Decile Class	Share of Total Population Falling in Decile Class and Primary Cooking Fuel as Biomass	Cumulative Share of Population up to the Decile Class (for Preceding Column)	Share of Total Population Falling in Decile Class and Primary Cooking Fuel as LPG	Cumulative Share of Population up to the Decile Class (for Preceding Column)	Share of Total Population Falling in Decile Class amd Principal Fuel for Lighting as Electricity	Cumulative Share of Population up to the Decile Class (for Preceding Column)
1	10	0.060	0.060	0.036	0.036	0.081	0.081
2	20	0.043	0.103	0.067	0.103	0.092	0.173
3	30	0.029	0.131	0.086	0.189	0.096	0.269
4	40	0.023	0.154	0.098	0.288	0.096	0.365
5	50	0.015	0.169	0.111	0.399	0.098	0.462
6	60	0.010	0.179	0.118	0.517	0.097	0.560
7	70	0.006	0.185	0.120	0.637	0.097	0.657
8	80	0.004	0.189	0.121	0.758	0.099	0.756
9	90	0.002	0.191	0.122	0.880	0.099	0.855
10	100	0.001	0.192	0.120	1.000	0.099	0.954

Source: Author's own estimations based on NSSO data of 68th NSS Round Report of the MOSPI, Government of India.

Notes: Households with biomass as principal fuel for cooking are classified as poor for cooking energy.

Households with fuel other than electricity as principal fuel for lighting are classified as poor for lighting energy.

Poverty ratio for cooking energy (urban) is 0.19.

Poverty ratio for lighting energy (urban) is 0.05.

or cooking services due to very different technologies of the appliances used for the purpose make such a definition of energy poverty extremely difficult for the rural and urban areas separately. Although, our definition of poverty is based on the qualitative category of fuel use in terms of cleanliness, the non-poor for cooking energy would be using anything other than biomass, which is mostly inefficient and unclean. The consumption of the non-poor would include kerosene as well as LPG, although the two differ in terms of both efficiency as well as cleanliness. Since LPG is the most efficient cooking fuel as mostly used among others excluding electricity (whose share in cooking fuel used would be very limited due to the relative higher costs), the share of the population using LPG as the principal cooking fuel has been 13 per cent in rural area and 88 per cent in urban areas as observed in the survey under reference.

Alternatively, if one considers a household to be cooking energy poor if its principal cooking fuel is anything other than LPG, then the cooking poverty ratio would become as high as 87 per cent in rural areas, while there would be practically no such poverty in terms of deprivation of principal clean-fuel use in urban areas (see Tables 6.5 and 6.6). There is thus a huge urban-rural gap in the use of LPG as cooking fuel.

In order to get a more precise idea about inequality in the distribution of the major cooking and lighting fuels, we have derived the specific concentration curve for each major fuel used and juxtaposed it to the Lorenz Curve for overall consumption distribution. The specific concentration curve plots the cumulative share of the total use of a given cooking or lighting fuel against the cumulative share population from the lower end of the scale of per head or per household income or consumption expenditure. Its position vis-à-vis the 45-degree line is indicative of inequality in sharing the fuel for cooking vis-à-vis the inequality of similar distribution of total consumption expenditure on all items together. The comparative position of the Lorenz Curve and the specific concentration curve indicates if the concerned fuel may be considered as a necessity or luxury item by the concerned segments of households. If the specific concentration curve lies between the 45-degree line and the Lorenz Curve, it is considered to be a necessity by households in the concerned range of income or per capita expenditure variation, while it would be considered a luxury item if it lies outside the Lorenz Curve but above the axes (see Figures 6.1 and 6.2). These figures present these curves of inequalities or concentration in the distribution of household-level total consumption expenditure as well as in that of individual fuels in the rural and urban segments of the Indian economy. This would provide useful policy insights for abating any social tension arising from inequality or poverty resulting from absolute or relative deprivation of clean fuels.

Figures 6.1 and 6.2 show the degree of inequality in the distribution of fuels. The concentration curve of biomass lying partly or wholly above the 45-degree line indicates the inferior nature of this good for the urban segment of the population as considered by the households, while the relative position of the concentration curves for LPG for cooking and electricity for lighting vis-à-vis the Lorenz Curve show these to be luxury goods; those of kerosene for rural lighting and electricity for urban lighting are seen to be necessities for the respective rural and urban populations. These characterizations have depended upon the preference structure of the households of various income-expenditure classes as revealed through their behaviour. However, we have to also remember that the pattern of fuel consumption has mostly depended on its availability and therefore often been constrained by the supply-side situation. The absolute and relative deprivation of fuels for

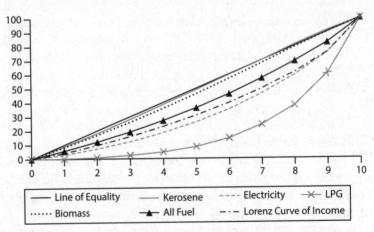

FIGURE 6.1   Specific Concentration Curve for Fuels and Lorenz Curve for Income (Rural)

Source: Author's own presentation.

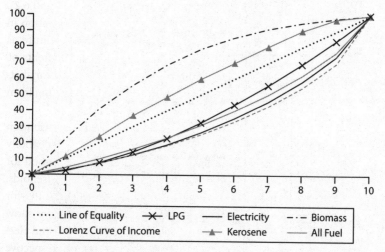

FIGURE **6.2**   Specific Concentration Curve for Fuel and Lorenz Curve for
Income (Urban)
Source: Author's own presentation.

households have been forced more by the conditions of their availability
rather than those of their incomes inducing the choice. This leads to
the importance of policy thrusts in respect of making fuels, particularly
electricity for lighting and LPG for cooking, available to the households
irrespective of their ability to pay. Besides, greater consumption of electricity for lighting and LPG/kerosene for cooking as facilitated by the
greater availability of these respective fuels would reduce lighting- and
cooking-fuel poverty arising from the deprivation of the clean fuels for
these purposes. Table 6.7 further shows how the price actually paid by
the people of different expenditure classes is different in terms of price
per unit of oil equivalent kg across fuels and how they are different
between urban and rural areas. A close analysis of this table indicates
how far household energy prices are redistributive or regressive.

Fossil Fuel, Climate Change, and the Challenge of Sustainable Development

The other very big issues relating to sustainable development and use
of energy resources are concerned with climate change largely due
to open GHG emissions mostly from the use of fossil fuel in energy.

TABLE 6.7 Price Variation (Rural and Urban) in INR per Kgoe

Decile Class of MPCE	Rural						Urban						Rural–Urban Differential in Price
	Electricity	Biomass	LPG	Kerosene	Total Fuel		Electricity	Biomass	LPG	Kerosene	Total Fuel		
1	3.0	6.6	30.7	213.0	6.6		3.6	7.9	26.8	220.1	7.1		0.48
2	3.1	7.4	26.6	218.3	7.0		3.6	8.3	26.2	234.4	7.2		0.24
3	3.1	7.3	26.2	215.5	6.8		3.6	8.2	26.7	258.9	7.2		0.37
4	3.2	7.2	27.1	214.1	6.6		3.7	8.0	26.4	256.9	7.1		0.47
5	3.2	7.0	27.2	213.2	6.4		3.7	7.4	26.1	276.4	6.8		0.36
6	3.2	6.8	26.8	212.5	6.2		3.8	7.2	26.0	277.9	6.6		0.38
7	3.3	6.8	26.5	210.0	6.1		3.8	7.3	26.1	317.0	6.5		0.37
8	3.4	6.8	26.1	210.4	6.2		3.9	7.5	26.1	341.9	6.4		0.20
9	3.4	6.9	26.3	211.4	6.2		4.0	6.0	26.1	423.7	6.1		-0.14
10	3.4	6.6	26.3	222.0	6.0		4.3	6.1	25.8	298.7	5.6		-0.37
Total	0.3	6.9	26.4	213.9	6.3		4.0	7.8	26.1	282.4	6.4		0.07

Source: Author's own estimations based on NSSO data of the 68th NSS Round Report of the MOSPI, Government of India.

In spite of the recognition of interdependence of the human economy and the earth's ecosystems and the fact that the carbon footprint from fossil fuel constitutes more than 50 per cent of the share in the total ecological footprint of human society, there has been scant regard for the consequences of consumption prevalent in our consumerist society on our natural heritage. Consumerism has evolved as the major cultural force for boosting the effective demand for our capitalist market, the prime motive for which has been indefinite accumulation of wealth as an end in itself, leading to the reckless pursuit of pecuniary profit or material gain. As a result, we are not only depleting our fossil fuels and other non-renewable resources, but also exhausting our renewable resources by overexploitation at rates exceeding their respective rates of regeneration as driven by the dynamics of the ecosystems. The ecosystem's ability to absorb waste, including GHGs, by degrading them is also a renewable fund service resource of our global commons. This common resource is being degraded by our habit of over-injecting GHGs into the atmosphere at a rate that's faster than what the forests and ocean can absorb by the processes of carbon sequestration and drive of ocean currents. The limited nature of our planetary resources determine the capacity of resource regeneration and that of waste absorption of the ecosystem, which are exceeded by the respective rate of resource extraction and that of flow of wastes into the sink of ecosystems in present times. The biggest challenge that the modern human economy ever faced in respect of sustainability in all its dimensionalities has in fact been climate change, which is going to be the case of the greatest market failure in the history of human economy. It is now amply clear that the capitalist institution of the market, in spite of policy intervention, cannot generate enough forces that can contain the hugely adverse effects of this market failure. The capitalist values which drive the market-based system and its institutions, left to themselves, make us oblivious of the finiteness of our ecosystems and their capabilities and of the impact of entropy law on our economic and social processes.

It is therefore not surprising that the Fifth Intergovernmental Panel on Climate Change (IPCC) Assessment (2014) affirms that it is far too late to 'stop' climate change—even if 'stopping' such change were within the capacity of humans. Indeed, even if all fossil fuel use (an entirely hypothetical presupposition) were to stop now, the GHGs already extant in the atmosphere from human activity over the last 150 years will continue to bring rapid mutations in the health of the biosphere. The IPCC's synthesis report for policymakers[1] makes it abundantly clear that the best chance of taking meaningful action is long behind us. In effect, their report tells us that we cannot prevent catastrophic climate change because we cannot turn back the tide of industrial history. Yet, even as we move vigorously to curb CO_2 emissions and find ways to adapt to inevitable climate change, a pivotal challenge remains: how to fundamentally change the way our species uses fossil fuels, our ways of life, and our value system, which would change our scale and pattern of demand and use of natural resources. We have to also look for ways of finding out how the gains of fossil fuel use in terms of rental flow can be used for the transition to make it least costly (Das and Sengupta 2015). It is, in fact, high time that we now consider how we can transit from a fossil fuel–based system to one based on renewable energies, some of which have tremendous potential and can bring about a Third Industrial Revolution (Rifkin 2011) with new technologies, and try to draw up the roadmap for it. That is going to be the thrust of this and subsequent chapters. We discuss these in the context of development of the Indian power sector with our own projections over the time horizon up to 2041–42.

Difference in the Perspectives of Developed and Developing Countries: Growth for Inclusion versus Climate Control

It is already well known that an event such as climate change, in fact, any event of environmental degradation, affects the poor and the vulnerable more adversely than the rich. Yet there arises a great deal of tension between the developed and the developing countries at any summit on climate change in arriving at a consensus regarding an action plan for its containment and for adaptation to it. The rich countries refuse to address the fundamental problem of global inequity and to view that the issues of poverty removal and those of controlling climate change

---

[1] Intergovernmental Panel on Climate Change, 2014. 'AR5 Synthesis Report: Climate Change 2014', available at: http://www.ipcc.ch/report/ar5/syr/ (accessed 9 December 2019).

have important complementarities and are not fundamentally conflicting. The fast removal of poverty through high growth in developing countries would soon have a high-income effect on demand for higher environmental quality, including environmental standards for controlling climate change on the one hand and also enhance the ability of mobilizing financial resources to fund such control on the other. However, first, in the stage of transition and development, developing countries have a serious choice problem of allocation of financial resources between growth and environmental protection. Second, developed countries, on the other hand, stubbornly resist any change to their way of life, which is dominated by wasteful consumerism. Third, the pre-existing capitalist market also has a vested interest in keeping up the effective demand for such consumerist market-promoted goods and their wasteful use irrespective of their long-run impact on the environment due to its essentially myopic view on societal well-being.

At another level, as development promotes per capita income, the people's social rate of discounting the future declines, as does the macroeconomic interest rate. The latter is induced by the decline in the marginal productivity of capital, with a greater-scale deployment of capital on the one hand and a decline in the rate of pure time preference on the other. This lowering of the discount rate facilitates higher scale of investment at the level of micro-management as it would facilitate the clearance of investment projects, including the ones for making the environment greener through mitigation of GHGs and adaptation to climate change. Lowering of the interest or discount rate would, in fact, contribute to the improvement of the net present value of projects as well as raise the probability of their internal rate of return (IRR), exceeding the cut-off discount rate for investment. This effect of the lowering of the discount rate would be reflected in the acceptability of a higher payback period by financiers and a higher credit rating of such green environmental and infrastructural projects.

As both the developed and the developing countries need to realize the complementarities between high growth and control of climate change, the moral suasion of the individual countries for coming together and taking cooperative action become important. We can, in all probability, reduce the total financial needs for such sustainable programmes of development through greater international cooperation in research in science and technology, technology transfer, and financial cooperation. Financial resource flow from the UN or any country-level climate fund can release the financial resources for other apparently competing but fundamentally complementary uses for growth and infrastructure development and expansion of human capability through better education and public health services. The logic of such reallocation of global resources would be that the benefit of the climate fund would accrue to the global community while the national development process would largely benefit the people at the country level.

We would like to elaborate here that we do not mean an either-or approach in our fuel choice during the transition from a fossil fuel to a green-energy regime. These should include both the optimum use of fossil fuel for generating the resource rent arising from their exploitation and their mobilization for investment in the development of the backstop technology of renewable energy as well as in various energy-conservation technologies across the carbon-intensive sectors of the economy through their modernization. We propose the conversion of the fossil fuel assets into clean energy resource developing assets not by altogether stopping extraction of fossil fuel but by using the capital fund created out of their resource rent arising from their extraction for the purpose of development of the new renewables. There should, of course, be every effort made to convert the existing fossil fuels through beneficiation and other technical measures into cleaner ones, particularly for the generation of electrical energy. The fossil fuel production and use and the development of renewable and alternative energy should occur simultaneously, and in a planned coordinated manner, making the two tracks of the energy sector development processes complementary (see Hartwick 1977) for the conceptual foundation of such strategy of sustainable development applicable in the context of energy using resource rent from fossil fuel. See also El Sarafi (1994) for the required proper accounting of income from non-renewable exhaustible resources which would warrant such investment use of resource rental for generating income in perpetuity or benefit in terms of sustained energy supply in the future.

The need for transforming the global economy and society to control climate change and clean up the environment at the local and global levels has led to the development of the vision of a new industrial era based primarily on the development of renewable and hydrogen to replace fossil fuels in the electricity and the transport sectors. Since the sources of supply of renewables (particularly the new renewable, that is, excluding large-storage hydro) and the load centres of demand are widely dispersed and subject to fluctuations, the development of energy internet for the flow of power from new renewables along the smart grid of power transmission is an imperative and such development can be facilitated by such sources of finance out of resource rent realizable from fossil fuels.

Role of Renewables and the Third Industrial Revolution

In order to appreciate the economy–energy–sustainability connection and explore the options to get out of the current state of unsustainable growth of energy, it is important to look back very briefly at the history of development since the Industrial Revolution in Western Europe. That experience can be viewed not merely as a process of explosion of labour productivity facilitated by the use of machines and technology permitting the division of labour, but essentially as a process triggered by the discovery of new energy resources along with the associated transport and communication technologies which had a great revolutionary impact on the process of division of human labour and the social organization of production. All these had radically transformed human society by reducing spatial distance and effecting wide diffusion of knowledge, information, and technology. The first revolution revolved around coal and steam power while the second one around hydrocarbons—oil and gas—and electricity, the latter as a converted, clean, and highly efficient energy for final use as fuel. The First Industrial Revolution gave us steam power and the steam engine, which led to the emergence of railways, the factory economy, and steam-powered printing technology. The Second Industrial Revolution was characterized by the discovery of the use of hydrocarbons leading to the innovation of the internal combustion engine. This converged with the development of electrical communication. The two together brought about the automobile revolution and clean electric power replacing the steam power in industry, commerce, and transport. All these further led to the emergence of the power grid, with telecommunication networks such as the telegraph, telephone, radio, television, and so on, having a vast impact on the organization and efficiency of society and economy in delivering human welfare.

Both the First and Second Industrial Revolutions have, however, been driven by the development of fossil fuels, which are non-renewable in the human time scale and involve a high intensity of pollution arising due to their essentially highly entropic nature of economic processes of production. In view of the implication of climate change, desertification, physical and chemical degradation of soil and water bodies, and air and atmospheric pollution, the concern has developed for saving the world and humanity by creating an ecologically sustainable economic order. The search and thrust of research in science and technology are now for the discovery and development of carbon-free or carbon-neutral renewable resources and that of communication technologies such as the internet which can ultimately permit phasing out of fossil fuels, GHGs, and other harmful emissions altogether in a Third Industrial Revolution. This revolution would essentially involve shifting from fossil fuel to renewable energy resources such as solar, wind, geothermal, tidal, biomass, water, among others, organizing such energy production in a decentralized manner and medium-scale enterprises, and sharing the energy output through a wide energy internet network. The latter would require the development of a wide network of a smart grid aided by wide information flow through the energy internet and their digitized coordination for demand–supply matching and automated energy sharing (Rifkin 2011).[2]

While clean energy production and use have been growing fast in recent years, the world is still grappling with the problems of the Second Industrial Revolution. It resolves them mainly through focusing on the issue of energy efficiency both in its end use in the non-energy sectors (energy conservation) and in the supply of primarily electrical energy by reducing conversion loss, auxiliary loss, and transmission and distribution (T&D) losses. The other way by which countries are trying to get out of the current problem of pollution and unsustainable fossil fuel use has been by reducing the share of fossil fuel (coal and oil) in gross electricity generation, and by raising the generation of the natural gas or coal-bed methane (cleanest of the fossil fuels), nuclear, micro-hydroelectricity, biomass and wastes, and other abiotic renewables like wind, solar, geo-thermal, tidal, and so on. People are

---

[2] 'The Third Industrial Revolution', available at: https://en.wikipedia.org/wiki/The_Third_Industrial_Revolution (accessed 9 December 2019).

resisting the development of new hydro-storage because of its adverse impact on river ecosystems, although it uses a clean energy resource like water. The development of bio-liquids and electric vehicles has also been initiated in some countries, and thier governments are setting goals to support the advancement of new vehicle markets in order to replace the use of fossil fuels. Finally, there is also the initiative of the development of carbon capture and storage technology, which would prevent the emission of CO_2 to enter into the atmosphere.

Although the growth of deployment of clean technologies in the first decade of the present century shows the decadal growth rate to be varying across countries, mostly in the range of 27 per cent to 56 per cent as per the 2011 Global Carbon Capture and Storage Institute (GCCSI) database, the world is still largely dependent on fossil fuels to satisfy growing energy demand. In the last decade, fossil fuel has supplied 50 per cent of the new energy demand, oil has supplied 9 per cent of the total fuel requirement of the transport sector, and non-hydro power from renewables has supplied only 6 per cent of total gross electrical energy produced in 2014 at the global level (see IEA Energy Balances of Developing Non-OECD Countries, 2016).[3]

This trend of development has resulted in the steady rise in CO_2 emissions at the global level over the last decade. The emission level in 2010 reached a record high of 30.6 gigatonnes. In fact, the world recently reached a grim milestone, with the cumulative CO_2 emissions by humans since 1750 (the beginning of the Industrial Revolution) touching 2,000 gigatonnes, the atmospheric concentration at the Mauna Loa Observatory in Hawaii has now hit the 400 parts per million mark due to ever-increasing global CO_2 emissions.[4] The major sources of the emissions have been coal (34 per cent), oil (25 per cent), cement (2 per cent), and land use change (29 per cent). The three major sinks for absorbing this 2,000 gigatonnes

[3] See also, https://www.iea.org/statistics/relateddatabases/energybalance sofnon-oecdcountries/.

[4] The Mauna Loa Observatory is a premier atmospheric research facility that has been continuously monitoring and collecting data related to atmospheric change since the 1950s. Their observations regarding change in CO_2 emission and in concentration of CO_2 is globally recognized as authentic and reliable for the purposes of information and policy action.

have been the atmosphere (44 per cent), land with vegetation and forest cover (26 per cent), and the ocean (30 per cent), through its acidification at obvious ecological cost. These sinks have absorbed a share of CO_2 emissions, without which the concentration would have been well above the 500 parts per million, raising serious threats of climate change and environmental collapse in certain parts of the global ecosystem (see 'Global Carbon Emissions and Sinks since 1750'[5]).

It is now to be further noted that 80 per cent of the projected emissions in the near future are to arise from the infrastructural investments that have been already made. In view of this, the ushering of a Third Industrial Revolution as conceptualized and described in this chapter at an early date has to be induced by deliberate policy initiatives and international energy cooperation. This can be achieved mainly through energy conservation and accelerated introduction of non-hydro renewables, and the development of energy internet for efficient energy sharing through a smart grid, among others. At this stage, it is important to review how a large developing country like India is trying to incorporate new energy technologies in the power sector in order to transit to a green regime of energy technology.

[5] www.shrinkthatfootprint.com/carbon-emissions-and-sinks (accessed 9 December 2019).

The Electrical Energy Scenario in India

Chapter 7 describes the power and energy scenario in India in terms of both the primary energy resource mix and the technology-wise gross generation mix of electrical energy in 2015–16. It also describes in detail the potential of all renewable energy resources, including storage hydro. So far as the carbon-free solar and wind power potentials are concerned, this chapter discusses the basis of the estimates of the new power-capacity potentials and also provides the power factor and the cumulative capacity built till 2012 utilizing the resources. These comparative figures indicate the huge potential of new capacity creation in the future for such technology-based power. The chapter also discusses the natural resource requirement of these new renewables-based technologies on the one hand and gives comparative estimates of the environmental cost and the true total resource cost for coal thermal power on the other.

India's Energy Scenario: Towards an Ecologically Sustainable Energy Economy

India is, however, still a long distance from reaching the stage of ushering in a Third Industrial Revolution, unless it is supported by the kind of funding that would be available from some climate fund, and a global technological collaboration for its transfer. While there has been the emergence of renewables, which are now beginning to play a more-than-negligible role in supplying the growing demand for new power, the most challenging task in the revolutionary era is going to be the development of energy internet through a smart grid of power and information flow. The development of new renewables has been particularly significant as a source of off-grid power generation in remote areas as it could substantively save the transmission and distribution costs of power supply. India has, however, made important progress in conserving energy by raising the end-use efficiency and efficiency of energy conversion and supply by reducing losses. While such efficiency gain would make the power sector economically sustainable, it would also contribute to the reduction of the carbon intensity of the GDP and to the saving of capital requirement in a capital-scarce country like India. The country's energy system primarily consists of energy carriers such as fossil fuel, hydro and nuclear resources, and biomass, combustible biomass, and wastes, the last one being largely a non-traded resource having a share of 24.5 per cent in the total primary energy supply in 2013. There are also other new renewable resources whose current use has a relatively small share in the total energy balance, but which can emerge as significant resources in the not-so-distant future in India's future energy balance in view of the recent decline in their costs of investment and the trend in the growth of their capacity.

The primary commercial energy supply of India has grown from 675 million tonnes of oil equivalent in 2009 to 851 million tonnes of oil equivalent in 2015 at an annual average rate of growth of 3.9 per cent as per the energy balance sheets of the International Energy Agency (IEA) for the different years to support the country's GDP and population growth during this period. The growth of electrical energy on the other hand grew from 906 billion kwh in 2009–10 to 1,336 billion kwh in 2015–16 at an annual average rate of 6.69 per cent as per the government's energy statistics for 2017. The composition of fuel mix of primary energy and that of the energy resource mix for gross generation of electricity are given in Tables 7.1 and 7.2 respectively for the year 2015–16.

The most important feature of this composition of mix for the overall energy system or the electricity generation in India has been the dominance of fossil fuel which has a high carbon footprint. The driving force behind the observed pattern of growth of the power sector, which

TABLE 7.1   Composition of Primary Commercial Energy in 2015 for the Entire Indian Economy

	Total Fuel (in mtoe)	Share (Per Cent)
Coal	378.91	44.52
Oil	206.91	24.23
Natural Gas	43.21	5.08
Total Fossil Fuel*	628.31	73.82
Hydro	11.87	1.39
Nuclear	4.82	1.15
New Renewables	4.82	0.57
Total Carbon-Free Fuel	196.35	23.07
Total	851.1	100

Source: The Energy Balance of Non-OECD Countries, IEA.
Note: *This includes the share of non-utility in thermal power.

TABLE 7.2   Technology-wise Gross Generation Mix of Electrical Energy in 2015–16

Fuel Resource	Total Gross Generation (Billion kwh)	Utility	Non-utility	Composition (Per Cent Share) of Fuel Mix of Generation
Coal	1,032.061	895.340	136.721	77.25
Gas	68.205	47.122	21.083	5.11
Oil	8.963	0.551	8.412	0.67
Hydro	121.487	121.377	0.110	9.09
Nuclear	37.414	37.414	—	2.8
Other Renewables	67.827	65.781	2.046	5.08
Total	1,335.957	1167.583	168.372	100

Source: Central Statistics Office, Ministry of Statistics and Programme Implementation, Energy Statistics 2017, Government of India.

provides the major opportunity of fuel substitution, has been energy security to provide support to India's high growth of GDP and to provide energy security to households in terms of access to electricity by supply-side initiatives in the energy industry. The relative endowments of availability of alternative fuels and their cost competitiveness have been the major determinants of such choice of fuel composition. The environmental unsustainability has, however, driven the search for an alternative to fossil fuel, which has led to the present policy thrust on the accelerated introduction of new renewables as alternative energy resources.

A Case for Carbon-Free Abiotic Conventional Energy Resources: Hydro and Nuclear

It may, however, be noted here that nuclear and hydro resources in large storage are two options that can contribute to the development of green energy. The prospect of taking a nuclear route to energy development depends on India's success at the stage of the breeder reactor and in developing a thorium–uranium cycle so that we can use our huge stock of thorium reserves. The availability of a suitable site for nuclear reactors is an important constraining factor. The capacity forecasts for this sector have chronically erred grossly on the higher side than what could be achieved. The analysts of the Department of Atomic Energy (DEA) claimed that the total capacity would require to be raised to 275 gigawatt (GW) by 2052 from the current level of 4.78 GW in 2013–14 to wipe out all the shortages of power supply from all other sources together. This is unlikely to happen unless there is a breakthrough in technology development and application in the Indian nuclear industry. The recent projections based on the current ongoing nuclear project capacities gives an additional 4.8 GW, while pre-project activities have started for 10.5 GW from domestic sources and for another 8 GW from the sources of foreign collaboration (particularly the Russian collaboration). In view of these developments, the Twelfth Five Year Plan had boldly set the target of raising the share of nuclear in the gross electricity generated from 3.17 per cent in 2011–12 to 5 per cent in 2016–17 and 12 per cent in 2031–32. While it is too early to assess the situation of a successful prospect of nuclear development, we need to engage in trade in uranium and light-water reactor market so that we are in a position to successfully experiment with a uranium–thorium reactor in the next phase of the cycle of nuclear power development.

So far as hydro energy is concerned, India has the potential to generate 150 GW from large storage of hydro resources and another 15 GW of small hydro-generation potential as per the assessment of the CEA and the Ministry of New and Renewable Energy (World Institute of Sustainable Energy Report 2014, Chapter 11) respectively. The actual hydro capacity installed has, however, been 40.53 GW in 2013–14. The share of all kinds of thermal power (steam, gas, diesel, and so on) together in the total gross generation of power in the utility system increased from 51 per cent in 1950 to 70.6 per cent in 1990–91, 82 per cent in 2011–12, and 83 per cent in 2015–16 (including the non-utility shares), while that of hydroelectricity declined from 49 per cent in 1950 to 27.1 per cent in 1990–91, 12.4 per cent in 2011–12 and 9.09 per cent in 2015–16. As the non-utility power generation has been mostly thermal based, there has thus emerged a serious imbalance of a hydro-thermal mix from the point of view of efficiency for meeting the varying load of power demand, hydro power being known to be the most convenient and efficient resource in meeting fluctuating peak loads by quickly ramping the load generation up or down.

The reasons for the declining share of hydro have been due to the long gestation lag of storage dam projects and various socio-ecological constraints of such projects, such as the displacement of human settlements, the degradation of the ecological landscape due to inundation of the catchment and dam area, disturbances in the riverine water flow with a consequent adverse impact on flora and fauna in the upstream as well as the downstream ecosystems. These options are, in fact, fraught with too many socio-political and political–economic problems arising from too much disturbance in the local and regional ecosystems due to environmental externalities as well as from the destabilization of human settlements.

New Renewable Energy Resources

Carbon-Neutral Biomass and Combustible Wastes as New Renewables

If all the conventional sources of commercial energy resources have limitations in providing environmentally and macro-economically sustainable electrical energy supplies, we have to look for other options of biotic and abiotic renewable resources. Biomass constituted about 23 per cent of the total primary energy supply in India as late as 2015. It was only a negligible fraction of approximately 0.69 per cent of such biomass, including wastes, that was converted into electricity in 2009. Most of the biomass fuel is used in a conventional country *challah* (oven) for combustion required in cooking, causing a huge problem of indoor air pollution which constitutes a serious health hazard for women and children in lower income households who are exposed to such emissions. These biomass resources themselves are, however, also used to some extent in rural industries to produce process heat and raise steam for supplying mechanical energy. The resource can alternatively be converted into biogas by way of gasification in a bio-digester. Such gaseous fuel can be further converted into electricity to meet household requirements or in agricultural operations of the rural sector. It is possible to organize, for example, both family-sized and community-sized plants if a critical minimum level of animal dung or other biomass can be mobilized for the plant, involving voluntary cooperation of all the stakeholders through incentives (Parikh and Parikh 1977), for local power supply in rural areas in a decentralized off-grid mode.

There are, in fact, two important biotic resources of power that need to be considered for the supply of electricity: (*i*) Biomass and bagasse (the fibrous matter that remains after sugarcane or sorghum stalks are crushed for juice extraction) and (*ii*) other wastes for conversion into electrical energy. Biomass resource, Atlas India, and a 2011 report by the World Institute of Sustainable Energy (see WISE, 2014: Table 11.4), show the biomass generation and its surplus potential to be 54 million tonnes and 13.9 million tonnes per year respectively. This would permit about 18 GW of biomass power. The waste resource of bagasse from the sugar industry has an additional potential of power co-generation of 5 GW. Apart from these, the master plan of the National Bio-Energy Board, in 2012, put a further power generation potential of 386 MW of electric energy from urban liquid waste, which was predicted to go up to 462 MW by 2017 and another 4566 MW from urban solid waste by 2017 (see Table 7.3).

Abiotic Source of New Renewable Energy

Finally, it is the abiotic energy resources of wind and solar radiation, geothermal heat, and tidal waves, which would constitute the major energy resources in the new industrial era. Both biomass resources

TABLE 7.3   Potential of Green New Renewable Power (in GW)

Technologies	Potential GW	Capacity factor	Generation Billion kwh	Cumulative Capacity GW March 2012
Solar Photovoltaic	850	0.2	1489.2	1.579605
Solar Photovoltaic Pump and Panel over Banks of Canal	322	0.2	564.144	
Wind Onshore	2006	0.25	4393.14	15.864622
Wind Offshore	15	0.25	32.85	
Biomass	18	0.6	94.608	3.99187
Cogeneration from Bagasse	5	0.6	26.28	
Waste to Energy	7	0.6	36.792	0.078368
Other Sources: Geothermal and Ocean	16	0.2	28.032	
Small Hydro <25 MW	15	0.2	26.28	2.975535
Total New Renewables	3254		6691.326	24.49
Large Hydro >25MW	150	0.2	262.8	38.99
Total Green Power	3404		6954.126	63.48

Source: WISE (2014).

Note: The table does not show the rooftop solar power potential of 254 GWP and concentrated solar power (CSP) of 710 GW as separate items.

and abiotic wind, solar light energy, and micro-hydroelectricity can not only help to fill any shortfall of power supply from the conventional sources to meet the demand, but may also constitute a major source of supply of electricity for supporting economic growth and universal access to electricity. The major shortcoming of our rural electrification programme has, however, been the suffering induced by the lack of infrastructure for electricity distribution, lack of strength of the grid extended to cover villages in large areas, and inadequate supply of power to flow along the distribution infrastructure. As the generation of power based on both biotic and abiotic renewable resources can be decentralized, these technologies may permit both supply to the grid in case such generation is grid connected or can provide off-grid supply to local consumers if the grid development or extension to the concerned areas become unfeasible due to physical or logistical constraints or high costs. The new renewables can, in fact, be a source of not only greater energy security by providing wider access to power and thereby greater equity in its distribution, but also facilitate improvement in the quality of power supply in rural India and greater competitiveness and efficiency in the power industry.

Solar Power Potential and the Challenges of Its Realization

As India is endowed with abundant sunshine, solar radiation has emerged as an important source of both electrical and thermal energy. Solar thermal heating of water had emerged as an economically viable competitive option for quite some time in India, while the solar photovoltaic electricity had been quite costly until 2016–17. While its cost of generation was varying in the range of INR 10 to INR 13 per kwh in 2012, it has recently come down quite rapidly due to technological improvement through R&D and increasing deployment of solar photovoltaic technology. A 2012 KPMG report predicted that both solar photovoltaic and solar rooftop power technology would be cost competitive with the grid power by the end of the Twelfth Plan, that is, by 2016–17. The latest estimate of generation cost of solar photovoltaic is shown to be INR 2.44 for any future plant from now onwards as per the expert opinion of the CEA, based on the latest bids for setting up such generation capacity. Most parts of India, however, receive solar radiation of 4 to 7 kwh per square metre per day. As several parts of India receive good radiation, the Expert Group on Low Carbon Strategies for Inclusive Growth of the Planning Commission (see Planning Commission 2014b) set the solar potential at over 500 GW, assuming 1 per cent of land area available for such use involving some diversion of land for the erection of solar panels. There are other expert views like that of WISE, which puts the estimate of potential in the range of 700 to 1,000 GW, assuming additional possibility of setting up grid-connected solar power capacity in several states, rooftop solar power generation, and solar pumping of water facility. Unlike in the case of wind, solar power generation would, however, involve land for constructing the solar panels that may cause some diversions of land use. The potential of solar power would therefore depend on the temporal and spatial distribution of strength of solar radiation and the land-space availability for solar power for uses other than rooftop generation, solar pumping, and so on.

In order to pre-empt any problem of food security due to diversion of land use, the WISE assumed in its estimates of solar energy potential the use of only wasteland for solar power generation. Land requirement for solar photovoltaic plants has been estimated to be 2.013 ha/MW of installed capacity and that for CSP has been taken to be 2.43 ha/MW of capacity. Given that solar radiation in terms of measures of the Global Horizontal Irradiance (GHI) with the productivity of 5.2 kwh/m^2/day and direct normal irradiance (DNI) with the average productivity of 4.73 kwh/m^2/day in India, such estimates of solar irradiance or availability of light energy in short waves are supposed to provide economically viable power with potential of 851 GW of solar photovoltaic power or that of 710 GW of CSP power. We assume here that a given area of land can be used for either of the solar technologies, but not for both at the same time. However, such estimates of solar power potential varies widely across states depending on the land area available and the measures of solar irradiance, that is, the availability of solar short-wave light energy for conversion into electric power. While Rajasthan and Jammu and Kashmir have solar photovoltaic potential of 137 GW and 124 GW respectively, West Bengal and Bihar have potentials of 4.5 GW and 9.3 GW respectively. It may further be noted here that the rooftop solar photovoltaic power panels and solar pumps would be able to generate power in addition to what can be obtained by the utilization of the waste land.

It may not be necessary to fully utilize the waste land, as significant development potential of solar power can be harnessed by rooftop solar photovoltaic systems and solar projects on irrigation canals. Gujarat developed a 1 MW solar photovoltaic project on the Narmada canal near Chandrasan in 2012. Such projects optimize land use by installing solar panels on the land available on the banks of the irrigation canals, and thereby also reduce the evaporation of canal water by 30 per cent.

The success of the Gujarat project warrants exploration of further lengths along the banks of canals for harnessing solar photovoltaic power in India. In off-grid solar power development, the rooftop solar photovoltaic panels for commercial and residential sectors and the solar pump set for agriculture are going to be the two most important applications of solar technology. The potential of total rooftop solar photovoltaic has been estimated to be 254 GWp and that of the water pump set more than 37GWp. The recently assessed solar potential of power development as indicated in the literature is given in Table 7.3.

It is also to be noted here that apart from solar photovoltaic, solar thermal technologies of CSP technologies of various kinds (such as a solar tower, parabolic solar trough, solar dish stirling, and so on) have been developed and are currently in practice globally, though not in India. These thermal solar power technologies essentially provide thermal energy, which can either be used for generating power by raising steam or for space and water heating, transferring the thermal energy harnessed from sunlight using these technologies through heat exchangers. Since the potential of solar power and that based on other new renewables as well is a function of the state of technology and the extent of their deployment, which brings down the plant and equipment costs, it is an ever-changing and dynamic concept. Table 7.3 provides estimates of potentials in terms of electrical power capacity as assessed by the experts on the basis of the state of technology development and costs.

A major source of constraint in the way of development of solar power potential has, first of all, been that CSP technology is not available in India. Second, it is the constraint of manufacturing capacity of solar photovoltaic cells, which poses a major constraint in the way of development of solar photovoltaic technology. We reached an annual capacity of production of solar cells of 3.1 GW and solar modules of 11 GW in 2018 in India. As a result, the actual installed capacity of solar photovoltaic power in India rose from 1 MW in 2010 to 29 MW in 2018. In view of the high potential of solar photovoltaic development of 852 GW in the long run, the equipment manufacturing sector for solar photovoltaic power technology and innovations in the development of more efficient solar cells made out of new materials on a larger scale would require high priority in financial resource allocation and policy thrust in providing the right incentives for such development. Promotion of this new material-based cell technology is imperative for India's utilization of the full potential of solar photovoltaic power.

Wind Energy Potential and Challenges of Its Development

Wind energy potential depends on the strength of wind flow and the hub height of the wind tower at which the wind energy can be harvested. India has a long coastal line of more than 7,600 km, where wind flow is favourable for wind power generation. Such power can be generated both onshore and offshore. For wind energy, the estimates of potential would obviously depend on the hub height and the spatial distribution of strength of the wind flow and that of its power generation potential per unit of land area across the different regions of India, although onshore generation of wind power does not as such cause any major land use diversion. While the Eleventh Five-Year Plan document showed the wind power potential to be 45,195 MW as assessed for 31 March 2007, this has been reassessed by the Centre for Wind Energy Technology (C-WET) to be 49,130 MW in 2010 at a 50 m hub height, with 9 MW/km^2 land requirement and 2 per cent of land availability for this purpose for all states other than the Himalayan ones, and 0.5 per cent land availability for others. The Lawrence Berkeley Laboratory, USA, gave separate independent estimates to be 2,006 GW at an 80 m hub height and 3,121 GW at a 120 m hub height and higher land availability in the range of 7 per cent to 11 per cent in various Indian states. For a higher capacity-utilization factor greater than 25 MW, the potential would, however, be in the range of 543 GW to 1,033 GW. The offshore wind potential can further provide an additional 15 GW at less than a 60 m hub height. In Table 7.3, we present the potential of such power capacity based on wind and other renewables-based on the estimates of various expert groups. Table 7.3 also provides the cumulative achievement of installing power capacity till March 2012 along with their respective capacity-utilization factors. In spite of all the limitations of the new and renewable energies, the total potential of generation of electrical energy from such sources is thus tremendous, while only a miniscule fraction of it has been really exploited.

The geographic distribution of wind energy potential is quite unevenly distributed over space, seasons, and time of the day. Tamil

Nadu and Gujarat have a substantial share of the total potential of wind power of the country, which was originally underestimated by the C-WET and officially published statistics. While the Energy and Resources Institute (TERI) estimated Gujarat's onshore potential to be 1,162 GW at an 80 m hub height, taking the availability of both crop and non-crop land together for setting up wind power installations, WISE, on the other hand, estimated Tamil Nadu's wind power potential using (Geographic Information System) data to be 196 GW at an 80 m hub height. These two states would thus generate around 1,300 GW at the full utilization of their onshore potential. Besides, India has long coastal line of 7,600 km, where wind flows make abundant wind energy resource available. The relatively low labour costs along coasts make also offshore power generation a favourable option; the high cost of offshore construction, on the other hand, pushes up the cost.

So far as equipment manufacturing capability is concerned, India has emerged as a manufacturing hub of wind energy equipment with a number of foreign firms participating in the industry here. The industry achieved a consolidated production capacity of equipment for the development of 34,000 MW of wind power in 2017–18. The country has, in fact, set a target of installed capacity of 60,000 MW of wind power by 2022. The turbine capacity in India ranges between 225 Kw and 2,500 Kw compared to 7,580 Kw as the global maximum. The hub height in India ranges from 41 m to more than 120 m, the global maximum being 135 m. The rotor diameter ranges between 28 m and more than 110 m, the global maximum being 127 m. As larger-sized plants and equipment will be deployed in the future, equipment efficiency is expected to go up and the costs of both installation and generation per unit of gross generation of electrical energy are expected to go down, making the wind option further competitive.

It is further expected that innovations in wind turbine technology, both onshore and offshore, would continue to take place the world over, to reduce material requirement for plant and equipment, making them lightweight, raising the life of the equipment, and improving the operation of the control system of the plant. A greater development of skill and knowledge of wind turbine manufacturing and operation are also important to further drive the dynamics of wind energy in the renewable energy industry.

Overall Potential of New Renewables and Green Electrical Energy

As already mentioned in the light of the discussions of the preceding sections, we have chosen to present in Table 7.3 the currently assessed potential, which may increase in the future because of the dynamic nature of the whole concept of potential, as argued earlier. The estimates of the potential of wind and solar power, which we have used for our further analysis as given in the Table 7.3, do not include the CSP potential of solar power and are based on only solar photovoltaicpotential on the assumption that the same land cannot be used for both solar photovoltaic and CSP technologies. The estimate of solar potential goes up to 1,050 GW as per WISE 2014 if we allow land to be shared between the two technologies. However, we have not used these latter estimates for our future projections, as CSP technology is not available in India. Besides, WISE 2014 has presumed the offshore wind energy potential to be 380 GW, which we have ignored because of high costs and risks in its development as a reliable energy source. The total estimates of potential new renewables-based power and green power has accordingly been taken to be 3,254 GW and 3,404 GW respectively (see Table 7.3). We have further provided in Table 7.4 the investment and generation costs of all the technologies for estimating the financial resource requirements and assessing relative competitiveness of the different technologies, although these are undergoing changes on the lower side for the renewables over time.

The estimates of the potential of renewable resources in terms of power capacity are also provided in the government's 2017 energy statistics, which are somewhat lower than the estimates of WISE 2014. The NITI Aayog, in its document of the Energy Policy Draft, 2017, has, on the other hand, provided estimates not of the potential of renewable resources as such, but has given the estimates of ultimate gross generation potential that can be realized in the time horizons up to 2020 and 2040 using all renewable and conventional fossil fuels, nuclear energy, and other resources. This takes account of both resource availability and the respective power factor for plants based on such technology. We have used the fuel- or energy-resource mix of the BAU scenario and the ambitious scenario of this NITI Aayog document of draft energy policy to develop various scenarios of energy resource–based generation mix

TABLE 7.4   Capacity Factor, Investment, and Generation Cost

Technologies	Capacity Utilization Factor	Capital Cost as per 2016–17 Prices (INR/MW)	Capital Cost in 2016–17 (USD Million/MW)	Unit Cost of Generation (INR/kwh)	Unit Cost of Generation (US Cents/kwh)
Coal	0.80	8.00	1.23	4	6.15
Gas	0.70	3.53	0.54	4.36	6.71
Hydro	0.20	10	1.54	5.51	8.47
Nuclear	0.60	8.8	1.36	2.35	3.62
Solar photovoltaic	0.20	5.3	0.82	2.44	3.75
All Solar	0.20	5.3	0.82	2.44	3.75
Wind	0.25	4.1	0.63	3.46	5.32
Other Renewables	0.60	5.45	0.84	5.19	7.99
Small Hydro, Ocean, Geothermal	0.20	5.45	0.84	5.19	7.99

Source: CEA contacts and interviews along with NITI Aayog's Draft Report of National Energy Policy, 2017.

Note: For the super-critical boiler, the capital cost would be INR 15.7 crore/MW or USD 2.42 Million/MW.

for our purpose of futuristic projection in this book: BAU scenarios, high-energy efficiency scenarios, and the accelerated introduction of new renewables in the resource technology-wise generation mix, and the latter two combined on a baseline of energy efficiency and energy resource mix (Tables 7.6 and 7.7).

Natural Resource Requirements of the New Renewables and Pressure on Ecosystems

We have, in Chapter 8, generated different scenarios of electrical energy supply in the future based on a model with the twin objectives of (*i*) providing energy security to India's growth process and (*ii*) speeding up the process to green India's power sector. To combine these two objectives, we have considered an alternative fuel-mix for power generation in different scenarios, along with alternative levels of energy consumption in view of a much higher environmental impact of coal thermal power vis-à-vis the options of an increase in the share of new renewables effected through policy initiatives, balanced by a corresponding decline in the share of coal thermal generation of power and other conventional energy resources as per the assumptions of the NITI Aayog for the coming decades. In this context, we have reviewed not only the comparative environmental impact of coal vis-à-vis new renewables, but also reviewed the true socio-economic cost of coal thermal power following WISE 2014, which is substantially higher than its financial cost. Our model, as followed in the next chapter, is based on this comparatively higher physical impact of coal thermal power and higher true resource cost of coal than the financial one. We therefore review the comparative requirements of natural resources and the environmental pressure on the ecosystems of the different power-generating technologies and the true cost of coal thermal power generation.

Land Use

All modes of power generation involve some use of land, which is a scarce and politically sensitive natural resource today in India. However, the land requirement of coal thermal projects has been substantively greater than that of the new renewables-based power generation technologies. Saving on the area of land resulting from switching to renewables from coal is an important environmental benefit of such fuel substitution. The land requirement would vary between 0.25 hectares to 0.4 hectares/MW of coal thermal power generation for the project site itself. Given the projected growth of capacity addition of 66.6 GW in the five-year period 2012–17 to that of 158.6 GW in the time horizon 2017–32 (assuming 8 per cent growth in capacity per annum), the total requirement of land for acquisition over this 20-year period would thus be varying in the range of 19,647 hectares to 46,703 hectares in the respective periods as worked out by WISE (2014). These do not include any share of land requirement for coal mining and the transportation of coal to power plants. Renewable energy–based generation, on the other hand, would involve much less land use when we compare the total life cycle requirement for the different technologies. Besides, the renewable energy–based generation causes no irreversible damage of land as in the case of mining and land can be reused after the life of the project in 25 years, with the same level of primary productivity as before.

Besides, unlike coal thermal generation, abiotic resource–based power generation— solar or wind—have no environmental impacts like those of emission, deforestation, damage to crops, grasslands, or forests, and no requirement of additional land for activities such as coal handling at ports, transport, townships, and so on. As renewable energy–based generation (wind or solar) is modular, it does not require contiguous pockets of land. Rooftop solar generation or solar pump sets would not require additional land. Even if we think of scaling up solar or wind energy generation, we may focus on harvesting the resources of solar radiation or wind on a large scale in areas where they are more abundantly available. For example, the environmental and social costs of solar power development in arid and semi-arid areas would be low, as population pressure and the opportunity cost of land-use diversion are both low due to low primary productivity of land in such areas. In the case of wind power, one has to identify location, season, and the time of day when there is abundant wind flow onshore as well as offshore, which may have low opportunity costs in terms of diversion of land use, warranting scaling up of wind generation. It may also be noted that as modern technology permits the operation and maintenance of such renewable energy technology-based projects from distant locations, no additional land is required on a significant scale for the purpose of housing and the attendant infrastructure. Besides, as renewable energy generation takes place in small dispersed units, there is no large-scale requirement of land involving diversion of its use and ownership, which might otherwise cause a source of social tension (WISE 2014).

Impacts on Water, Forests, and Pollution

The renewable energy–based generation of power—particularly based on solar and wind—does not require any significant quantity of water as compared to the requirements of coal thermal generation. Wind power is water-neutral, while water is required for cleansing solar photovoltaic panels, but such a requirement is small except in desert areas where dust storms pollute the panels.

While coal-based thermal projects get delayed because of the constraint of forest clearance for the development of linked mines, there is no environmental impact on forest for solar or wind–based generation if these projects are located outside the forests as these have no externalities leading to pollution, noise, or thermal effects creating any damaging impact on wildlife habitats. In case any such projects are developed inside a forest, the adverse impact may be controlled by conditions of the grant of forest clearances. In the case of wind turbines, there would be some requirement of such clearances for transportation of large blades and heavy-duty cranes for the setting up of or dismantling the plant. The counterpart requirements for setting up solar photovoltaic panels are minimal or negligible. The environmental impact of any large solar thermal electricity projects for power generation would also be of much smaller order as there would be no requirement of transportation of energy resources like coal or evaluation of waste like fly ash, hot water, and so on. Besides, renewable energy–based technologies can supply power to forest-based communities through micro-grids which would have no adverse impact on the forest ecosystem.

Air Pollution

Finally, renewable energy–based technologies have no environmental impact through air pollution, particularly in the cases of solar photovoltaic panels, solar thermal, wind, or small hydro projects. In the case of biomass combustion or gasification-based power generation, there would be some adverse impact on air quality. This can be controlled if there are non-overlapping areas of biomass supply.

Besides, there are technologies like bio-methanation, which have a far lower particulate emission as in the case of natural gas–based power generation.

Saving of Financial Costs as a Relative Advantage of Renewable Energy Technologies vis-à-vis Coal Thermal

One of the major environmental-cum-financial benefits of substitution of fossil fuels by new renewables is going to be in the form of substantive reduction in the requirements for transportation of fossil fuels by railways and roads and therefore, substantive saving of capital investment for the development of mines, railways, ports, and other infrastructure that would have been otherwise required.

Besides, the secondary fuel requirement of oil for the current 1,16,000 MW of coal thermal power generation yielding 693 billion units of electricity requires an expenditure of INR 6,300 crores per annum only on oil at the assumed subsidy rate of diesel at INR 45 per litre, while the renewables do not require any such subsidiary fuel. The savings out of such costs of transport and oil are, in fact, important benefits of such substitution, which are not recognized in the current methodological practice of cost-benefit analysis. This becomes particularly important when the pricing of oil and railway tariffs contain substantive subsidy elements, since the tariff of power based on such subsidized input prices would not reflect the true cost of the concerned technology.

Comparing the True Resource Costs of Technology Options

The correct methodology on which is based the choice of technology among alternatives requires the comparison of the true socio-economic costs of power generation, that is, the one that does not contain any hidden subsidy and internalizes all costs of environmental externalities over the lifetime of projects which are substantive in the case of coal vis-à-vis any renewable energy technology. It is, in fact, the stream of net differences between the true costs of coal thermal and any competing alternative renewable energy technology which is to be considered as the stream of net savings of costs or net benefits arising from the technology substitution over the life of the project. The net present value of the stream of such cost savings at an assumed rate of discount (say 10 or 12 per cent) is going to be the deciding criterion of the merit ordering between the two. By all such binary merit comparisons, we can finally arrive at the complete merit ordering of all the renewable energy options along with the coal thermal technology, the latter being the dominant generation technology of power in India today.

Hidden Costs of Subsidy of Thermal Coal

The real challenge here involves in the estimation of both the hidden subsidy in coal thermal power and in the replacing technology, on the one hand, and the costs of environmental and social externalities of the different power generation technologies on the other. The subsidies in a technology route may take the forms of under-pricing of the fuel input, capital subsidy, tax waiver, concessional tax rate on capital equipment, and so on, by way of government interventions and regulations (for example, price control) in the fuel, finance capital or equipment market, or into the other markets of sectoral products linked through input–output relationships. As the range and forms of subsidy—direct and indirect—are quite large in India, it is a difficult task to ascertain the hidden subsidies precisely. The World Institute of Sustainable Energy (WISE) at Pune made an attempt to calculate the hidden subsidy for 19 thermal power projects in India (WISE 2014).

The method of calculating the hidden subsidy has been to calculate (i) the levelized cost of power generation without internalizing any benefit of subsidy, (ii) adjusting for all the monetized values of all incentives levelized for the unit of power generation provided by the central and state governments, and finally, (iii) comparing the total cost of generation without internalizing any benefit of subsidy with the actual cost of power generation with the impact of subsidy as per the books of account. The difference between the two would provide an estimate of the hidden cost of subsidy per unit of generation. The levelized cost of the thermal power station at Kota was, for example, found to be INR 2.63/kwh as per the actual internalization of benefits of subsidy per unit of generation, and escalated to INR 3.08 with its internalization. The subsidy was thus estimated to be INR 0.45 per unit of generation for the project at a 10 per cent discount rate for Kota. The same was found to be INR 0.94 per kwh of gross generation of energy for the Talcher Super thermal power plant. For the 19 power projects in the 2014 WISE study, the weighted average subsidy was estimated to be INR 0.68 per kwh of gross generation. For the current installed capacity of coal thermal power generation, the total amount of hidden subsidy would work out to be INR 561 billion per annum or USD 10 billion per annum without taking any share of subsidy to the railways for coal transportation.

Costs of Environmental Externalities

Besides the cost of the hidden subsidy, the internalization of the cost of environmental externalities is another important step for arriving at the true comparative costs of the various technological options of power

generation, including coal thermal and the renewables. The monetization of the environmental damage cost is difficult because of the non-
traded character of eco-services whose gain or loss is to be captured in
such costs of externalities. In recent years some international studies
such as the External Costs of Energy (Extern E) method (Bickel and
Friedrich, 2004) made some advancement in this direction, particularly
in the context of power generation. Paul Epstein et al. (2011) showed the
methodology of working out the costs of environmental impact over
the entire life cycle of coal from the stage of coal mining, extraction,
transportation, washing, and combustion for power generation causing damages to the landscape, massive deforestation, degradation of
air quality due to emissions of methane, nitrogen oxide (NO), sulphur
dioxide (SO_2), PM2.5, CO_2, mercury, and other carcinogenic substances.
Besides, local hydrology would also incur damage due to the arising of
effluents containing sludge and drainage of other highly acidic wastes.

All these externalities are identified as per the Extern E methodology
and then classified into three categories: (*i*) can be quantified and monetized, (*ii*) can be quantified but difficult to monetize, and finally, (*iii*)
those which are qualitative. Different methods are employed for estimating the different types of damage impacts. These are further grouped
into (*i*) impacts of the use of energy resources in power generation on
the climate and (*ii*) the direct impact on public health. The cost implications of these two types of impacts in value terms of loss of income or
asset are worked out, which are then finally internalized to obtain the
true resource cost of power generation. All public health impacts due to
mortality are to be estimated using the mortality-adjusted statistical value
of life (SVL). Similarly, the public health impact due to increased morbidity
is to be estimated by the disability-adjusted life expectancy and the
SVL. Since accidents in mines and coal transportation, and increased
morbidity due to health hazards to which mines workers are exposed are
to be recognized in the estimates of the social cost of power generation,
these estimates are to be based on the risk of accident or morbidity to
which workers are exposed and the SVL. Since the mortality risks are
particularly uncertain there has to be high and low estimates of such
elements of social cost deriving alternative scenarios for simulation.
Epstein and his colleagues have found the estimate of the cost of the
environmental externalities of coal thermal power generation in 2008
to be 17.8 cents/kwh or INR 8.39 per kwh as a point estimate in the

entire range of possible variations from INR 9.36 per kwh to INR 26.89 per kwh. In the Indian context, P.R. Shukla and D. Mahapatra (2011) estimated such costs of externality only due to air and water pollution in coal thermal power generation over the life cycle of coal to be INR 3.15 per kwh, the components of air and water pollution damage costs being respectively INR 2.09 and INR 1.09 per unit of kwh.

There is, however, a wide variation in the estimates of such studies on the costs of externalities, because of the variations in assumptions depending on the country or case specificities of the plant or project contexts. However, there is unanimity between the results of the different studies in respect of the dominance of the cost of health as it has been found to be the single largest element in the total cost of externalities.

It is, however, to be noted that the earlier estimates by Epstein and his colleagues (2011) suffer from the limitations of assigning numerical values to impacts that cannot be monetized such as the choice of discount rate in the valuation of ecosystem damage, among other aspects. Such imperfections are inevitable. The greater the volume of data available for a wide range of case- specific situations, the easier it is to make a better choice of the cost-price factor in the context of evaluation of a specific new project, and for ascertaining the true cost competitiveness of coal vis-à-vis other renewable-based technology.

However, as an illustration of the application of the methodological principle of obtaining the true cost of coal thermal generation, which can be used as a benchmark for the assessment of the relative merit of any new renewable–based generation technology, we may point out that such a normative benchmark price of a coal-based power tariff should be the sum of the following three components.

1. A base tariff of power comprising the fuel cost, which, in turn, comprises the conventional fixed and variable (mainly fuel) cost on a normative basis (see Table 7A.1 in the Appendix 7A for the details of assumptions of the tariffs for alternative assumptions of the blend of the domestic and imported power-grade coal).
2. The hidden cost of subsidy at the alternative discount rates.
3. The cost of externalities.

Assuming a range of coal blend varying between all domestic coal and 90 per cent imported coal in the blend, we obtain the estimates of tariff ranging between INR 3.78 per kwh and INR 5.86 per kwh in the Indian context. The cost of the hidden subsidy as estimated by WISE (2014) for a set of Indian coal thermal projects has been found to be in the range of INR 0.45 per kwh and INR 1.55 per kwh for private sector plants at a 10 per cent discount rate, the weighted average estimates being INR 0.58 per kwh. From the study of Epstein and co-authors (2011), we obtain, on the other hand, the cost of externalities of a coal thermal plant to be lying in the range of INR 4.43 per kwh to INR 12.65 per kwh. The true socio-economic cost is thus estimated to be lying between INR 8.79 to INR 19.09 per kwh. The component of the cost of environmental externalities thus constitutes a major share of 50 to 66 per cent of the economic resource cost of power generation (see Table 7.5).

TABLE 7.5   True Cost of Coal Thermal Power: The Range of the Genuine Cost of Coal Thermal Electrical Energy

Items	Lower Limit	Upper Limit	Mean Value (Un-weighted Average of Minimum and Maximum)
Share of Imported Coal (per cent)	0	90	
Variable Cost (INR/kwh)	2.2	4.2	
Fixed Cost (INR/kwh)	1.58	1.66	
Total Estimated Cost-Based Tariff (INR/kwh)	3.78	5.86	4.82
Variable Cost as Per Cent of Tariff	58.2	71.67	
Hidden Cost of Subsidy on Sample Observation of 19 Power Projects (Private Ownership Basis), Discount Rate 10 Per Cent, (INR/kwh)	Min. over sample 0.45	Max. over sample 0.94	0.695
Cost of Externality (INR/kwh)	4.40	12.64	8.52
Total True Cost (INR/kwh)	8.63	19.44	14.035

Source: WISE (2014).

Note: Assuming 1 cent = Rs 0.47 (wherever conversion was required).

The tariff estimates of the earlier table have been estimated on the basis of the assumptions given in Table 7A.1.

It is not surprising that a comparison of the range of variation of the true cost of coal thermal power with the normative cost of generation based on new renewable, as given in Table 7.5, makes it clear that the new renewables-based power technology should be the preferred social choice as it involves lower socio-economic resource costs. The major reason behind this true cost competitiveness of renewable-based power is the opportunity of saving of substantive costs of externalities and of the hidden subsidies of coal thermal generation that such technology substitution offers. This clearly emphasizes the need for a new policy direction in reducing our dependence on coal for power generation and raising the share of new renewables in the gross generation of power.

One may, however, argue that the quoted costs of renewables-based on the tariffs fixed by the Central Regulatory Commission (CRC) may contain some hidden costs of subsidies in these emerging technologies. While there may be some elements of hidden subsidies, the costs of environmental externalities are supposed to be negligible, at least in the case of abiotic resources of wind, solar, and micro-hydroelectricity. It is only biomass-based power generation that would involve some external-ities, which are still likely to be quite small as compared to coal thermal because of the advantage of carbon recycling in the case of the former.

The actual choice of fuel or energy-resource mix in technology and generation would depend on relative costs of the different resources as well as their relative availability, while the levels of respective generations would be determined by the level of final demand for alternative levels of efficiency of energy use. Tables 7.6 and 7.7 provide us the percentage-wise composition of the different energy resource–based power generation for the BAU level of energy efficiency combined with that of the BAU and higher share of new renwables use as being forced by policies.

The Current Technology Scenario of India's Power Sector

The landscape of the power industry and its growth in the post-liberalization and economic reform era is depicted in Table 7.8. In the first decade of this century, when the Electricity Act of 2003 was passed and the new electricity policy was issued by the government, an

TABLE 7.6 Technology-wise Gross Generation Mix Share in Percentage
(Business as Usual Fuel Share)

2021–22	2031–32	2041–42	
65	60.75	56.50	Coal
11	7.50	4.00	Gas
2.5	3.00	3.50	Nuclear
13.3	9.35	5.40	Hydro storage
0.19	4.64	9.100	Solar photovoltaic
0.00	1.15	2.30	CSP
0.00	1.80	3.60	Distributed solar photovoltaic
0.19	7.59	15.00	Total solar
3.00	5.75	8.50	Onshore wind
0.00	0.65	1.30	Offshore wind
3.00	6.40	9.80	Total wind
4.73	5.31	5.90	Other renewables

Source: Author's own estimates.

TABLE 7.7 Technology-wise Gross Generation Mix Share in Percentage
(Accelerated Share of Renewables)

2021–22	2031–32	2041–42	
62.60	51.76	42.80	Coal
6.50	6.50	6.50	Gas
3.70	4.34	5.10	Nuclear
9.00	7.94	7.00	Hydro storage
4.20	6.65	10.50	Solar photovoltaic
0.60	1.55	4.00	CSP
2.30	3.11	4.20	Distributed solar photovoltaic
7.10	11.52	18.70	Total solar
5.50	7.07	9.10	Onshore wind
0.30	0.77	2.00	Offshore wind
5.80	8.02	11.10	Total wind
5.35	6.86	8.80	Other renewables

Source: Author's own estimates.

institutional framework was provided for the creation of large capacities
in thermal, gas, and hydro projects. Coal was allocated for captive use to
such large plants. The civil nuclear deal with the USA (2008) facilitated
the prospect of growth of large-scale nuclear capacities as well. All

these were premised on the fast growth of the power sector based on conventional energy resources and technology so that the requirement of faster economic growth for poverty removal could be provided with energy support (Maithaini and Gupta 2015). As P.C. Maithani and D. Gupta correctly observe, such growth along the conventional route faced serious problems over these years since 2003, due to environmental and forest clearances, infrastructure and logistical constraints, lack of adequate financial resource flow—particularly bank credit—increasing costs of imported fossil fuel energy, and the popular perception of high accidental and health risks of nuclear power particularly in the post-Fukushima years. People's resistance made the locational choice of such nuclear technology–based power plant politically quite a difficult task. All these have caused slippage in the actual realization of the targeted growth in power capacities in the Tenth and Eleventh Plans and in the subsequent periods. The main source of difficulty as we notice later has been the inadequate availability of the concerned primary resources of fossil fuels and people's resistance against both hydro and nuclear projects for environmental reasons. Before going into the discussion on possible future-relative roles of the conventional and the new renewable resources over the time horizon up to 2031–32 or 2041–42, we now have a look at the capacity structure and resource-wise composition of the country's electricity industry for working out the roadmap towards a radically different capacity and technology structure as would be envisaged by the Third Industrial Revolution for India.

Table 7.7 shows the distribution of the installed capacity of the Indian electricity industry across technologies as of March 2016 and their pattern of growth between 2006–07 and 2015–16. Figure 7.1 shows the technology-wise composition of such capacities as of March 2016. It is important to note that the installed capacities of both the thermal power (utility and non-utility together) and those of new renewables power reached the level of 259.24 GW and 42.85 GW respectively in March 2016, both improving their respective shares to 72 and 14.2 per cent in the total installed power capacity of the country as of March 2016 (see Table 7.8). The total renewable power capacity is mostly grid-interactive power of 42.8 GW. In grid-connected power, the major share has been that of wind energy amounting to 62.7 per cent of the total of such capacity (see Table 7.9a), followed by solar, which had a share of 15.78 per cent in the same year (these capacity estimates take

TABLE 7.8   Installed Capacity of India's Electric Power Industry (in GW)

Sector and Mode	March 2014–15	Share in March 2014–15	March 2015–16	Share in March 2015–16	Compound Annual Growth Rate (CAGR) 2006–07 to 2015–16
Total Utility (a+b+c+d)	**271.72**	**85.9**	**302.08**	**86.2**	**8.60**
a) Hydro	41.26	13.0	42.78	12.2	2.13
b) Thermal	188.89	59.7	210.68	60.1	9.38
c) Nuclear	5.78	1.8	5.78	1.6	4.01
d) Renewables Grid Interactive	35.77	11.3	42.85	12.2	18.63
Non-utility	**44.66**	**14.1**	**48.28**	**13.8**	**8.01**
Grand Total	316.38	100	350.67	100	8.52

Source: Author's estimation based on Government of India (2017).

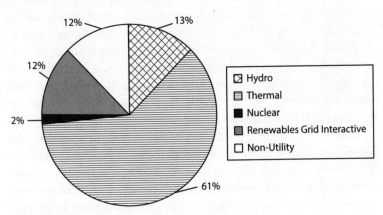

FIGURE 7.1   Source-wise Composition of Installed Capacity of India's Power Industry, March 2016
Source: Derived from Table 7.8.

into account the limited data that was available on off-grid power). The share of biomass-based power reached a level of 11.54 per cent and that of micro-hydel, 10 per cent (see Table 7.9a and Figure 7.2). This scenario has been, however, fast changing due to substantive fall in cost of solar photovoltaic power and it's becoming competitive with conventional

TABLE 7.9A   Growth of Installed Capacity of New Renewables Power (in GW)

	March 2014–15	March 2015–16	Growth Rate (per cent) 2014–15 to 2015–16
Biomass	4.41	4.83	9.1
Waste to Energy	0.12	0.12	–
Wind	23.44	26.87	14.6
Small Hydro	4.06	4.27	5.1
Solar	3.74	6.76	80.7
Grand Total New Renewables	35.78	42.85	19.7

Source: Government of India (2017).

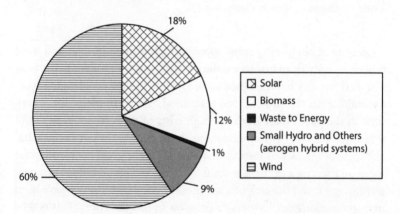

FIGURE 7.2   Resource-wise Composition of New Renewables-Based Installed Power Capacity
Source: Derived from Table 7.9b.

resource–based grid power. This is reflected in the fact that the solar power capacity grew at the rate on 80 per cent between March 2015 and March 2016 (see Table 7.9a) while the capacity of both wind and biomass and combustible waste–based power increased at the rate of 14.6 and 9.34 per cent respectively in the same one year period (see Table 7.9b). The small micro-hydel capacity has grown at a moderate rate of 5.4 per cent in that year. As a result, both capacity and gross generation of new renewables-based power has grown at the rate of 20 per cent approximately in that year (see Table 7.9a).

TABLE 7.9B   Total Installed Capacity and Resource-wise Composition
of New Renewables in India (in MW)

	Grid (in MW), March 2016	Off-Grid (in MW), March 2016	Total in March 2015–16 (in GW)
Solar	6,762.87	1,221.26	7,984.13
Biomass	4,831.33	843.15	5,674.48
Waste to Energy	115.08	154.48	269.56
Small Hydro and Others (Aerogen Hybrid Systems)	4,273.48	2.69	4,276.17
Wind	26,866.66	–	26,866.66
Total	42849.42	2,218.89	45,071

Source: Government of India (2017).

In spite of such very recent apparent high growth in solar and wind power capacity from low bases, the share of new renewables in the total installed capacity has remained quite low due to slow progress in capacity build-up in the new abiotic resource–based technology for a long time in the past. Apart from the high costs of such technologies until recently, the lack of entrepreneurship in the deployment of such capital and technology, lack of institutional support at the grass-root level, poor focus on training and management for using and maintaining such new technologies, and the lack of awareness of rural community have been important additional barriers to progress in this direction. This is why I consider the idea of a climate fund based on resource rent extracted from fossil fuel as a valuable instrument in accelerating the pace of such progress by providing finance for removing those constraints. Since the power sector is the largest user of fossil fuels in a developing country like India, we focus here on projection of the future sustainable development of the sector using a quantitative (econometric-regression-cum-spreadsheet) model for simulating alternative scenarios based primarily on the substitution of coal thermal power by new renewables.

Appendix 7A: Normative Estimation of Coal Thermal Tariff

TABLE 7A.1 Basic Assumptions for Normative Coal Thermal Tariff Calculation

No.	Items	Values
1	Capacity Utilization Factor	80 per cent
2	Auxiliary Consumption	10 per cent
3	Capital Cost of Power Project	INR 507 lakh
4	Salvage Value	10 per cent of capital cost
5	Debt Fraction	70 per cent
6	Interest Rate on Term Loan	13.50 per cent
7	Depreciation for the First 12 Years	5.28 per cent
8	Depreciation for the Next 13 Years	2.05 per cent
9	Discount Rate	11.08 per cent
10	O&M Cost	INR 14.59 lakh/MW
11	O&M Cost Escalation	5 per cent a year
12	Return on Equity	15.50 per cent
13	Interest on Working Capital	12 per cent
14	Station Heat Rate	2,425 kcal/kwh
15	Calorific Value of Fuel (Imported)	5,500 kcal/kg
16	Calorific Value of Fuel (Domestic)	4,000 kcal/kg
17	Fuel cost (Imported)	INR 6,000/tonne
18	Fuel Cost (Domestic)	INR 2,200/tonne
19	Escalation in Fuel Cost	5 per cent a year

Source: WISE (2014).

8

Transition from Fossil Fuel–Based Power to Renewable Energy

Finally in Chapter 8, we will conclude by summarizing what big bang changes are required to meet the challenges of green energy development for transitioning from a power system based on fossil fuel to one that is based on new renewables. We have elaborated here the requirements of technological development for the storage of electric power, the development of flexibility in operations of thermal technologies for ramping up and down the intensity of generation and of smart grid development.[1] We have also elucidated what kind of financial support and human resource development measures may have to be arranged within the framework of a social perspective of investment for facilitating the revolutionary development of eco-efficiency of India's economic system for the impending Third Industrial Revolution.

Model-Based Projections of Different Future Power Energy Scenarios and the Role of New Renewables

The potential of power generation by the alternative resources of solar, wind, and other new renewable energy technologies along with their

---

[1] The smart grid development is important for facilitating efficient flow of both information relating to power demand and resource availability, and power flows at various nodal points.

costs of investment and generation as assessed by experts have been given in Tables 7.3 and 7.4 of the preceding chapter, while Table 7.5 from the same chapter specially points out the true cost of coal thermal power. In view of such alternatives to coal thermal power, we have developed a model of sustainable development of electrical energy in India as described later. The considerations of economic, social, and environmental dimensions of the sustainability of power sector development would turn the focus of creating a model based on evolving strategies that would transform the country's energy economy with the following objectives:

1. Energy security for supporting India's high and inclusive growth and to provide universal access to electricity.
2. Macroeconomic sustainability by reducing the import dependence of India's energy sector.[2]
3. Environmental sustainability by transitioning from fossil fuel to a new renewables-based regime of electricity generation.

The first two objectives take care of the sustainability of macroeconomic growth without compromising on the conditions of macroeconomic balances. They further take account of the issue of equity in the form of universal access to electricity, which is critical for social sustainability. The third objective focuses on the environmental sustainability of development with the prime objective of climate control. As climate change is likely to occur due to the adverse global externalities arising from fossil fuel use, we suppose India is to share at least some moral responsibility of saving the planet.[3]

Demand Model for the Future Projection of the Requirement and Supply of Gross Electrical Energy

We now develop a quantitative model for projection of growth of the Indian economy's future demand for energy, which would support

[2] The issue of import dependence may not be important for the electricity industry, but as such is critical for the sustenance of the Indian transport sector.

[3] In order to fulfil the national commitment of achieving some targets of controlling CO_2 emissions, the Indian government has fixed some emission norms to be attained by 2022.

certain basic economic targets on both the demand and supply sides to enable the achievement of the objectives enumerated earlier. These projections will be contingent upon the following:

1. Some given growth rate of GDP with its structural composition.
2. Targeted technical change for energy conservation as induced by the progress in R&D.
3. Policy targets for accelerating the introduction of new renewables replacing coal at the margin of additional generation of power in the development process of the power sector.

In Table 8.1, we describe the different scenarios of the model of projection of electricity requirement, or the demand and supply. All scenarios assume an overall GDP growth rate of 8 per cent and alternative rates of energy-conserving technical change and the introduction of carbon-free new renewable fuels. We have developed an econometric model (see Appendix 8A for the basic model and methodology for future

TABLE 8.1 Scenarios of Projections of Commercial Energy Requirements in the Form of Electricity for an 8 Per Cent Gross Domestic Product Growth Rate with Base Year 2014–15

Items	Description
Scenario 1: Baseline or BAU	Baseline efficiency of electrical energy use and baseline share of new renewables in the gross generation of electrical energy.
Scenario 2: Higher energy efficiency	Higher and rising trends of efficiency of energy use and the baseline share of new renewables in gross generation of electrical energy.
Scenario 3: Accelerated share of new renewables	Baseline efficiency of electrical energy use and accelerated introduction of new renewables in gross generation of electrical energy.
Scenario 4: Higher energy efficiency and accelerated share of new renewables	Higher and rising trends of energy efficiency, accelerated introduction of new renewables in gross generation of electrical energy.

projections) for ascertaining the final energy demand at the sectoral level for the basic BAU scenario (BAU Scenario 1), while the other scenarios are obtained by combining either high energy efficiency or a higher rate of introduction of new renewables-based power (or both) vis-à-vis this BAU Scenario 1 (see Tables 8.3a and 8.3b). Table 8.4, on the other hand, gives the share of electricity in the sectoral final energy demand and from which we derive the demand or requirement of electrical energy at the sectoral and aggregative levels for the purpose of such projections (see Table 8.5). It may be noted that Table 8.4 also shows the share of

TABLE 8.2A Aggregate Gross Domestic Product Elasticity of Sectoral Income and Projected Sectoral Rate of Growth

Sector	Sectoral GDP Growth Rates (per cent)	Elasticity of Sectoral GDP with Respect to Aggregate GDP
Agriculture	7.68	0.75
Commercial	8.16	0.62
Residential	8.32	0.72
Transport	6.96	0.88
Industry	7.92	0.82

Source: Author's own estimates.

TABLE 8.2B Per Capita Final Electricity Use (in kwh)

Time Period	BAU Scenario	High Energy Efficiency Scenario
2011–12	880	880
2021–22	1,657	1,485
2031–32	3,223	2,738
2041–42	6,068	5,029

Source: Author's own estimates.

TABLE 8.2C Energy Intensity (Grams per INR)

Time Period	BAU Scenario	High Energy Efficiency Scenario
2011–12	0.81	0.81
2021–22	0.74	0.73
2031–32	0.22	0.16
2041–42	0.005	0.004

Source: Author's own estimate.

TABLE 8.3A Final Sectoral Energy Demand (in Ktoe, Scenarios 1 and 3)

Time Period	Agriculture	Commercial	Residential	Transport	Industry	Total
2014–15	24,518.00	14,272.00	48,559.00	78,354.00	1,61,267.00	3,26,970.00
2021–22	46,674.94	17,815.63	80,490.54	1,00,746.33	2,57,943.94	5,03,671.38
2031–32	97,572.94	25,502.72	1,55,407.82	1,54,115.75	4,95,777.79	9,28,377.02
2041–42	1,85,902.67	37,994.80	2,88,601.69	2,50,721.94	9,42,148.48	17,05,369.58

Source: Author's own estimate.

TABLE 8.3B Final Sectoral Energy Demand (in Ktoe, Scenarios 2 and 4)

Time Period	Agriculture	Commercial	Residential	Transport	Industry	Total
2014–15	24,518.00	14,272.00	48,559.00	78,354.00	1,61,267.00	3,26,970.00
2021–22	42,814.92	16,251.42	69,664.56	94,479.91	2,31,582.07	4,54,792.88
2031–32	80,452.41	22,665.71	1,29,986.55	1,41,663.79	4,25,319.79	8,00,088.25
2041–42	1,51,176.04	31,611.67	2,42,540.87	2,12,411.63	7,81,135.30	1,418,875.50

Source: Author's own estimates.

TABLE 8.4   Share of Electricity in Total Final Energy Demand (in Per Cent)

Time Period	Agriculture	Commercial	Residential	Transport	Industry
2014–15	60	27	32	2.1	26
2021–22	60	35	35	3	30
2031–32	60	42	38	4	34
2041–42	60	50	42	5	36

Source: Author's own estimate.

electricity in the final demand rising over time because of the dynamics of penetration of electricity in the different sectors, which has been far from complete. Given such demand for electrical energy, the model projects the required gross generation of electrical energy and plant capacities of various technologies to meet the above-mentioned objectives of energy security for economic growth and social sustainability on the one hand and the reduction of the carbon footprint for ecological sustainability on the other. We assume the planning horizon for the projection of our model to be the terminal years of 2021–22, 2031–32, and 2041–42, with 2014–15 (actual) as the base for the demand side of the model. The growth of the power industry as per our projection is intended to affect the transition from fossil fuel to renewable-based electricity, the transition being based on the assumptions regarding realizable targets of new renewables resources on the one hand and India's experience and current state of development of such energy technologies on the other. We will also address the critical question of financing such a transition.

The econometric model of demand as per the BAU trend assumed the demand of the sector to be a function of sectoral income (or consumption expenditure in the case of the household sector) and the real energy price faced by the concerned sector. For high energy efficiency scenarios, it was assumed that the government, by policy forcing, would reduce the demand of each sector from the level as obtained to be the BAU demand from our econometric model. The extent of such reduction in proportionate terms was taken to be the same as the proportionate saving of electrical energy as considered achievable by energy conservation, according to the ambitious BAU scenario envisaged by the NITI Aayog in its document of the 2017 Energy Policy Draft. For the purpose of estimation of the model, the time-series data of consumption of electricity, sectoral GDP and overall GDP, and real energy prices faced by the different sectors over the period 1993–94 to 2014–15 were used. The real energy price for a sector has been the nominal energy price as applicable for the sector as per wholesale price index data as deflated by the GDP deflator for the concerned year.

As a first step, the time series of aggregate and sectoral GDP data were used to estimate a double-log regression model to obtain the aggregate GDP elasticity of the sectoral GDP or the sectoral gross value added and also that of private final consumption expenditure after ensuring stationarity properties of the concerned series of sectoral income or expenditure by way of augmented Dickey Fuller unit root test (Table 8A.1). Additionally, we estimated the co-integration relationship using the series of differences of the appropriate order of the concerned variables. The co-integrated relation yielded the required elasticity of the sectoral GDP with respect to total GDP. These elasticities, along with the sectoral growth for the overall GDP growth of 8 per cent, are given in Table 8.2a.

We have further estimated multi-variable regression models using sectoral total final energy consumption as the dependent variable and the sectoral GDP and real energy prices faced by the concerned sector as independent ones, using the time-series data as mentioned earlier. The regression model was estimated after verifying stationarity of the concerned time series by making use of the Augmented Dickey Fuller unit root test and identifying the order of integration of each time series of the concerned variables. We set up the model for the estimation of the co-integrated relationship in terms of the logarithm of the differences of appropriate order (if not zero) of the basic concerned variables. The regression coefficients of such a relationship as estimated yielded the partial elasticity coefficients of energy demand for any sector with respect to the sectoral GDP or private final consumption expenditure for the household sector. It would also yield the partial elasticity coefficients of energy demand with respect to the relevant real energy prices facing the concerned sector. See Table 8A.2 in Appendix 8A for the derivation of the expression for the prediction of final energy demand from the estimated co-integrated relationship and for the given sectoral GDP and real energy price facing the concerned sector. It was, however, found that the partial elasticity coefficients of the model with respect to real energy prices were either statistically insignificant or of such order of magnitude (even if it is statistically significant) that the predicted values of energy demand in the domain of relevant price variation (as considered by us, between a 0 and 3 per cent annual increase in the real energy prices from the base year 2014–15) do not make much of a difference. In view of this, we have worked out the projections of final energy demand for a sector for variation in sectoral GDP from year to year but for no variation in real energy price over the base year 2014–15. In other words, we have carried out the projections of demand for the future presuming the insignificance of the impact of variation in relative prices on energy consumption at the macro level.

Table 8.6 provides us the assumptions regarding energy conservation for the different sectors in the different terminal years. This has been taken to be the savings in any sector or year as indicated by the comparison of final energy consumption between BAU and higher efficiency in use for the same GDP or level of driving activity (as reflected in the comparative values of the BAU and ambitious scenario of the Draft Report of NITI Aayog on Energy Policy, 2017).

We present in Table 8A.2 of Appendix 8A, the results of the time series regression models of sectoral energy demand with estimates of all its relevant parameters or coefficients as referred to earlier. Tables 8.3a and 8.3b further present the projected values of sectoral final energy demand in the three terminal years concerned covering the time horizons up to 2041–42 using the estimates of the co-integrated relation. As our basic data on energy demand is all in ktoe, the results of the tables are also in the same unit. Since the focus of the present analysis is on the future development of electrical energy, we next assume the share of electricity in the final energy demand of the different sectors, which should be increasing in the future due to the rising penetration of electricity—the cleanest and most efficient fuel but whose penetration in the different sectors is far from being complete in India as of now. While Table 8.4 provides the dynamics of increasing penetration of electricity in the different sectors in terms of share in total final energy over time, Table 8.5 presents the projection of the sectoral final electricity demand (in Twh units) for the different terminal years for the BAU Scenario 1. We then present in Table 8.7, the aggregate final electricity demand for all the four years over the time horizon 2011–12 to 2041–42, for all the four scenarios. However, the focus of our analysis is the fuel choice and required plant capacities to be created. Searching ultimately for appropriate policies for their realization, we have next derived the required gross generation requirement of electrical energy from the final use by

TABLE **8.5** Sectoral Electricity in Total Final Energy Demand (in Twh) as per
Business as Usual

Time Period	Industry	Residential	Transport	Commercial	Agriculture
2014–15	487.63	180.72	19.14	44.82	171.09
2021–22	899.97	327.64	35.15	72.52	325.69
2031–32	1,960.40	686.81	71.69	124.57	680.86
2041–42	3,944.58	1,409.70	145.79	220.94	1,297.23

Source: Author's own estimates.

TABLE **8.6** Savings Coefficient and Conservation Efficiency Factor

Sectors	Savings due to Higher Efficiency		Conservation Efficiency Factor	
	2021–22	2041–42	2021–22	2041–42
Agriculture	8.27	18.68	0.917	0.8132
Commercial	8.78	16.8	0.912	0.832
Residential	13.45	15.96	0.866	0.8404
Transport	6.22	15.28	0.938	0.8472
Industry	10.22	17.09	0.898	0.8291

Source: Author's own estimates based on the Draft Report of NITI Aayog on
Energy Policy 2017.

TABLE **8.7** Aggregate Electricity Demand for Different Concerned Scenarios
(in Twh)

Time Period	Scenarios 1 and 3	Scenarios 2 and 4
2014–15	903.395	903.395
2021–22	1,660.970	1,489.437
2031–32	3,524.343	2,994.274
2041–42	7,018.254	5,817.418

Source: Author's own estimates.

accounting for auxiliary and T&D losses by adding such total loss on
top of the final demand at the consumer's end.[4] Table 8.8 describes how
these losses will be reduced over the periods of the planning horizon

[4] The T&D loss includes the share of commercial loss for 2011–12 and
2021–22.

TABLE 8.8   Phasing of Auxiliary and Transmission and Distribution Losses

Time Horizon	Auxiliary Loss as Per Cent of Gross Generation	T&D Loss as Per Cent Dispatch at Bus Bar	T&D Loss as Per Cent Gross Generations 4	Auxiliary + T&D Loss as Per Cent Gross Generations
2011–12	6.1	23.64	22.16	28.26
2021–22	6	21	20	26
2031–32	5.5	18	17	22.5
2041–42	5	15	14.25	19.25

Source: Author's own estimates.

due to a rise in the supply-side efficiency. These estimates were based on the recommendations of the Planning Commission Report by the Expert Group on Energy Policy (2006) and NITI Aayog's Draft Report on Energy Policy (2017) on the concerned issue. Accordingly, Table 8.9a gives the total gross generation requirement of electrical energy in the different terminal years for the different scenarios. Table 8.9b gives the compound average annual growth rate of the gross generation of electrical energy over the different time horizons for the four scenarios.

Although we have not considered variation in real energy prices over the base of 2014–15 for the reasons stated earlier, we have considered forcing of the higher energy efficiency vis-à-vis the BAU scenarios by policy interventions.

We assume for our model two alternative levels of policy forcing efficient use of electrical energy use—a BAU scenario, and a high energy efficiency and conservation scenario. The comparative final electricity

TABLE 8.9A   Technology-wise Gross Generation Requirement

	Gross Generation Requirement (in Twh)					
	All Technologies		New Renewables		Solar and Wind	
	Scenario 1	Scenario 4	Scenario 1	Scenario 4	Scenario 1	Scenario 4
2011–12	1,106.529	1,106.529	82.423	82.423	35.030	35.030
2021–22	2,293.841	2,055.242	379.034	354.685	294.586	266.014
2031–32	4,908.018	4,174.830	1,055.224	1,185.652	858.903	889.239
2041–42	9,642.062	7,888.638	2,855.493	2,908.826	2,424.835	2,417.317

Source: Author's own estimates.

Table 8.9b   Compound Annual Growth Rate of Gross Generation of
Electrical Energy (in Per Cent)

	All Technologies		New Renewables		Solar and Wind	
	Scenario 1	Scenario 4	Scenario 1	Scenario 4	Scenario 1	Scenario 4
2011–12 to 2021–22	7.562	6.387	16.483	15.712	23.730	22.474
2011–12 to 2031–32	7.7326	6.864	13.596	14.260	17.347	17.551
2011–12 to 2041–42	7.483	6.766	12.543	12.613	15.170	15.158

Source: Author's own estimates.

demand between Scenaries 1 or 3 and Scenarios 2 or 4 as presented in
Table 8.7 have been based on the energy saving and conservation in
percentage as given in Table 8.6. Such saving would be targetted by a
policy drive for different terminal years vis-à-vis final energy consumption in those years as per the BAU scenario. We have taken these to be
the energy saving indicated by the comparative values of final energy
consumption as per the BAU scenario and the ambitious scenario in
the same year of the NITI Aayog's Draft on the National Energy Policy
Report (2017). Our projections of final energy consumption as per the
BAU scenario has, however, been taken to be the ones yielded by the
basic econometric model of our final energy demand and has nothing
to do with NITI Aayog's assumptions on BAU. The high efficiency scenario of our model has been generated by adjusting such final energy
demand projection by the targeted improvement of sectoral energy
efficiency in terms of the saving of final energy use (as indicated in
Table 8.6) in any terminal year for any given sector.

Summary Observation of the Final Energy Demand Projection of Electricity in India

The results of the demand for final energy as yielded by our econometric model and assumptions of energy efficiency improvement as

aggregated over the sectors in ktoe are presented in Tables 8.3a and 8.3b. These are found to vary between 800 and 928 mtoe in 2031–32 and between 1,418 and 1,705 mtoe in 2041–42 for the respective scenarios of high efficiency of energy use and BAU. These imply the GDP elasticity of the final energy demand as lying between 0.675 and 0.791 in the time frame from 2014–15 to 2031–32 and in the range between 0.698 and 0.788 in the long run from 2014–15 to 2041–42.

The projections of sectoral final energy demands as presented here are premised on an overall GDP growth of 8 per cent over the time horizon up to 2041–42. They further anticipate the final energy intensity of GDP to decline from 0.81 gm/INR in 2011–12 to 0.0.22 gm/INR in 2031–32 and to 0.005 gm/INR in 2041–42 as per the BAU scenario (see Table 8.2c). On the other hand, the energy intensity would be projected to decline from the same 0.81 in 2014–15 to 0.16 gm/INR in 2031–32 and to 0.004 gm/INR in 2041–42 as per the high energy efficiency scenario. The results for 2041–42 may appear to be unrealistically low. This has been due to the assumption of a persistently high 8 per cent rate of growth over the time horizon. The estimate of energy intensity would, however, rise for any deceleration of the rate of growth at some stage in our time horizon. In any case, such a trend of a decline of energy intensity of the GDP as estimated in Table 8.2c would, in fact, facilitate India's meeting it national commitment regarding mitigation measures of abating climate change.

The growing share of electricity in the total final energy as envisaged for the future has further given the projections of the final demand for electrical energy at the consumer end to be lying between 2,994 and 3,524 Twh in 2031–32 and between 5,817 and 7,018 Twh in 2041–42 for the respective scenarios of high energy efficiency of use or the BAU level of efficiency dynamics.

This would again imply an overall GDP elasticity of long-term electricity demand to be 0.893 and 0.986 in the time horizon from 2014–15 to the year 2031–32 as per the high efficiency and BAU scenarios respectively. The same elasticities would be 0.912 and 1.042 as per high energy efficiency and BAU scenarios for the time horizon from 2014–15 to 2041–42. The per capita final electricity use would, on the other hand, be projected to rise from the level of 880 kwh in 2014–15 to that of 2,738 and 3,223 kwh in 2031–32 and to 5,029 and 6,068 kwh in 2041–42 for the high efficiency and BAU scenarios respectively (see

Table 8.2b). The combined results of a declining final energy intensity of GDP and rising per capita use of electricity in the long-run projections point to India's potential of achievement of higher energy efficiency as combined with higher per capita use of electricity, the latter having clear implications in respect of the rise in the social well-being due to higher accessibility to the cleanest and most efficient fuel of electricity.

The gross generation requirement of electrical energy as necessitated by the projections of growth of electricity demand at the consumer end has finally been projected to be lying between 2,055.242 and 2,293.841 Twh in 2021–22, between 4,174.83 and 4,908.01 Twh in 2031–32, and between 7,888.638 and 9,642.062 Twh in 2041–42 for the different scenarios of energy efficiency (see Tables 8.9a and 8.9b). The growth rates as given in Table 8.9b would imply the GDP elasticity of gross electrical generation to vary between 0.85 and 0.95 over the long-run horizon up to 2041–42 with 2014–15 as the base year.

Future Projection of Energy Resource and Technology for India's Power Scenario: Carbon Dioxide Emission Implications for Changing Technology

Let us turn our attention to the changing fuel or resource composition of power technologies in the development of India's electricity industry. We present in this and the following sections the results of BAU (Scenario 1) and those of the most eco-efficient scenario (Scenario 4). Tables 8.10a and 8.10b give the resource-based technology-wise breakup of gross generation requirement (that is, into coal, gas, nuclear, storage hydro, and new renewable—solar, wind, biomass, and micro-hydel) over our time horizon from 2014–15 till 2041–42 for the two scenarios. These projections show the gross generation by coal thermal technology to rise from 826 Twh in 2014–15 to 2945 Twh in 2031–32 and to 5,528 Twh in 2041–42 as per the BAU scenario. The same will rise to comparatively moderate levels of 2,200 Twh in 2031–32 and 3,470 Twh according to Scenario 4, which combines the impact of both high energy efficiency and fuel substitution. These tables further show that the total gross generation of new renewables-based power will rise from 93.36 Twh in 2014–15 to 1,055 Twh in 2031–32 and 2,855 Twh in 2041–42 as per BAU. The same will rise to comparatively

TABLE 8.10A Technology-wise Gross Generation Mix (Scenario 1)

	Gross Generation (Twh)				
	Scenario 1/Scenario 4 2011–12	Scenario 1/Scenario 4 2014–15	Scenario 1 2021–22	Scenario 1 2031–32	Scenario 1 2041–42
Coal	729.443	826.280	1498.459	2,944.811	5,528.540
Gas	118.483	134.210	125.690	319.021	383.985
Nuclear	27.818	31.510	80.520	147.241	347.920
hydro storage	148.361	168.050	210.138	441.722	526.124
Solar Photovoltaic	2.061	2.330	97.213	245.401	895.259
CSP	0.000	0.000	10.801	73.620	222.754
Distributed Solar Photovoltaic	0.000	0.000	54.007	147.241	347.920
Total Solar	2.061	2.330	162.022	466.262	1,465.933
Onshore Wind	32.969	37.350	126.672	343.561	827.372
Offshore Wind	0.000	0.000	5.892	49.080	131.531
Total Wind	32.969	37.350	132.564	392.641	958.903
Other Renewables	47.393	53.680	84.448	196.321	430.658
Imports	5.150	5.840	0.000	0.000	0.000
Total					
Total New Renewables	82.423	93.360	379.034	1,055.224	2,855.493
Total Solar and Wind	35.030	39.680	294.586	858.903	2,424.835
Total All Technologies excluding Imports	1,106.529	1253.410	2,293.841	4,908.018	9,642.062
Total Requirement Including Imports	**1,111.679**	**1,259.250**	**2,293.841**	**4,908.018**	**9,642.062**

Source: Author's own estimates.

TABLE 8.10b   Technology-wise Gross Generation Mix (Scenario 4)

	Gross Generation Twh					
	Scenario 1/Scenario 4 2011–12	Scenario 1/Scenario 4 2014–15	Scenario 4 2021–22	Scenario 4 2031–32	Scenario 4 2041–42	
Coal	729.443	826.280	1,301.097	2,200.135	3,470.301	
Gas	118.483	134.210	135.202	271.364	528.241	
Nuclear	27.818	31.510	76.380	183.693	414.547	
hydro storage	148.361	168.050	187.878	333.986	566.723	
Solar Photovoltaic	2.061	2.330	86.915	304.763	855.331	
CSP	0.000	0.000	12.291	96.021	323.592	
Distributed Solar Photovoltaic	0.000	0.000	48.286	137.769	337.585	
Total Solar	2.061	2.330	147.493	538.553	1,516.508	
Onshore Wind	32.969	37.350	113.253	304.763	739.888	
Offshore Wind	0.000	0.000	5.268	45.923	160.921	
Total Wind	32.969	37.350	118.521	350.686	900.809	
Other Renewables	47.393	53.680	88.671	296.413	491.509	
Imports	5.150	5.840	0.000	0.000	0.000	
Total						
New Renewables	82.423	93.360	354.685	1,185.652	2,908.826	
Solar and Wind	35.030	39.680	266.014	889.239	2,417.317	
Total All Technologies excluding Imports	1,106.529	1,253.410	2,055.242	4,174.830	7,888.638	
Total Requirement including Imports	**1,111.679**	**1,259.250**	**2,055.242**	**4,174.830**	**7,888.638**	

Source: Author's own estimates.

higher levels of 1,186 Twh in 2031–32 and to 2,909 Twh in 2041–42 as per Scenario 4. Thus, while the share of coal thermal generation as a percentage share of total gross generation will decline from 66 per cent in 2014–15, 60 per cent in 2031–32, and 57.3 per cent in 2041–42 as per the BAU scenario, the share of new renewables will rise from a 7 per cent share in 2014–15 to 21.5 per cent in 2031–32, and further to 30 per cent in 2041–42 in the same scenario. According to Scenario 4, the share of coal is supposed decline to a comparatively lower level of 52.7 per cent in 2031–32, and to 44 per cent in 2041–42, while the share of new renewables should rise to a comparatively higher level of 28.4 per cent in 2031–32, and 36.9 per cent in 2041–42. We finally present the total impact of change in resource-wise generation shares between 2014–15 and 2031–32 in the form of two pie charts in Figures 8.1 and 8.2 for Scenario 1.

We now need to study the overall implications of the projection of such gross generation requirement of power in terms of requirement of the capacity of different technology-based plants and the financial resource requirement to create such capacities on the one hand, and the CO_2 emission implications on the other. The results of the projections

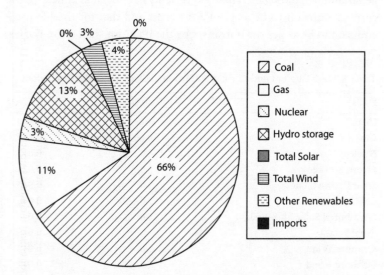

FIGURE 8.1   Resource-wise Generation Shares in 2014–15 in Business as Usual Scenario

Source: Based on data in Table 8.10a.

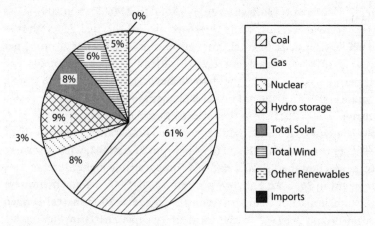

FIGURE 8.2   Resource-wise Generation Shares in 2031–32 in Business as Usual Scenario
Source: Based on data in Table 8.10a.

indicate the relative physical benefit and financial cost of CO_2 emission reductions. Table 8.11a provides the normative CO_2 emission coefficients—current as well as life cycle—for the different power generation technologies. These coefficients have been assumed for the current emission to be as per CEA norms and that for the life cycle emission to be as per the norms set by the IPCC for such technologies.

TABLE 8.11A   Current and Life Cycle Carbon Dioxide Emission Coefficient

Fuels	Current	Life Cycle
Coal	1.04	0.820
Gas	0.60	0.490
Nuclear	0	0.012
Hydro Storage	0	0.024
Solar Photovoltaic	0	0.048
CSP	0	0.048
Distributed Solar Photovoltaic	0	0.048
Total Solar	0	0.048
Onshore Wind	0	0.012
Offshore Wind	0	0.012
Total Wind	0	0.012
Other Renewables	0	0.230

Source: Government of India (2014).

TABLE 8.11B   Total Carbon Dioxide Current and Life Cycle Emissions (in Million Tonnes)

Time Period	Total CO_2 Current Emissions		Total CO_2 Life Cycle Emissions	
	Scenario 1	Scenario 4	Scenario 1	Scenario 4
2014–15	829.711	829.711	671.984	671.984
2021–22	1,633.812	1,434.262	1,334.493	1,175.972
2031–32	3,254.016	2,450.959	2,682.772	2,075.592
2041–42	5,980.073	3,926.058	5,001.152	3,403.312

Source: Author's own estimates.

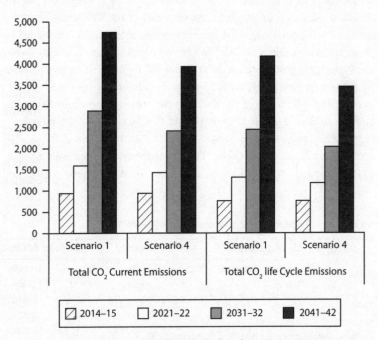

FIGURE 8.3   Total Current and Life Cycle Carbon Dioxide Emissions
Source: Based on data in Table 8.11b.

Table 8.11b presents the total current CO_2 emissions for the different terminal years for the different scenarios of projection and the same for a total life cycle emission for the same terminal years. Figure 8.3 presents the same in the form of a bar chart.

Projected Requirements of Installed Capacities of Generation of Power and Financial Resources

For any given generation scenario from our projection, the requirement of installed capacity would depend on the capacity utilization
factors, which would vary across energy resources and technologies.
This factor further varies widely for the new renewables because of the
uncertain time distribution of availability of energy resources vis-à-vis
that of load demand. The capacity utilization factors of the different
technologies have been assumed to be as given in Table 7.4 and the
same set of values of such utilization factors have been used for
the purpose of projection of the installed capacity requirement for the
different scenarios in the different terminal years. These are reported
for the total system, and for the new renewables-based subsystem of
generation in Table 8.12. Within the renewables, this table also shows
the capacity requirement of solar and wind together. The implications
of these capacity projections in respect of financial resource requirements for the build-up of the capacity over the different time horizons,
such as 2012 to 2022, 2012 to 2032, and finally, 2012 to 2042, have been
respectively presented in Tables 8.13a and 8.13b in the units of INR
and USD billion, respectively. The investment cost per unit of generation capacity for the various technologies and also their levellized

TABLE 8.12   Installed Capacity Requirement (in GW)

	All Technologies		New Renewables		Solar and Wind	
	Scenario 1	Scenario 4	Scenario 1	Scenario 4	Scenario 1	Scenario 4
Base Capacity	238.631	238.631	25.248	25.248	16.231	16.231
Cumulative Addition to Installed Capacity (GW)						
2011–12 to 2021–22	300.026	246.020	143.829	129.928	136.779	122.074
2011–12 to 2031–32	996.511	869.069	457.524	498.671	429.189	451.293
2011–12 to 2041–42	2,335.884	2,115.478	1,331.264	1,345.181	1,258.344	1,260.684

Source: Author's own estimates.

Table 8.13A Cumulative Requirement of Capital Resource for Capacity Build-up (in INR Billion)

Duration	All Technologies		New Renewables		Solar and Wind	
	Scenario 1	Scenario 4	Scenario 1	Scenario 4	Scenario 1	Scenario 4
2011–12 to 2021–22	20,316.439	16,119.700	7,087.796	6,429.161	6,703.572	6,001.145
2011–12 to 2031–32	67,508.241	55,633.359	22,320.449	24,759.739	20,776.204	22,177.628
2011–12 to 2041–42	1,48,826.529	1,30,667.226	65,592.739	66,666.065	61,618.632	62,060.979

Source: Author's own estimates.

Table 8.13B Cumulative Requirement of Capital Resource for Capacity Build-up (in USD Billion)

	All technologies		New Renewables		Solar and Wind	
	Scenario 1	Scenario 4	Scenario 1	Scenario 4	Scenario 1	Scenario 4
2011–12 to 2021–22	312.561	247.995	109.043	98.910	103.132	92.325
2011–12 to 2031–32	1,038.588	855.898	343.392	380.919	319.634	341.194
2011–12 to 2041–42	2,289.639	2,010.265	1,009.119	1,025.632	947.979	954.784

Source: Author's own estimates.

generation cost per kwh have been based on the data as presented in Table 7.4.

However, we want to make it clear that these projections are not predictions of India's future energy scenario, but represent certain alternative energy scenarios which may be considered to be quite feasible for India to attain under reasonable conditions, particularly in view of the very high potential of abiotic new renewables resources that exist as indicated in the preceding sections. These model-based results also indicate how India's growth and energy development can be made low carbon and environmentally sustainable within the time horizon up to 2041–42, depending mainly on energy conservation through enhancing the efficient use of electrical energy and accelerated use of abiotic new renewable energy resources. These also broadly support the targets of the present government regarding the creation of generation capacity of new renewables-based power—particularly solar and wind—by 2021–22 and 2031–32.

One issue may, however, be raised regarding the technical and project feasibility and financial viability of such a pattern of growth of electrical energy in the Indian context, as it contains a large component of addition of power capacity based on new renewables. Such capacity addition over the base capacity of 24.5 GW in 2012 is projected to be in the range of 130–144 GW over the time horizon up to 2021–22, 457 GW to 498 GW for the horizon up to 2031–32, and in the range of 1,331 to 1,345 GW for the horizon up to 2041–42, depending on the scenarios. The corresponding financial requirement for the creation of such generation capacity would vary in the range of INR 22,320 to 24,760 billion, or USD 343 to 380 billion over the time horizon up to 2031–32, and in the range of INR 65,593 to 66,666 billion or USD 1,009 to 1,025 billion in the time horizon up to 2041–42 from the base year of 2011–12. A comparison of projections between BAU Scenario 1 and the eco-efficient Scenario 4 of Tables 8.13a (or Table 8.13b) on the financial requirement for generation capacity investment and of Table 8.10b on current or lifetime CO_2 emission shows that the low-carbon strategy as represented by Scenario 4 in comparison with BAU Scenario 1 will cause a saving of life-cycle CO_2 emissions of 607 million tonnes in 2031–32 for an additional investment of INR 2,440 billion for cumulative capacity addition for the time horizon up to 2031–32. A similar comparison of results between Scenarios 1 and 4 for the extended time horizon up to 2041–42 shows that the life-cycle CO_2 emissions will be reduced by approximately 1,600 million tonnes in 2041–42 for an additional investment of INR 673 billion for capacity addition. It is thus observed that in the Indian cost situation, the marginal investment requirement goes down for CO_2 reduction over a longer time horizon, justifying the adoption of an eco-efficient strategy such as that of Scenario 4 for the sustainable development of the Indian power sector.

It may, however, be pointed out here that the estimated projections of financial resource requirement as given in Tables 8.13a and 8.13b represent only the requirement of investment generation for the purpose of building up the required installed capacity and do not include any share of the financial resource requirement of the corresponding required strengthening of the T&D system. The latter would inevitably involve costs of smart grid development as it is almost a basic prerequisite of the development of the new renewables due to the variability of both the load demand and instantaneous supply of non-storable renewable resources (wind and solar). Besides, our cost projections of the different scenarios do not include the share of investment for energy conservation, which is supposed to follow any policy forcing in respect of energy-efficiency improvement in our present model of power development. The financial burden of such energy conservation investment, however, is to be borne by the consumer sectors as the benefit of such investment would accrue to them. We therefore do not include this issue of investment requirement for energy conservation here in the power sector model of financial resource mobilization.

However, it may be further noted that the normative ratios for the required investment in generation, transmission, and distribution would be 4:2:2 as per the CEA norm's thumb rule. This would imply that the total investment requirement in a greenfield plant set-up, including the share of T&D capacity expansion, would be double the investment cost of the generation plant. The aggregate capital resource requirement for the capacity build-up over the base of 2011–12 in new renewables-based power, including the T&D shares, would then be in the range of INR 44,640 to 49,520 billion in the planning horizon up to 2031–32 and in the range of INR 1,31,185 to 1,33,332 billion in the planning horizon up to 2041–42. A comparison of projections of results for BAU Scenario 1 and Scenario 4 would thus imply that the total additional system investment cost (including T&D share) to be INR 4,880 and 1,346 billion for the respective time horizons up to 2031–32 and 2041–42 against the same respective saving of the life-cycle CO_2 emissions of 613 million tonnes in 2031–32 and 1,600 million tonnes in 2041–42.

Our projections of investment requirement as presented earlier for the build-up of the capacity of a renewable-based power system should not as such pose any big constraint in these days of globalization, when global capital is crossing national boundaries with greater ease. The real challenge would arise in attracting entrepreneurship and funds in the generation technology of choice, because of the low credit ratings of many such projects in India—at least to begin with. Such ratings may be affected not only by the risk involved due to the project's technology and business environment, but also by the macroeconomic and country-level policies in the context of attracting foreign capital. To overcome such constraints, it may be important to develop new initiatives for alternative sources of finance, such as regional infrastructural banks, multilateral banks, and climate funds. Apart from direct financing of electricity projects based on renewables, all these sources including the illustrative climate fund as proposed here in the following section of this chapter may help the concerned projects by extending credit-enhancing facilities by appropriate guarantee or counter-guaranteeing the rating enhancement for the proposed investments.

Financing from the Resource Rent–Based Climate Fund: Projection of Resource Rent due to Fossil Fuel Extraction

In order to project the resource rent arising from the extraction of fossil fuel for the power sector, we assume the coal or gas price to be linked with the internationally traded price of oil. In other words, the price of coal has been taken to be the value of the kgoe per unit of coal in terms of the globally traded oil price for the purpose. We take a notional value of the price of coal on the basis of its energy content in kgoe and the OPEC oil price as predicted for the concerned years of rent estimation. We have further taken 15 per cent of such an oil-linked price of coal or gas to be the resource rent component of the fuel price or value in view of the prevailing 14 per cent rate of royalty on coal in India. The other assumptions related to resource rent calculations have been reported in Table 8.14.

TABLE 8.14   Assumptions for Resource Rent Calculations

	2011–12	2021–22	2031–32	2041–42
Price of Oil (USD/barrel)	50	58	78	105
Oil Equivalent Factor of				
Coal	0.4	0.4	0.4	0.4
Gas	0.9	0.9	0.9	0.9
Oil-Linked Prices (USD/Tonne)				
Coal	154	178.64	240.24	323.4
Gas	346.5	401.94	540.54	727.65
Oil-Linked Prices (INR/Tonne)				
Coal	10,010	11,611.6	15,615.6	21,021
Gas	22,522.5	26,126.1	35,135.1	47,297.25
Conversion Efficiency into Power (Per Cent)				
Coal	29	32	35	38
Gas	42.5	44	45	46
Fuel Cost of Power (USD/mwh)				
Coal Thermal	113.96	119.69	147.55	182.94
Gas Plant	77.89	87.27	114.76	151.13
Fuel Cost of Power (INR/mwh)				
coal thermal	7,407.40	7,779.77	9,590.71	11,891.32
gas plant	5,063.00	5,672.83	7,459.44	9,823.27
Resource Rent Generated (USD/mwh) at 15 Per Cent of Fuel Price				
Coal Thermal	17.09	17.95	22.13	27.44
Gas Plant	11.68	13.09	17.21	22.67
Resource Rent Generated (INR/mwh) at 15 Per Cent of Fuel Price				
Coal Thermal	1,111.11	1,166.97	1,438.61	1,783.70
Gas Plant	759.45	850.92	1,118.92	1,473.49
Coal Cess Cost (INR/mwh) of Power				
Coal Thermal	296.50	268.70	245.67	226.28

Note that 1 tonne = 7.7 barrel of oil

Exchange Rate: 1 USD = INR 65

Coal Cess = INR 400 per tonne of coal

Source: Author's compilation and estimates.

For coal-thermal and gas-based power generation, the projection of gross generation for any terminal year has yielded the oil equivalent fuel requirement depending on their respective conversion efficiency which would, however, be changing over time in future as per our assumption of technical changes. The value of the oil-linked price of the fossil fuel would then immediately yield the projected volume of the total resource rent that would be generated from resource use in the power sector in each year in the future on the basis of the levy of 15 per cent ad valorem.

We propose here such resource rent to be taxed whenever the fuel resources are being extracted for the power sector and put in a climate fund (Das and Sengupta 2015). The total resource rent at zero interest rate that would accumulate over time (we assume zero interest rate for our hypothetical exercise here) is estimated for any time of our time horizons. We assume a linear phasing of growth of resource flow over each decade of 2011–12 to 2021–22, 2021–22 to 2031–32, and 2031–32 to 2041–42. Such linear phasing leads to the result that the amount of such a flow of resource rent will grow in arithmetic progression over the individual years of each decade. The projections of the accumulated amount of resource rent over each decade are then derived by the formulae of the sum of arithmetic progression series. The further estimate of accumulated resource rent for any terminal year of our planning horizons from the base year of 2011–12 can then be derived from this data of decadal resource rent estimates and the current flows of terminal years. These estimates of projections of resource-rent flows and accumulation are all given for coal and gas in Tables 8.15a and 8.15b for BAU Scenario 1 and eco-efficient Scenario 4 respectively. These projections can then be compared with the estimates of resource requirement for a cumulative capacity build-up for the same time horizons. While these two need not balance, their comparison would tell us if and to what extent such resource rent can provide adequate finance for the capacity build-up based on new renewables over the same time horizons of planning. The results of such comparisons are given in Table 8.15c. One can, however, introduce interest earning by such a climate fund, and find out what interest rate would be enough for the basic fund along with its interest earnings to finance the required growth of power capacities based on the new renewable resources.

One may, however, argue that if the resource rent is to be mobilized as a tax and is to be passed on to the consumer through higher tariffs, power will be high cost and unaffordable for millions of Indians. In the interest of equity and social sustainability of development, part of this

TABLE 8.15A   Resource Rent Calculations: Scenario 1

Resource Rent (at 15 Per Cent	Resource Rent (INR Billion)	Resource Rent (USD Billion)	Cumulative Rent (INR Billion) from Base Year (INR Billion)	Cumulative Rent (USD Billion) from Base Year (USD Billion)
Coal			**Coal**	
2011–12	810.4470073	12.4684155	810.4470073	12.4684155
2021–22	1,748.650705	26.90183443	12,795.48856	196.8512496
2031–32	4,236.425718	65.17455705	40,972.21998	630.3313726
2041–42	9,861.245741	151.7086661	96,177.3137	1,479.623516
Gas			**Gas**	
2011–12	89.9769641	1.384279213	89.9769641	1.384279213
2021–22	106.9526376	1.64540779	984.6480083	15.14843502
2031–32	356.9577012	5.491627494	3,197.247065	49.18820365
2041–42	565.7980577	8.704555965	6,576.372787	101.1744662
Coal + Gas			**Coal + Gas**	
2011–12	900.4239714	13.85269471	900.4239714	13.85269471
2021–22	1,855.603343	28.54724222	13,780.13657	211.9996846
2031–32	4,593.38342	70.66618455	44,169.46704	679.5195762
2041–42	10,427.0438	160.4132221	1,02,753.6865	1,580.797983

Source: Author's own estimates.

resource rent may have to be used for subsidizing the targeted poor by the direct transfer for power consumption for offsetting the high cost. It will be important to verify if the balance of resource rent mobilized would suffice to finance the expansion of the new renewables-based power capacity.

Coal Cess in India: Comments and Observations

The Government of India currently imposes a coal cess at the rate of INR 400 per tonne. This was originally introduced in 2010 at the rate of INR 50 per tonne and later enhanced in 2016 to the current level. This was imposed as a carbon tax on the production and import of coal, lignite, and peat whose proceeds were to flow to the National Clean Energy & Environment Fund (NCEEF). This was supposed

Table 8.15b   Resource Rent Calculations: Scenario 4

Resource Rent (at 15 Per Cent)	Resource Rent (INR Billion)	Resource Rent (USD Billion)	Cumulative Rent (INR Billion) from Base Year (INR Billion)	Cumulative Rent (USD Billion) from Base Year (USD Billion)
Coal			**Coal**	
2011–12	810.4470073	12.4684155	810.4470073	12.4684155
2021–22	1,518.335962	23.35859444	12,795.49033	167.0947805
2031–32	3,165.130202	48.69339689	33,542.9097	516.0364119
2041–42	6,189.968985	95.22853024	67,027.69655	1,031.176195
Gas			**Gas**	
2011–12	89.9769641	1.384279213	89.9769641	1.384279213
2021–22	115.0466266	1.769929382	1,025.117954	15.77104298
2031–32	303.6334655	4.671259035	3003.471788	46.20705568
2041–42	591.0577373	11.97470395	6263.223009	110.764498
Coal + Gas			**Coal + Gas**	
2011–12	900.4239714	13.85269471	900.4239714	13.85269471
2021–22	1,633.382588	25.12852382	13,820.60828	182.8658235
2031–32	3,468.763667	53.36465593	36,546.38149	562.2434676
2041–42	6,781.026723	107.2032342	73,290.91956	1,141.940693

Source: Author's own estimates.

to be a non-lapsable fund, the unutilized portion of the cess revenue being transferable to the following year for utilization. This is to be routed through the Consolidated Fund of India (CFI) but earmarked for clean energy development initiative. The fund is meant for financing research and innovative development projects in clean energy technologies. The cess thus had a dual objective—penalizing the production and import of coal and its variants and encouraging a shift towards renewables. Since this is supposed to serve the purpose of resource rent, which I propose should be imposed as tax to be mobilized for financing clean energy development, I give my observations and comments on the adequacy of this cess and in that context, discuss the required rate and form of resource taxation for the development of new renewables-based green power, as envisaged in the era of the Third Industrial Revolution.

TABLE 8.15c Adequacy of Resource Rent for Financing Capacity Build-up from the Base of 2011–12

Period	Scenario 1: BAU with Respect to Energy Efficiency and Fuel Mix			Period	Scenario 4. High energy Efficiency-cum-Accelerated. Introduction of New Renewables		
	Cumulative Rent (USD Billion) from Base Year 2011–12	Cumulative Capital Requirement for Capacity Build-up over 2011–12 (USD Billion)	Adequacy (Per Cent)		Cumulative Rent (USD Billion) from Base Year 2011–12	Cumulative Capital Requirement for Capacity Build-up over 2011–12 (USD Billion)	Adequacy (Per Cent)
2011–12	13.853			2011–12	13.853		
2011–12 to 2021–22	212.000	109.043	194.418	2011–12 to 2021–22	182.866	98.910	184.881
2011–12 to 2031–32	679.520	343.392	197.885	2011–12 to 2031–32	562.243	380.919	147.602
2011–12 to 2041–42	1,580.798	1,009.119	156.651	2011–12 to 2041–42	1,141.941	1,025.632	111.340

Source: Author's own estimates.

However, after the introduction of the goods and services tax (GST) in India, the coal cess has been replaced by a GST cess (as a cess on some demerit goods) for compensating revenue loss of states which suffered from the shift to GST from the earlier tax regime. The coal cess was abolished when this new GST cess was introduced and was supposed to be subsumed by it. This was followed by a transfer of the accumulated fund of the unutilized coal cess to the CFI, out of which most of the government expenditure is made. Although the fund of coal cess is supposed to be made available for the purpose for which it was set up, the actual historical record of fund utilization for this cess has been very poor. Firstly, only a mere 37 per cent of the total coal cess collected was transferred to the NCEEF. Out of this, 81 per cent has been used for financing projects for clean energy development. Thus only a share of 30 per cent of the coal cess was applied for the purpose for which it was originally meant.

Such meagre utilization is a matter of concern if the government is serious about using the coal cess fund for the objective of developing new technologies for clean energy. This is particularly important as the coal cess has been now subsumed under the GST cess and unused money from the NCEEF has been siphoned off to fund GST compensation to industrially advanced states of the past to placate their disgruntlement over the loss of revenue due to the regional redistributive impact of GST reform. Such diversion of use of fund of coal cess, though not illegal, is surely immoral from the environmental ethics perspective.

One may raise the issue if the current coal cess of INR 400 per tonne is adequate as an eco-tax either for the purpose of internalizing the environmental external cost of use of coal in the context of its use in the power sector. With reference to the assumptions of our thermal coal–based power as stated in Table 8.14, such coal cess would imply a hike in the cost of power only by INR 0.30 in 2011–12, which will come down to INR 0.27 in 2031–32, and INR 0.23 in 2041–42, due to improvements in the efficiency of thermal power generation. This is, in any case, negligible in comparison to the cost of environmental externality of coal thermal generation whose estimate varies between INR 4.40 and INR 12.64, the mean value being INR 8.52 (see Table 7.5). There seems to be thus no relation between such cess and the environmental externality of the use of coal in power generation. This is not surprising in view of the fact that this cess was conceived not as an eco-tax to internalize costs of externalities of coal use for power generation, but as a compensatory GST cess for revenue loss of states due to the transition to a GST tax regime.

However, one may still wonder if such cess of INR 400 per tonne would be adequate for meeting the requirement of capacity building in new renewable based power development in India in future over the planning horizon up to 2031–32 or 2041–42.

Table 8.16 shows how coal cess at the rate of INRs 400 per tonne would generate a cumulative revenue of INR 3,094 billion for the time horizon up to 2021–22, INR 8,322 up to 2031–32, and INR 14,779 up to 2041–42, assuming a linear phasing of cess revenue growth over time between the terminal years of any decade according to the baseline Scenario 1. When these are compared with the requirement of financial resources for the cumulative generation capacity build-up from the same base year as projected for the same scenario, we find the cumulative coal cess revenue will meet only 43.66 per cent of the capital requirement of creation of the generation capacity in new renewables-based power up to 2021–22, such coverage declining to 37.29 per cent in 2031–32, and to 22.53 per cent in 2041–42. For scenario 4 the level of adequacy of cess revenue is even lower for the different time horizons as compared to the one of BAU scenario 1.

However, it is also be to noted that coal cess revenue at the rate of INR 400 per tonne would generate substantially lower financial resources than the estimate of resource rent that would arise if we take the resource rent of a fossil fuel to be 15 per cent of the oil-linked price of coal or gas. Based on the average or marginal rate of resource rent, the total cumulative resource rent or equivalent tax proceeds that would arise over the time horizon from 2011–12 up to 2031–32 and up to 2041–42 would be respectively, 47.6 per cent and 11.34 per cent higher than the capital resource requirement for building up the generation capacity of new renewables over the same time horizon. Even if we put a tax on resource rent arising from the use of only coal, the total cumulative undiscounted tax revenue would balance with the capital resource requirement for the build-up of new renewables resource–based power capacity up to 2041–42. Although these observations are not based on the result of any truly dynamic multi-period model of revenue growth and capital expenditure, the undiscounted inter-temporal revenue total is found to be converging to that of the requirement of

TABLE 8.16 Coal Cess Revenue at INR 400 per Tonne of Coal and Its Adequacy

		Scenario 1: BAU with Respect to Energy Efficiency and Fuel Mix		
Period	Current Coal Cess Revenue (INR Billion)	Cumulative Cess Revenue from Base Year 2011–12 (INR Billion)	Cumulative Capacity Resource Requirement for New Renewables up to the Current Year (INR Billion)	Cess Finance Availability for Capacity Resource Requirement for New Renewables (Per Cent)
2011–12	216.268	216.268		
2021–22	402.636	3,094.520	7,087.796	43.660
2031–32	723.452	8,322.322	22,320.449	37.286
2041–42	1,250.998	14,779.235	65,592.739	22.532
		Scenario 4: High Energy Efficiency-cum-Accelerated Introduction of New Renewables		
Period	Current Coal Cess Revenue (INR Billion)	Cumulative Cess Revenue from Base Year 2011–12 (INR Billion)	Cumulative Capacity Resource Requirement for New Renewables up to the Current Year (INR Billion)	Cess Finance Availability for Capacity Resource Requirement for New Renewables (Per Cent)
2011–12	216.268	216.268		
2021–22	349.605	2,829.364	6,429.161	44.008
2031–32	540.507	6,930.319	2,4759.739	27.990
2041–42	785.260	10,538.888	66,666.065	15.808

Source: Author's own estimates.

capital expenditure with the extension of the time horizon to 2041–42, on the assumption of the linear phasing of their respective growth within each decadal period. This justifies that cess or fossil fuel resource tax be linked with oil-linked prices of fuels of coal or gas for taxing, not for internalizing the environmental externality into the cost, but for meeting the requirement of capital financing of transitioning to the new regime of new renewables-based power from a predominantly coal-based thermal regime.

One may, however, argue that the existing coal cess was imposed with the limited objective of capital financing only for the development of new technology and innovations—possibly mainly through R&D—and not for financing the building up of the entire new capacity embodying the new technologies. Besides, the adequacy of resource rent as shown in Table 8.15c is not considering the T&D investment requirement for setting up new capacities in the new renewables. If one is to include the supporting T&D investment requirement into the total financial requirement for the expansion of the power system to supply the new renewables-based power, the estimate of such requirement would be double of that shown in Table 8.15C, for the reason already mentioned in a preceding section. This would, in fact, imply a deficit in financial availability from such resource rent–linked tax. One may, however, decide the financial policy in respect of what share of capital financing—for the development of new technology, its application in the creation of new generation, and supporting T&D capacity—should be mobilized from within the energy (fossil fuel) industry, and what balance should be mobilized from domestic or international bonds and other financial instruments. The fuel cess rates can then be arrived at accordingly. In any case, what I want to focus on here is the importance of fossil fuel–based thermal power and backstop technology-based (new renewables-based) power playing complementary roles, from the viewpoint of meeting the challenge of financing new technology development in the power industry.

Other Recent Comparative Studies for the Potentials of a Low-Carbon Economic Growth for India

Before we conclude this chapter we refer to other studies on the future prospects of a low-carbon economic growth for India. The present author himself (Sengupta 2010) analysed the past patterns of India's GDP growth, energy use, and CO_2 emissions and identified the respective roles of scale, structural patterns of economic growth, and technology (through energy efficiency and fuel mix) in determining such growth of CO_2 emissions. A decomposition analysis was carried out for the growth of CO_2 emissions for both the pre-reform (1971–90) and post-reform periods (1990–2005) using conventional as well as the refined Divisia methods. Taking cues from these results, the monograph further developed econometric models for future projections of sectoral and aggregate energy-related CO_2 emissions in the economy for the time horizon up to 2030 (Sengupta 2010). It was reassuring to see from the results of these models of decomposition and econometric demand analysis that it is possible for India to significantly delink CO_2 emissions and economic growth, by making appropriate choices of price and fuel policies without compromising on the targets of economic growth. The policies considered for the purpose of attaining a low-carbon growth trajectory have been both price-induced energy conservation and the substitution of fossil fuel by new renewables.

This chapter uses a similar econometric model for the projections of structural patterns of growth, sectoral energy demand, and CO_2 emissions. However, while Sengupta (2010) considered the emissions from both direct use (in sectors other than power) and indirect use of fossil fuel through electricity, the present study focuses on the prospect of new renewables that can replace fossil fuels for lowering the carbon intensity of energy use only through a change in fuel mix in the electricity industry in the time horizon up to 2041–42. In view of this, the sectoral energy demand model of this chapter is an updated version of Sengupta's 2010 model, although the derivation of the projection of CO_2 emissions has been worked out only for the power sector. While the time-series database used for the purpose has been that of sectoral energy consumption from 1993–94 to 2014–15, the methodology of econometric estimation in this present work has involved a more updated method of time series analysis for the stationarity test for all the concerned variables and the use of a model of co-integration in the light of such test results for the estimation of the long-run partial elasticity of the final energy consumption with respect to sectoral income or real energy prices facing the sector. No such time-series analysis of the data had been carried out by Sengupta on the top of usual auto-correlation and heteroscedasticity tests and the usual measures of correction for such non-spherical disturbances in the random term, if any.

The other important report on the same theme, which came out between 2005 and the present one has been the one entitled, 'Final Report of the Expert Group on Low Carbon Strategies for Inclusive Growth' published by the Planning Commission in 2014(b). I review here the report in short, particularly its model structure in order to be able to appreciate its comparative merit vis-à-vis the model in this chapter. This 2014 Planning Commission study has provided a projection of inter-temporal resource allocation as yielded by the optimized dynamic path of macroeconomic variables of consumption, investments, and inflow of foreign resources along with exports and imports with their respective sectoral break-ups. The macroeconomic model used in the report for the Indian economy has been a multi-sector one of the generalized Leontief type of sectoral inter-dependence through the relationship of input–output flows. It is a 25-sector model, the product of each sector being produced by one basic activity or technique of production, except for electricity, which has been considered to be produced by 14 alternative activities involving the use of different energy resources and associated technologies. This gives a total of 38 activities for the model whose input coefficients would determine all intermediate uses of sectoral products.

The model under reference subsumes a model of an endogenous income distribution and a model of a linear expenditure system to determine the private consumption use of sectoral products by all income classes and also at the aggregate level of all classes together. Government consumption is exogenously determined and given to be growing at the rate of 7 per cent per annum over time. It is supposed to reflect the policies initiated for the inclusive growth of the Twelfth Plan, although the model does not contain any fiscal policy and inter-temporal budgetary constraints.

The treatment of investment is also made endogenous in the model—the investment-by-destination sector being determined by the year-to-year sectoral increase in gross output and incremental capital output ratio and the investment by use or origin of the sectoral product being determined by the commodity-wise composition of investment expenditure giving the estimates of incremental stock use of sectoral products in a given period. The trade and balance of payments block of equations of the model allows an endogenous choice of commodity-wise imports and exports subject to the constraints of upper and lower limits of year-to-year sectoral import growth, the upper limit of sectoral export growth and the upper-limit constraints on the current account deficit as yielded by total imports minus total exports at a realistic level. The model solves for such choices of inter-temporal paths of imports and exports that sectoral demand-supply balances and macroeconomic savings—investment balance—are ensured for every period, and the discounted present equivalent value of the inter-temporal stream of consumption is maximized.

The model is solved for two scenarios: (*i*) Baseline Inclusive Growth (BIG) and (*ii*) Low Carbon Inclusive Growth (LCIG). The comparison of the two results provides the impact of a low-carbon growth strategy. For both the scenarios, inclusive growth was defined in terms of various monitorable targets for the Twelfth Five Year Plan and has been common. These targets comprise, first of all, a certain reduction of poverty by way of employment growth by the end of the Twelfth Plan, which would affect the parameters of endogenous income distribution. It is, however, not clear from the report how this target of poverty alleviation has been concretely taken account of in the endogenization of income distribution. Besides, the objective of inclusive growth as per the model comprises certain targets of attainment of human development in terms of health and education, infrastructure, particularly rural infrastructure such as access to electricity, pucca housing, drinking water supply and sanitation, and improvement in service delivery including access to banking services and major subsidies implemented as cash transfers. The policies for achieving such an inclusive growth objective would possibly be partly reflected in the government consumption vector (though that is not clear from the report), and partly in the total expenditure in the form of various transfers and subsidies exogenously set aside from the total GDP or income by reduction in the marginal savings rate, which is treated as exogenous and whose estimation is supposed to be taken up as an offline exercise. (This part is also not enumerated and clarified in the report.)

However, given the baseline scenario, the Planning Commission study examines the impact of a low-carbon inclusive growth scenario on CO_2 emissions, among other aspects, by introducing two sets of additional measures over the baseline one:

1. Energy conservation by improvement in the efficiency of energy use in different sectors.
2. Introduction of various carbon-free or low-carbon power generation and transportation technologies as well as constraining coal thermal power generation as a share of total generation.

A low-carbon scenario includes enhancement of autonomous energy efficiency over time, with the benefit from the total factor productivity growth in all sectors, including power, remaining the same between the two scenarios. Besides, the penetration of carbon-free and low-carbon renewables in total power generation has been assumed to rise over time, driven by policy forcing. Besides, the low-carbon scenario has considered the rail–road modal shift, the introduction of electric vehicles, and so on, to reduce CO_2 emissions, not only through electricity, but also through fuel substitution in transport and other sectors. The capital cost of all such policy initiatives, both for energy- efficiency improvement and the introduction of carbon-free or low-carbon technology, are supposed to have been incorporated in the estimates of capital costs given in the report over time. The results show while the well-being indicators capturing the feature of inclusive growth have been forced to remain the same between the two scenarios, the GDP estimate and the number of poor are found to vary marginally between the two scenarios, the impact being primarily traced for CO_2 emissions and capital investment required for both the energy sector and the overall economy. It is important to note that while the path of CO_2 emissions has been lower for the LCIG scenario than the baseline one, the cumulative energy investment required has also been similarly lower for the low-carbon scenario. The low-carbon development strategy thus appears to be a win-win option.

The study based on the model of projection as presented in this chapter has a commonality with the 2014 Planning Commission report of low-carbon strategies for inclusive growth in the objective of exploring its scope in the future development of the entire Indian economy. Besides, the Planning Commission model took the inclusive growth as its baseline and was subsumed in both the scenarios of the study, while the model in this chapter takes a certain growth rate—8 per cent—and the removal of poverty by raising the share of the cleanest and most efficient fuel-share of electricity in the total energy consumption for all sectors over time in all the scenarios. As the prospective role of the new renewable for low-carbon growth has been the objective of the present study on the Third Industrial Revolution, unlike the Planning Commission (2014b), the model in this chapter has focused mainly on tracing the impact of an increased penetration of new renewables in the electricity industry in lowering the carbon intensity of India's economic growth. The scope and impact of a low-carbon strategy in transport and other sectors that have direct use of fossil fuel has, therefore, not been considered here.

Besides, the 2014 Planning Commission model has been one of optimization, defined in a 'fixed price, general equilibrium' framework of sectoral resource allocation based on a dynamic version of activity analysis or a generalized input–output model with the endogenization of income distribution and consumption, as well as investment and trade. It thus tries to capture the impact of a low-carbon policy initiative as worked out through the direct and indirect demand and supply of gross electricity and other fuels as induced by such policy. The model of this chapter is, on the other hand, a much simpler econometric one of sectoral energy demand-based projection of CO_2 emissions in the future for the different time horizons. This captures, more directly, the total impact of any policy on the sectoral demand for energy and electricity. The pathway of the impact of any measure of power conservation or change in the fuel mix for power would be more easily traceable through the working of the regression model of the present study and the derived carbon implication of the projected values of its dependent variables as well as that of electricity supply. In view of the different rounds of interaction among a whole range of variables, one cannot easily interpret the results of the Planning Commission model so as to understand the underlying process of interactive actions and their ultimate consequences. It is only through the estimates of its dual model, the shadow values of the constraints, and other results of sensitivity analysis that one could possibly separate the partial effects of change of any given policy from others in the Planning Commission model. The reference to any such analysis is missing in the report.

So far as the capital cost estimates are concerned, the model in this chapter has derived the cumulative capital resource requirement of the power sector and its component for new renewables-based power from the base of 2011–12 up to the horizon of 2031–32 and 2041–42. The Planning Commission model does not show separately the share of such costs of introduction of new renewables whose introduction is envisaged to bring about the Third Industrial Revolution. Besides, unlike the Planning Commission study, the model of the present chapter addresses the issue of financing the development of new renewables-based power through the mobilization of resource rent that can be extracted from fossil fuel and used for developing such backstop technology for power. The idea of making the use of fossil fuel and that of new renewables as a complementary one has been the new contribution of this chapter in the pre-existing literature of sustainable development of the power sector in the context of India.

In spite of the similarity of the broad objectives of the two studies, the methods of projection are quite different, as discussed earlier. However, it is interesting to see that although comparative results of gross electricity generation requirement and CO_2 emissions—the two critical variables as presented later—are at variance, the extent of

TABLE 8.17 Comparable Results of the Present Study and That of the Planning Commission (2014b)

Model/Scenario	GDP Growth Rate (Per Cent)	Gross Generation of Electricity (Twh) in 2031–32	CO_2 Emissions (Current)	CO_2 emissions (Lifetime)
Model of the Present Study BAU Scenario 1	8 per cent	4,908	2,886	2,683
Scenario 4 (Energy and Carbon Conserving Scenario)	8 per cent	4,175	2,410	2,076
Planning Commission (2014)				
(a) Baseline Model Scenario	7.03 per cent	3,371	5,271	
(b) Low-Carbon Scenario	6.87 per cent	3,466	3,830	

Source: Author's own estimates and Planning Commission (2014b).

savings of CO_2 emissions over the horizon 2031–32 are comparable and can possibly be explained.

It is, in fact, important to note that the comparative projections of gross generation requirement of electricity between Scenarios 1 and 4 of the present study show that the gross generation of electricity can be reduced by 15 per cent in 2031–32 by energy conservation along with an accelerated introduction of new renewables in the power sector. This would result in saving of 16 per cent and 23 per cent of CO_2 emissions as per current and lifetime emission basis respectively (see Table 8.17). The comparison of results of the BIG and LCIG scenarios of the Planning Commission (2014b), on the other hand, show that the requirement of the gross generation of power is higher by 2.8 per cent for LCIG vis-à-vis BIG. This result of change in the opposite direction for LCIG can possibly be explained by the greater access to electricity for households and the railroad model shift, and possibly also by the introduction of electric cars among others. However, the extent of CO_2 savings as per the model of this chapter is projected to be 28 per cent in 2031–32, which is higher by about a 3 per cent point above that of the Planning Commission estimations for that period. In any case, the impact on saving of CO_2 emissions is not at all widely different between the two studies. This establishes robustness of the result of the low-carbon strategy in abating emissions to control climate change.

Challenges of Generation and Transmission of Electricity in the Era of Renewables-Based Power

What would then be further required to introduce a big bang change in fuel policy for generating electricity by making a structural shift in technology in favour of new renewable resources?

Large solar and wind capacities need to be created for the faster transformation of India's fossil fuel–based electricity industry into a green one. The development of new renewables would require large-scale availability of financial resources of the order of USD 450 billion (Scenario 4) over a 30-year period. Additionally, the financial requirements of energy conservation as envisaged for the concerned scenarios have to be made available to the industries at large; this is in order to realize the full potential of more than 500 million tonnes of lifetime savings on CO_2 emissions vis-à-vis the BAU Scenario 1 in 2031–32.

In the area of R&D for technology development, there needs to be a policy thrust in favour of the development of CSP and offshore wind energy. India needs to accelerate its capacity to manufacture equipment required for new renewables-based technologies and also prioritize human resource development for the new renewable energy industry through a large-scale introduction of new renewables technology education, which is of crucial importance to realize the potential of India's renewable energy capacity.

The major challenge that arises from the abiotic renewable–based power development is that both the power output as well as the energy resources such as wind or solar irradiation are non-storable, unlike fossil fuels. In a conventional power system, the demand for power fluctuates, but fossil fuel resources such as coal and natural gas, as well as water in large hydro storage facilities, or nuclear fuel, are all storable and can be drawn upon as and when the load of generation needs to be raised. In view of the intermittent nature of supply of wind or solar radiation due to varying wind speeds or varying radiation depending on cloud cover or the time of the day, the availability of these resources fluctuate both spatially and temporally. In the interest of the sustainability of power supply, the focus needs to be on maximizing the mobilization and conversion of solar or wind resources, whenever they are available, into electric power while at the same time, matching the demand and supply of power along the network of the power grid serving the various load centres, by dispatching power from the generation sources—both conventional and new renewables-based. This challenge can be met in one of the following ways:

Storage Devices

1. When solar or wind power is available abundantly, it can be stored in a battery storage system for use at other time. A project is already being implemented in Puducherry, India, where experiments are going on with alternative battery technologies.
2. Pump storage is an option for hydro resources, in order to store water during off-peak hours and using the available solar or wind power to drive the turbine that releases the pumped water during peak hours.

Flexible Operation and Balancing Power Needs

This involves flexibility of load generation in a power plant with the aid of power electronics, which can ensure automated control of the production and supply of power. Technical progress in power electronics would intend to introduce flexibility in a coal- or gas-based power plant by ramping up or down the instantaneous rate of load generation to meet the fluctuating power demand of the load curve. The use of fossil fuel, nuclear energy resources, or storage hydro resources, as well as new renewable resources can be complementary in power generation to meet the load curve. In a flexible plant operation, the system operator can ramp up generation by using the wind and solar radiations in their hours of availability and ramp down the rate of load generation by the other conventional plants. Similarly, in the hours of non-availability of such new renewables, the operation of the load-generation rate in the conventional thermal or hydel plants can be ramped up to meet the total load demand of the system. This would minimize the use of fossil fuel, and at the same time, utilize the best wind or solar resources whenever they are available and also control the externalities of CO_2 emissions. This, of course, requires R&D work on technology alteration for making plants flexible by raising their ramp rate up or down with minimum damage to the plant life. The ramp rate is the rate at which the load generation, as a percentage of capacity generation, can be raised per unit of time. For a ramp rate of 5 per cent of capacity per minute, for example, the plant will take 20 minutes to reach the full capacity load generation, which is an index of operational flexibility. For a base-load plant such as a coal thermal plant, it is likely to remain low even after R&D efforts to bring in flexibility. One of the real resource costs of such flexibility of operation may be the reduction of plant life due to a higher rate of wear and tear brought about by such flexibility.

In India, R&D activities are trying to promote the operational flexibility of plants with minimum damage incurred by the equipment and machinery for the conventional power generation technologies. Besides, quite a large number of pump storage projects have been undertaken in different regions. For better utilization of renewable energy–based power, economic incentives in the form of lower or higher power tariffs are to be introduced in the hours of high or low availability of renewable energy–based power. Besides, the investment in pump storage development, or better utilization of the stranded gas-based power plants in India, for which there was, at some point in the past, over-investment relative to the actual availability of gas due to wrong market signals. There also remains the possibility of setting up some new greenfield gas-based plants for balancing the power need in times of low availability of power from renewable energy relative to demand.

Besides, it has to be noted that the grid balancing requirement for meeting the high demand for power-intensive industries such as steel, aluminium, cement, paper, railway traction, and so on, Would, in any case, require some constant supply from large point sources of hydro power and natural gas, which may only be supplemented by supply sources of new renewables-based power, which is intermittent in nature. Furthermore, the challenge of balancing load demand and supply is not just a matter of resolving a temporal mismatch of demand and supply, but also a matter of their spatial balancing due to divergence between spatial distribution of load demand and that of supply of renewable energy resources. All these require both grid-scale storage and upgradation of the T&D system.

For T&D, the upgradation of the power grid into a smart grid is a prerequisite for efficient utilization of renewable energy resources when introduced as grid connected. Such upgradation into a smart grid would essentially mean automated coordination for the smooth two-way flow of electricity and information regarding power demand and capacity of all kinds of power both conventional and new renewables ones. This is important for (i) avoiding congestion while evacuating power from a large number of sources of renewable-based generation, and (ii) for the relevant coordination of activities of the power sector across regions and state boundaries in the context of the transmission of power and load dispatches from the various nodal junctions.

A smart grid, in fact, represents an efficient and reliable power system with diverse energy resources for meeting fluctuating load demand, with both supply and demand for load being independently given over space and time. The system includes a variety of operational and energy measures such as the introduction of smart meters and smart appliances for the measurement and communication of demand and supply of the load. It is essentially a system of electronic power conditioning, by automated control of production and despatch of power generated from various sources for supply to a wide range of load centres.

In India, such a grid would require strengthening the information system for energy every 15 minutes, if not a minute-by-minute update on the demand for power and the availability of power capacity and basic renewable energy resources. While the existing power system is quite geared to making load forecasting and managing supply accordingly, the forecasting of supply from fluctuating and uncertain sources of wind and solar energy poses a challenge on demand-supply management.

The upgradation of the information system for efficient ways of electrical energy production and the sharing of power generated using renewable energy resources requires use of telemetry, which is nothing but an automated communications process by which measurements and other data are collected from remote or inaccessible points of locations and transmitted to a receiving equipment for monitoring. A telemeter is a physical device used to remotely measure any quantity. It consists of a sensor, a transmission path which may be wireless or hard-wired, and finally, a display, recording, and control device. The central government is setting up a National Optical Fibre Network, Bharat Net, which would provide connectivity to 2.5 lakh gram panchayats spread over 6,600 blocks and 641 districts of the country, for facilitating data transmission regarding power-load demand, renewable energy resources, and power availability at all the nodes of the power network. In fact, the objective is that all renewables-based generated power plants should be connected with the optical fibre network which can ensure their transmission of real-time data regarding generation and availability to the system operator. Such facilities' gathering of data can ensure a two-way flow of information and power and upgrade India's power grid in different regions into smart grids. The latter would, in turn, enable the integration of a range of new renewable resources into our energy system, which would contribute to the sustainable development of the Indian economy by providing energy security, universal access to electricity, and finally, abatement of the CO_2 emission that typically accompany economic growth.

However, all these would involve extensive use of power electronic devices for smooth and reliable operation when the system integrates a range of alternative renewable energy resources. A lot of work in the area is being done by the power grid of India. Besides, the rolling out of smart grid technology has essentially meant a fundamental re-engineering of the electricity servicing industry. The central government's Ministry of Power has allocated 14 smart grid pilot projects to be implemented by the various state-owned distribution networks in India.

It has to be further noted here that while we consider the balancing of power need and power supply from alternative sources—particularly renewables on the basis of the telemetric data capacity—we need to meet such balancing not only at the state level, but also at the national level, not to mention including, if possible, some of the neighbouring countries. This issue becomes important because some of the renewable resource–rich states may not have high power demand, while at a wider regional/national level these locally surplus resources can be best utilized by investing in a long-distance transmission arrangement of such power. The government is investing in the development of a green corridor in renewable energy–rich states to evacuate power from solar parks or wind parks, particularly where there is no pre-existing regular grid connectivity. These corridors are meant for transmitting the power from such renewable energy–based power plants and connect them to the main power grid. However, such investment costs should partly be socialized for power supply by pooling financial resources from the central government while rendering benefit due to some externalities of advantages to all the stakeholder states. The government, of course, should weigh the cost benefit of the development of such a corridor vis-à-vis the option of off-grid power development with storage facilities near a renewable energy generator pooling station.

However, the efficiency of operation of such a power system involving the use of diverse renewable energy technologies would depend on the choice of models for forecasting on the supply side. There are not only problems of uncertainty but also those of accuracy in the prediction of the new supply-side variables. Generally, the larger the area of such forecasts and the shorter the time horizon (gate closure time), the accuracy of forecasts is higher.

Besides, one major issue in this context would be the cost-effectiveness of the transition to the new industrial order through technological and socio-economic transformation. As new renewables-based technologies would be knowledge-intensive and as the patented knowledge market is highly imperfect and monopolistic, the capital cost may finally become quite high, standing in the way of cost-effectiveness and the distribution of capitalism in the new order. So far as the inclusiveness of the development process is concerned, wide sharing of knowledge, transfer of technology, and control of price of the knowledge capital by governmental intervention become important for both the sharing of benefit of the new industrial revolution between the rich and the poor and between developed and developing countries. International cooperation among the member countries of the United Nations Framework Convention on Climate Change in joint research on science and technology and in sharing and transferring technologies across borders would only enable developing countries to leapfrog to a higher stage of development characterized by the new order. The intellectual property right regime would be of critical importance in such knowledge sharing and delivering the R&D output to the users at affordable prices and in converting the knowledge into a global public good at the earliest. The financial cooperation through the UN Climate Fund at the global, regional, or national levels would be such an arrangement which can be catalytic for such required cooperation.

Concluding Remarks

The development of renewable resource–based power supply as per the projections would contribute towards sustainability by (i) expanding the use of domestic clean energy resources and augmenting the supply of electricity for greater removal of energy poverty, (ii) reducing the dependence on imports, and (iii) reducing the carbon footprint of the energy sector.

Second, it is also important to note that renewable energy technologies are ideally suited to distributed application and constitute a reliable and secure energy supply as an alternative to grid extension or as a supplement to grid power. In rural India, 30 per cent of the population lives without access to electricity because of remoteness. Renewable energy can provide an economically viable or sustainable means of power supply for greater energy security to Indian households by replacing fossil fuel, which is an exhaustible, non-renewable, and imported resource.

As new renewable resource–based power would be generated by large number of decentralized units, including possible innumerable rooftop ones, the capital, wealth, and economic power would tend to be less concentrated in the third phase of the Third Industrial Revolution and contribute towards greater economic equity on equality.

The evolution or revolution in technology that is required for the sustainable development of the power sector revolves around the replacement of fossil fuel by the new renewable, combined with the enhancement of efficient use of electrical energy so produced. The major technological challenges that have to be addressed in this connection are as follows:

1. The development of technology for the storage of electrical energy—for example battery, pump storage, and so on.
2. The introduction of a flexible operation of a renewable-based power plant, that is, ramping up or down of load generation for each type of technology.
3. Reconfiguring, restructuring, and upgrading the Indian power grid for integration with renewable resource–based power generation in the system.
4. The development of large solar or wind parks for power generation on a grid scale in remote areas and that of a green energy corridor for the evacuation of power in such energy-rich areas for feeding into the grid.

All these measures to make India's electricity industry green would require substantive effort and financial resources in R&D activities and human resource development. However, the substitution of fossil fuels by new renewables, which is the driving force of the Third Industrial Revolution, is to be viewed not as a short-term objective but as a long-term one, which is to be achieved by the conversion of the resources rent of the extracted fossil fuels into capital assets, as emphasized in the earlier section, created for the development of knowledge, human resources, and infrastructural capital along with new kinds of plant and equipment that serve as the vehicle of technical progress. Since developing countries are often constrained in their financial capability and technological resources, global cooperation is imperative for the required technology transfer and investment flows across boundaries of nations to bring about the necessary transformation of the global energy system at the least cost of transition and structural adjustment.

Appendix 8A: Basic Model of Demand Analysis and Projection—The Income and Price Model of Energy Demand

For analysing energy consumption behaviour at the sectoral as well as the overall economy levels, we pose a simple model, which assumes that demand for energy (EDD^i) of each sector i of the economy is a function of its income (I^i) and the real energy price (RPE^i) it faces. The partial income elasticity of demand and the partial price elasticity are assumed to remain constant over the projections period. This gives us a demand function of the form:

$$EDD^i = A(I^i)^\alpha (RPE^i)^\beta,$$

where i = overall economy, agriculture, industry, residential, commercial, and transport sectors.

Here,

α is the income elasticity of energy demand.

β is the price elasticity of energy demand.

A is the technology parameter.

α, β, and A are constant over the entire projection period.

For the purpose of econometric estimation, the earlier model can be transformed into a double-log linear model of the form:

$$\log(EDD^i_t) = \log(A) + \alpha * \log(I^i_t) + \beta * \log(RPE^i_t) + \varepsilon^i_t$$

where ε^i_t, is the random error component and conforms to the assumptions of the classical regression model.

Data and Sources

The econometric estimation of the model for the overall economy and for each sector requires data on energy demand, GDP that indicates the level of income or value added, and the real energy price index. The nominal energy price is calculated using the fuel shares and the corresponding wholesale price index of fuels faced by a given sector or by the aggregate economy. The real energy price is calculated by deflating the nominal price by the GDP deflator. The private final consumption expenditure (PFCE) is used as an indicator of income for the residential sector. The model is estimated using data from 1990 to 2015. The data for energy demand is obtained from the energy balances of the non-OECD countries published by the IEA and available on its website. The data for GDP and PFCE are obtained from the National Account Statistics, and the data for wholesale price index prices are obtained from the RBI database (in 'Handbook of Statistics on the Indian Economy') and the website of the Office of the Economic Advisor.

Estimation

We begin by applying the standard time series techniques. First to check the stationarity of the data, we use the Augmented Dickey Fuller Test, the results of which have been reported in Table 8A.1.

TABLE 8A.1 Unit Root Results

Variables (Order of Integration)	Augmented Dickey Fuller Test Statistic	Probability
Industry—GDP (2)	−5.28	0.00*
Industry—Energy Demand (2)	−6.38	0.00*
Industry—Real Energy Price (1)	−6.11	0.00*
Agriculture—GDP (2)	−13.37	0.00*
Agriculture—Energy Demand (2)	−6.72	0.00*
Agriculture—Real Energy Price (1)	−6.23	0.00*
Residential—GDP (2)	−6.46	0.00*
Residential—Energy Demand (2)	−5.26	0.00*
Residential—Real Energy Price (1)	−6.20	0.00*
Commercial—GDP (2)	−5.69	0.00*
Commercial—Energy Demand (2)	−9.16	0.00*
Commercial—Real Energy Price (1)	−6.24	0.00*
Transport—GDP (2)	−4.34	0.01*
Transport—Energy Demand (2)	−5.46	0.00*
Transport—Real Energy Price (1)	−6.27	0.00*
Overall—GDP (2)	−6.33	0.00*
Overall—Energy Demand (2)	−7.12	0.00*
Overall—Real Energy Price (1)	−4.23	0.01*

Source: Author's own estimates.
Note: *Represents significance at the 95 per cent level.

Given the unit root results and the order of integration, we estimate the following model:

$$\log(\Delta ED_0) = \beta \log(\Delta GDP_0) + \gamma \log(REP_0)$$

The model requires that the sectoral GDP and the final energy demand of the concerned sectors are integrated of the second order whereas the real energy prices faced by each of the sectors are integrated of the first order. For applying the Engel and Granger (1987) methodology of co-integration in single equation specification, we consider the following model:

$$\log(\Delta ED_i) = \beta \log(\Delta GDP_i) + \gamma \log(REP_i) + \epsilon \quad \text{where } i = A, I, T, R, C \quad \text{and}$$

where,

ΔED_i is the change in the energy demand of the ith sector, integrated of the first order 1.

ΔGDP_i is the change in GDP of the ith sector, integrated of first order.

REP_i is the real energy price faced by the ith sector, integrated of the first order.

The co-integration results deriving the long-run elasticity coefficients of sectoral energy demand and real energy price of different sectors have been reported in Table 8A.2.

In order to project the final energy demand at the original level, we make use of the following derivation:

$$\log(\Delta ED_t) - \log(\Delta ED_0) = \beta \left[\log(\Delta GDP_t) - \log(\Delta GDP_0) \right]$$
$$+ \gamma \left[\log(REP_t) - \log(REP_0) \right]$$

$$\frac{\Delta ED_t}{\Delta ED_0} = \left(\frac{\Delta GDP_t}{\Delta GDP_0} \right)^{\beta} \times \left(\frac{REP_t}{REP_0} \right)^{\gamma}, t = 2015, 2016, \ldots, 2041$$

or, $$\Delta ED_t = \left(\frac{\Delta GDP_t}{\Delta GDP_0} \right)^{\beta} \times \left(\frac{REP_t}{REP_0} \right)^{\gamma} \times \Delta ED_0 \quad \ldots\ldots\ldots \quad (1)$$

Now, projecting the energy demand at 2021, we do the following:

TABLE 8A.2   Long-Run Elasticity Coefficients: Results

Variables (Logarithm)	Elasticity Coefficients	Probability
Dependent Variable: Δ (Industry— Energy Demand)		
Δ (Industry—GDP)	0.83	0.00*
Industry—Real Energy Price	0.03	0.00*
Dependent Variable: Δ (Agriculture— Energy Demand)		
Δ (Agriculture—GDP)	0.75	0.00*
Agriculture—Real Energy Price	0.12	0.06
Dependent Variable: Δ (Residential— Energy Demand)		
Δ (Residential—GDP)	0.72	0.00*
Residential—Real Energy Price	−0.02	0.00*
Dependent Variable: Δ (Commercial— Energy Demand)		
Δ (Commercial—GDP)	0.62	0.00*
Commercial—Real Energy Price	−0.38	0.00*
Dependtent Variable: Δ (Transport— Energy Demand)		
Δ (Transport—GDP)	0.88	0.00*
Transport—Real Energy Price	−0.08	0.00*

Source: Author's own estimates.

Note: *Denotes significance at the 95 per cent level.

Calculate (1) for $t = 2015, 2016, 2017, 2018, 2019, 2020, 2021$ and then add up these to get the total change from 2014–21 and finally add it up with the base year value of 2014 to derive the final energy demand in the concerned year.

We do the same for 2031 and 2041.

Epilogue

The discussions within this book have analysed the interdependences among economic, social, and environmental dimensions of sustainability. The social and environmental sustainability of development requires the process of growth to be socially non-disruptive and it should not involve any serious environmental risk of the collapse of its ecosystem. The former would require a just distribution of resources and social products among its people so that there is no serious poverty or inequality due to absolute or relative deprivation of resources or income for some of its people, and therefore no economic source of social tension. The empirical findings using advanced econometric and quantitative methods on the interrelationships among poverty, inequality, social tension, social discrimination, and religious polarization on the one hand and their fallouts in the form of crime, riots, and insurgencies across Indian states on the other have been quite informative, not always stereotypical, and insightful from the point of view of policy planning for social sustainability. The environmental sustainability condition would, on the other hand, require the reduction of the ecological footprint and improvement of environmental protection through conservation of resources and control of pollution, including CO_2 emissions.

The conceptual arguments and empirical analysis of the book have shown that reduction of inequality and poverty promotes both growth and human development. The discussions and econometric analysis of inter-linkages among economic growth, a rise in the level of human development, and environmental conservation further point to the direct and significant impact of growth on human development and the environment, although the impact of human development on the environment is somewhat remote and relatively weak. These have warranted the combining of strategies of economic growth with a social perspective of investment for social and environmental infrastructure development, along with direct policy actions for environmental conservation.

However, as the discussion of the book has evolved around the role of entropy law in affecting economic processes, it would require either delinking or at least weakening of the link between resource use or emission and the product or GDP. In the context of climate change, the main strategy for the sustainable development of the energy sector particularly, the power sector, has to be one of energy conservation and fuel substitution. The focus of such policies has been thus one of eco-efficiency, particularly the minimization of CO_2 emissions per unit of energy or electricity. This has called for a revolutionary change in the energy technology in the form of a Third Industrial Revolution based on new renewables.

It is, however, important to note that the place of origin of waste or CO_2 emissions is the location of production or resource use. The country-wise distribution of waste or the arising CO_2 would thus be determined by the spatial distribution of production or fuel combustion across locations of fuel use. However, a country can outsource CO_2-intensive or any resource-intensive environment-degrading product by importing them from other country.

If a country is to be held responsible for emissions, one may argue that the share or extent of responsibility should be worked out not on the basis of production but on that of emissions imputable to consumption for which the country should be responsible and bear the cost of damage or of its abatement. The polluter should be the consumer of products rather than its producer and the incidence of the burden of polluter pays principle should accordingly be fixed for the consumer (Gough 2015).

So far as the policy is concerned in such cases, if we want to shift the accounting principle of waste arising or CO_2 emissions, and fixing its burden of cost from production to the consumption of goods and services, we have to have a different analytical approach altogether. In such a case, the factor analysis of emission arising would show the break-up of the total emissions imputable to consumption at the macroeconomic level as follows:

> Growth of emission = impact on it of changes in (a) population + (b) per capita consumption + (c) composition of consumption + (d) eco-efficiency or emission coefficients of production of the items of consumption, holding other factors constant for each component item. (Gough 2015)

The eco-efficiency of consumption would thus be determined by the composition of consumption as well as the technology of production of the consumption items. This would imply a necessity of recomposition of consumption on grounds apart from the considerations of technological eco-efficiency improvement in the production of individual goods for the overall reductions of emissions. However, there may arise here a conflict between the considerations of necessity and that of environmental conservation in recomposing macro-level consumption. It is quite possible that many necessities such as domestic energy and food are highly energy- and emission-intensive while some of the non-necessities may be low-emission intensive. Among the necessities there may also be some goods with low- emission intensities. If we have unit income elasticity of demand as the cut-off for the necessity–luxury distinction and a certain other cut-off for, say, the CO_2-intensity high or low distinction in units of kg/USD value of the product or value added, we can generate a matrix of a two-way classification of goods and services according to the degrees of necessity and that of emission intensity. Such a matrix showing the identity of the goods in terms of these two characteristics would, in fact, point to a fundamental contradiction between securing emission reduction and ensuring equitable distribution of real income if we choose to use emissions tax as a policy instrument.

Most of the international dialogue regarding the negotiation of a climate change policy revolves around controlling the level of production and the composition of its growth, technology, and country-wise sharing of responsibility accordingly, than that of consumption. Since consumption is the ultimate objective of production, the logic of making consumption as the basis of sharing responsibility of emissions is ethically and logically more justified. However, this would require further research to arrive at policies based on control of consumption (rate of savings) and resource intensity of consumption of different kinds, as well as private or public sources of spending on consumption, and so on—the last one being related with redistribution and welfare implications as well.

This issue of consumption-based pollution control would lead to wider issues beyond recomposition of consumption at the macro level. While capitalist economies would always argue for the promotion of market development, which runs counter to the idea of controlling the rise in entropy, these issues would raise a debate regarding how far we should promote market by wasteful or unproductive resource use, which is inevitable in a market-driven system without regulation. This raises more philosophical issues, such as what should be valued in life and what is meant by a decent living. Entropy law warns us about the upper limit of our planetary ecosystem to meet our demands. This reminds us of the great saying of Mahatma Gandhi: 'Earth has got enough to meet everybody's need, but not everybody's greed.'

In spite of the gloomy prospect of the entropy law–based dynamics of the human economic system, the Mahatma's message gives us a positive perspective regarding the prospect of development of well-being over time. The value system on which 'well-being' is founded in such a context is not one of indefinite growth of wants or accumulation of wealth by some for the sake of itself, irrespective of its relevance for the society as a whole. The desired value system has to be founded on a sufficiency theory of well-being, which continually searches for a sufficiency condition of making the economic system not necessarily larger but an improved one, with its changing stock of knowledge and a changing composition and structure of economy, and supporting institutional norms of sharing of resources and income and inclusiveness in development (Daly and Farley 2004). For attaining such sufficiency, the economy would require social investment of the type propagated by the Swedish School (see Chapter 1), than mere accumulative investment driven by market. It would again make welfare statism relevant to attain the goals. All this calls for further interdisciplinary research, not just involving physical and biological sciences with economics but also with ethics, philosophy, and sociology for understanding issues of values and well-being better in such a context.

References

Alkire, S., and M.E. Santos. 2010. 'Acute Multidimensional Poverty: A New Index for Developing Countries'. Human Development Research Papers (2009 to present) HDRP-2010-11. Human Development Report Office (HDRO), United Nations Development Programme (UNDP).

Alkire, S., J.E. Foster, S. Seth, and M.E. Santosh. 2014. *Multidimensional Poverty Measurement and Analysis*. Oxford Poverty and Human Development Initiative. Available at: https://www.ophi.org.uk/wp-content/uploads/OPHIWP086_Ch5.pdf (accessed 9 December 2019).

Anand, S., and A. Sen. 2000. 'Human Development and Economic Sustainability'. *World Development* 28(12): 2029–49.

Andreoni, J. 1995. 'Criminal Deterrence in the Reduced Form: A New Perspective on Ehrlich's Seminal Study'. *Economic Enquiry* 33(3): 476–83.

Arrow, K., P. Dasgupta, L. Goulder, G. Daily, P. Ehrlich, G. Heal, and B. Walker. 2004. 'Are We Consuming Too Much?' *The Journal of Economic Perspectives* 18(3): 147–72.

Ayres, R.U. 1978. *Resources, Environment, and Economics: Applications of the Materials/Energy Balance Principle*. New York: John Wiley and Sons.

Becker, G.S. 1968. 'Crime and Punishment: An Economic Approach'. *Journal of Political Economy* 76(2): 169–217.

Bickel, P., and R. Friedrich, eds. [2005] 2004. *Extern E: Externalities of Energy Methodology*. Luxembourg: Office for Official Publications of the European Communities.

Bourguignon, F. 2000. 'Crime, Violence, and Inequitable Development'. Annual World Bank Conference on Development Economics 1999 (December), 199–220.

Brown, L.R. 2001. *Eco-Economy: Building an Economy for the Earth*. New York: W.W. Norton & Company.

Clark, S., R. Hemming, and D. Ulph. 1981. 'On Indices for the Measurement of Poverty'. *The Economic Journal* 91(362): 515–26.

Cleveland, C.J. 1987. 'Biophysical Economics: Historical Perspective and Current Research Trends'. *Ecological Modelling* 38(1–2): 47–73.

Costanza, R., ed. 1991. *Ecological Economics: The Science and Management of Sustainability.* New York: Columbia University Press.

Costanza, R., and H.E. Daly. 1987. 'Towards Ecological Economics'. *Ecological Modelling* 38(1–2): 1–7.

Cronert, A., and J. Palme. 2017. 'Approach to Social Investment and Their Implications for Sweden and the European Union'. In Global Challenges, *Working Paper Series*, No. 4.

Daly, H.E., ed. 1973. *Towards a Steady State Economy.* San Francisco: W.H. Freeman.

———. 1991. *Steady-State Economics: With New Essays.* Washington, DC: Island Press.

———. 1999. 'Uneconomic Growth: In Theory, in Fact, in History, and in Relation to Globalization'. In *Ecological Economics and Ecology of Economics: Essays in Criticism*, 8–24. Cheltenham, Gloucestershire, UK: Edward Elgar Publishing.

Daly, H., and J. Farley. 2004. *Ecological Economics: Principles and Practice.* Washington, DC: Island Press.

Dasgupta, P. 2001. *Human Well-Being and the Natural Environment.* New Delhi: Oxford University Press.

Dasgupta, P., and K.G. Mäler. 2000. 'Net National Product, Wealth, and Social Well-Being'. *Environment and Development Economics* 5(1): 69–93.

———, eds. 2001. *The Environment and Emerging Development Issues*, Vol. 2. Oxford: Clarendon Press.

Ehrlich, I. 1996. 'Crime, Punishment and the Market for Offenses', *Journal of Economic Perspectives* 10(1): 43–67.

El Serafy, S. 1994. 'The Proper Calculation of Income from Depletable Natural Resources'. In *Environmental Accounting for Sustainable Development.* Edited by Y.J. Ahmed, S. El Serafy, and E. Lutz, 141–62. Washington, DC: United Nations Environment Programme, World Bank Symposium.

Engel, R.F., and C.W.J. Granger. 1987. 'Co-integration and Error Correction: Representation, Estimation, and Testing'. *Econometrica* 55(2): 251–76.

Epstein, P.R., J.J. Buonocore, K. Eckerle, M. Hendryx, B.M. Stout III, R. Heinberg, R.W. Clapp et al. 2011. 'Full Cost Accounting for the Life Cycle of Coal'. *Annals of the New York Academy of Sciences* 1219: 73–98.

Esteban, J.M., and D. Ray. 1994. 'On the Measurement of Polarization'. *Econometrica: Journal of the Econometric Society* 62(4): 819–51.

Fajnzylber, P., D. Lederman, and N. Loayza. 2002. 'Inequality and Violent Crime'. *The Journal of Law and Economics* 45(1): 1–39.

Flora, P., and A.J. Heidenheimer, eds. 1981. *The Development of Welfare States in Europe and America*. New Jersey: Transaction Publishers.

Foster, J., J. Greer, and E. Thorbeck. 1984. 'A Class of Decomposable Poverty Measures'. *Econometrica* 52(3): 751–66.

Glaeser, E.L., and B. Sacerdote. 1999. 'Why Is There More Crime in Cities?' *Journal of Political Economy* 107(S6): 1–34.

Global Carbon Capture and Storage Institute (GCCSI). 2011. GCCSI Database.

Georgescu-Rosen, N. (1971). *The Entropy Law and the Economic Process*. Cambridge: Harvard University Press.

Gough, I. (2015). *Macroeconomics, Climate Change and the 'Recomposition of Consumption'*. London: Prime.

Government of India. 2005. National Electricity Policy, Government of India. Available at: https://powermin.nic.in/en/content/national-electricity-policy (accessed 9 December 2019).

———. 2008a. Eleventh Five Year Plan, Planning Commission, Government of India.

———. 2008b. National Action Plan on Climate Change. Available at: https://www.ncbi.nlm.nih.gov/pmc/articles/PMC2822162/ (accessed 9 December 2019).

———. 2011–12. 'Household Consumption of Various Goods and Services in India 2011–12'. *National Sample Survey (NSS) Report of 68th Round on Consumption Expenditure*. Delhi: Ministry of Statistics and Programme Implementation. Available at: http://mospi.nic.in/sites/default/files/publication_reports/Report_no558_rou68_30june14.pdf (accessed 9 December 2019).

———. 2012a. Energy Statistics, Central Statistics Office.

———. 2012b. Regulation Regarding Tariff Determination (March) No L-1/94/CERC/2011, Central Electricity Regulatory Commission. Available at: http://www.cercind.gov.in/2012/regulation/CERC_RE-Tariff-Regualtions_6_2_2012.pdf (accessed 9 December 2019).

———. 2013. Twelfth Five Year Plan, Planning Commission, Government of India.

———. 2014b. *Energy Statistics 2014*. Delhi: Central Statistics Office.

———. 2015. Energy Statistics, Central Statistics Office.

———. 2017. 'Draft National Energy Policy'. NITI Aayog, Government of India. Available at: https://niti.gov.in/writereaddata/files/new_initiatives/NEP-ID_27.06.2017.pdf (accessed 11 December 2019).

Hartwick, J.M. 1977. 'Intergenerational Equity and the Investing of Rents from Exhaustible Resources'. *The American Economic Review* 67(5): 972–4.

Hawking, Stephen. 1988. *A Brief History of Time: From Big Bang to Black Holes*. UK: Bantam Dell Publishing Group.

Imrohoroğlu, A., A. Merlo, and P. Rupert. 2000. 'On the Political Economy of Income Redistribution and Crime'. *International Economic Review* 41(1): 1–26.

International Energy Agency. 2016. *Energy Balances of Non-OECD Countries 2016*. Paris: OECD. Available at: https://www.oecd-library.org/energy/world-energy-balances-2016 (accessed 11 December 2019).

IPCC. 2014. *Fifth Assessment Report of the Intergovernmental Panel on Climate Change 2013*. New York: Cambridge University Press, 2014.

Jones, C. 2006. *Introduction to Economic Growth*. London: W.W. Norton & Company.

Kakwani, N. 1988. 'Income Inequality, Welfare and Poverty in a Developing Economy with Applications to Sri Lanka'. *Social Choice and Welfare* 5(2–3): 199–222.

Kakwani, N., and H.H. Son. 2016. *Social Welfare Functions and Development: Measurement and Policy Applications*. New York: Springer.

Kelly, M. 2000. 'Inequality and Crime'. *Review of Economics and Statistics* 82(4): 530–9.

Khramov, M.V., and M.J.R. Lee. 2013. 'The Economic Performance Index (EPI): An Intuitive Indicator for Assessing a Country's Economic Performance Dynamics in an Historical Perspective'. No. 13-214. International Monetary Fund.

KPMG. 2012. 'The Rising Sun—Grid Parity Gets Closer: A Point of View on the Solar Energy Sector in India' (September). KPMG. Available at: https://natgrp.files.wordpress.com/2013/06/kpmg_rising-sun-2-full.pdf (accessed 9 December 2019).

Maithani, P.C., and D. Gupta. 2015. *Achieving Universal Energy Access in India*. New Delhi: Sage Publications.

Meadows, D.H., D.L. Meadows, J. Randers, and W.W. Behrens. 1972. *The Limits to Growth: A Report to the Club of Rome*. New York: Chelsea Green Publishing Company.

Montalvo, J.G., and M. Reynal-Querol. 2003. 'Religious Polarization and Economic Development'. *Economics Letters* 80(2): 201–10.

Morel, N., B. Palier, and J. Palme. 2012. 'Beyond the Welfare State as We Knew It'. *In Towards a Social Investment Welfare State*. Edited by Nathalie Morel, Bruno Palier, and Joakim Palme, 1–30. UK: The Policy Press.

Myrdel, G., and Alva Myrdal. 1934. *The Crisis in the Population Question (Kris i beforlkningsfragan)*. Sweden: Bonniers.

Parikh, J.K., and K.S. Parikh. 1976. 'Mobilisation and Impacts of Biogas Technologies'. *Energy* 2(4): 441–5.

Phadke, A.A., R. Bharvirkar, and J. Khangura. 2011. *Reassessing Wind Potential Estimates for India-Economic and Policy Implications*. Berkley: Lawrence Berkeley Laboratory, University of California.

Planning Commission. 2006. Report of the Expert Committee on Integrated Energy Policy, Planning Commission, Government of India. Available at: http://planningcommission.gov.in/reports/genrep/rep_intengy.pdf (accessed 9 December 2019).

————. 2014a. Databook Compiled for Use of Planning Commission. Available at: http://planningcommission.nic.in/data/datatable/data_2312/comp_data2312.pdf (accessed 11 December 2019).

————. 2014b. 'The Final Report of the Expert Group on Low Carbon Strategies for Inclusive Growth'. Planning Commission, Government of India. Available at: http://planningcommission.nic.in/reports/genrep/rep_carbon2005.pdf (accessed 11 December 2019).

Rajan, A. 2017. 'Diversion of Clean Energy Funds to GST Is a Problem—but a Bigger Problem is the Coal Cess Itself'. *Scroll.in.*, 3 August. Available at: https://scroll.in›India›Counterview (accessed 9 December 2019).

Ranis, G., and F. Stewart. 2005. *Dynamic Links between the Economy and Human Development*. Working Paper No. 8. Department of Economic and Social Affairs, United Nations.

Rifkin, J. 2011. *The Third Industrial Revolution: How Lateral Power Is Transforming Energy, the Economy, and the World*. New York: Palgrave Macmillan.

Romer, P.M. 1990. 'Endogenous Technological Change'. *Journal of Political Economy* 98(5, Part 2): S71–S102.

————. 1993. 'Idea Gaps and Object Gaps in Economic Development'. *Journal of Monetary Economics* 32(3): 543–73.

Sen, A. 1974. 'Informational Bases of Alternative Welfare Approaches: Aggregation and Income Distribution'. *Journal of Public Economics* 3(4): 387–403.

————. 2000. 'Social Exclusion: Concept, Application and Scrutiny'. Social Development Papers, 1 June, Office of Environment and Social Development, Asian Development Bank.

Sengupta, R. 2010. 'Prospects and Policies for Low Carbon Economic Growth of India'. National Institute of Public Finance and Policy, New Delhi.

————. 2013. *Ecological Limits and Economic Development: Creating Space*. New Delhi: Oxford University Press.

————. 2015. *Challenges of Transition from Fossil Fuels to Green Regimes*. New Delhi: Asian Institute of Transport Development.

Sengupta, R. and S.B. Das. 2015. *From the Fossil Fuel Present to a Low Carbon Future: How Alberta's Oil Wealth Can Help Our World Adapt to Climate Change*. Edmonton, Canada: Cambridge Strategies.

Shukla, P.R., and D. Mahapatra. 2008. 'Fuel Life Cycle for India'. Costs Assessment for Sustainable Energy Markets, Deliverable No. D 7.1, Project No. 518294 SES6. Available at: www.feem-project.net/cases/index.php (accessed 9 December 2019).

————. 2011. 'Dynamic Life Cycle for India's Electricity System'. *International Energy Journal* 12(1): 1–14.

Singhal, R. and R. Sengupta. 2012. 'Energy Security and Bio-diesel: Implications for Land Use and Food Security'. *Economic and Political Weekly* 47(40).

Solow, R.M. 1986. 'On the Intergenerational Allocation of Natural Resources'. *The Scandinavian Journal of Economics* 88(1): 141–9.

———. 1991. 'Sustainability: An Economist's Perspective', 14 June. Paper presented at the 18th J. Seward Johnson Lecture to the Marine Policy Center, Woods Hole Oceanographic Institution, Woods Hole, Massachusetts.

———. 1996. *Growth Theory*. New York: Routledge.

Suri, T., M.A. Boozer, G. Ranis, and F. Stewart. (2011). 'Paths to Success: The Relationship between Human Development and Economic Growth'. *World Development* 39(4): 506–22.

United Nations (UN). 2002. 'Report of the Summit. Doc. A/Conf. 199/20, Chapter 1, Resolution 1, Annex Point 5. Available at: https://www.un.org/ga/search/view_doc.asp?symbol=A/CONF.199/20&Lang=E (accessed 13 December 2019).

Wiener, Norbert. 1954. *The Human Use of Human Beings: Cybernetics and Society*. Boston: Da Capo Press.

World Bank. 2015. World Development Indicators. 'Statistical Tables'. Oxford: Oxford University Press.

———. 2016. World Development Indicators. 'Statistical Tables'. Oxford: Oxford University Press.

World Commission of Environment and Development (WCED). 1987. *Our Common Future*. Oxford, New York: Oxford University Press.

World Institute of Sustainable Energy. 2011. 'Achieving 12% Green Electricity by 2017', p. 19 (Table 3.1), WISE Report, World Institute of Sustainable Energy, Pune. Available at: www.wisein.org/pdf/Final_12_RE_Report.pdf (accessed 13 December 2019).

———. 2014. 'Coal in India: Time for a Verdict'. Pune: WISE Report, World Institute of Sustainable Energy.

Index

About the Author

Ramprasad Sengupta is emeritus professor of economics at the Centre for Economic Studies and Planning at the School of Social Sciences, Jawaharlal Nehru University (JNU), New Delhi. Before this, he was professor of economics for almost four decades, held the Sukhamoy Chakravarty Chair of Planning and Development, and was dean of the School of Social Sciences at JNU. He has also been the Mahatma Gandhi National Fellow of the Indian Council for Social Science Research (ICSSR) at the Centre for Studies in Social Sciences, Kolkata. He started his teaching and research career at Presidency College, Kolkata, and since then has been visiting professor or distinguished fellow at many institutes, including the Indian Institute of Management Calcutta; Ambedkar University, Delhi; National Institute of Public Finance and Policy, New Delhi; and India Development Foundation, Gurgaon, as well as at a number of universities in Germany, Japan, USA, UK, Canada, and the Netherlands. Besides his teaching stints, he has also been advisor to the Planning Commission, Government of India, and a part-time independent director on the governing board of the Steel Authority of India for several years.

His areas of interest and specialization are energy, ecological/environmental economics, development economics and planning, and quantitative policy modelling of infrastructural sectors (including power, energy, transport, and steel). His previous book with Oxford University Press was *Ecological Limits and Economic Development: Creating Space* (2013).